MASTERING

MARKETING

D0453236

MACMILLAN MASTER SERIES

Banking
Basic Management
Biology
British Politics
Business Communication
Chemistry
COBOL Programming
Commerce
Computer Programming
Computers
Data Processing
Economics
Electronics
English Grammar
English Language
English Literature
French
French II
German

Hairdressing
Italian
Keyboarding
Marketing
Mathematics
Modern British History
Modern World History
Nutrition
Office Practice
Pascal Programming
Physics
Principles of Accounts
Social Welfare
Sociology
Spanish
Statistics
Study Skills
Typewriting Skills
Word Processing

OTHER BOOKS BY THE SAME AUTHOR

Managing for Growth
Managing for Profit
Marketing Imperative
Planning for Products and Markets
Successful Management in Developing Countries, vols 1–4
The Management Quadrille

MASTERING

MARKETING

SECOND EDITION

DOUGLAS FOSTER

MACMILLAN

© Douglas Foster 1982, 1984
Line-drawings © The Macmillan Press Ltd 1982

First edition 1982
Second edition 1984
Reprinted 1985

Published by
MACMILLAN EDUCATION LTD
Houndmills, Basingstoke, Hampshire RG21 2XS
and London
Companies and representatives
throughout the world

Printed in Hong Kong

British Library Cataloguing in Publication Data
Foster, Douglas
Mastering marketing. – (Macmillan master
series)
1. Marketing
I. Title
658.8   HF5415
ISBN 0–333–37195–X

To E L I Z A B E T H

without whose love, encouragement and
support this book would not have been
written.

'Devote yourself patiently to the theory
and conscientiously to the practice . . .'

Confucius (551–479 B.C.)

CONTENTS

CONTENTS

CONTENTS

Appendices

PREFACE TO THE FIRST EDITION

Marketing is accepted as a major discipline of management. As such it features prominently in most courses on business education and management development. This book defines and explains the basic concepts while avoiding unnecessary jargon. It draws upon the author's experience and practice of marketing and management in Britain, Europe, North America and some developing countries. The book highlights the extent to which successful marketing management must consider other, non-marketing, aspects of management.

The book treats marketing as an activity that can be applied equally successfully to manufacturing industry, services and non-profit-making organisations, whether at home or abroad, for both large and small enterprises. While dealing with the obvious differences encountered in each sector and showing how basic techniques are adapted for them, it avoids the excessive differentiation that has been drawn in earlier books. The cases mentioned will help all readers to appreciate the practical implications of marketing.

The work is aimed primarily at students on BEC National and Higher courses (certificate and diploma) but will also be useful reading for other similar courses. It will be useful too to all executives, being a handy 'refresher course' or reference work on their bookshelves.

Woking, 1982   DOUGLAS FOSTER

PREFACE TO THE SECOND EDITION

The contents of the original edition of this book have been thoroughly reviewed and brought up to date. New material has been added to take account of changes in marketing thought since the first manuscript was prepared. This edition brings the subject of marketing in line with present concepts, appropriate for the objectives originally set for this book.

Woking, 1983   DOUGLAS FOSTER

ACKNOWLEDGEMENTS

The author and publishers wish to thank the following who have kindly given permission for the use of copyright material: The Financial Times Ltd, for a figure from 'Most New Products Die Young' by D. W. Foster published in the *Financial Times*, 29 July 1969. *Harvard Business Review*, for a table from 'How to Organize for New Products' by Samuel C. Johnson and Conrad Jones (May/June 1957). Copyright © 1957 by the President and Fellows of Harvard College. Longman Group Ltd, for tables from *Planning for Products and Markets* by D. W. Foster. Prentice-Hall Inc., for the adaptation of an extract from *Marketing Management: Analysis, Planning and Control*, 4th ed., p. 39, by Philip Kotler, © 1980. Every effort has been made to trace all the copyright-holders, but if any have been inadvertently overlooked the publishers will be pleased to make the necessary arrangement at the first opportunity.

INTRODUCTION TO

MARKETING

A great deal of jargon has been written about marketing. This seems to have been the fate of every so-called 'new' management technique. The amount of nonsense appearing in print seems to increase in direct proportion to the fashionable rating of the technique. Yet, stripped of all jargon, marketing is simply the total commercial activity of an enterprise (excluding purchasing). Put another way, it is concerned with the 'four Ps' of product, price, promotion and place.

1.1 THE MARKETING CONCEPT

In general terms marketing requires executives to be in a frame of mind that realises if there are no customers there is no business. It does not matter how fancy, complex or academic marketing and other management systems may be, if a company cannot attract customers' business it will eventually be forced into liquidation or merger.

The marketing concept acknowledges that a business geared to serve the needs and requirements of customers will achieve better results over a longer period of time than a company whose executives are not so motivated. The jargon phrase is that the company is *marketing-orientated*. It has placed its customers and their needs or wants at the very centre of its business decisions. The company strives always to identify these needs as accurately as possible so that it can match them more precisely with the products or services it is offering, within its resources and capabilities. It is no longer a case of 'we make only these sizes of pumps (or egg-cups or whatever), take it or leave it', but rather 'what size and type do you require?'

The company will then have ceased to be preoccupied with keeping production facilities loaded in the way *it* wants. Thus it does not produce products which meets *its* own standards but which ignore customers' needs and are not required or cannot be afforded by potential customers.

Marketing also involves all the actions necessary to fit a business, its resources, capabilities and experience, to these customer needs. It must therefore identify both potential customers and their needs or wants. As stated, it embraces all the commercial activities and these include techniques such as marketing research, statistical methods of forecasting and the application of knowledge of human behaviour drawn from the behavioural sciences.

The main point to be understood here is that 'marketing' seeks to achieve more effective and profitable selling by looking ahead, discovering potential customers or applications and their wants and then devising products or services which match these requirements as closely as possible. Old-style 'selling' was preoccupied with the need to 'make a sale' in the present, without considering the precise nature of customers' needs and longer term developments and changes. The customers a company wishes to serve may also have to be selected from a wide range of possibilities. All these factors, especially the need to consider both the present and the future, makes it necessary to formalise marketing as a specific, integrated activity, if sustained success is to be ensured.

Also, Marketing is the name given to the department responsible for carrying out the activities involved in identifying customers and their needs or wants, promoting the products or services offered to them and achieving sales. In more sophisticated companies, it is also responsible for the physical distribution of the products and whatever aftersales services are necessary. However, where physical distribution is a critical activity, or is complex or extensive, it can be assigned to a separate department. In this case there is vital need for close co-operation and communication at all times between Marketing and Physical Distribution management. (In this book 'Marketing' with a capital 'M' will be used to denote the department, rather than the management activity.) Like all other departments of a company, Marketing's responsibilities, powers and authority are delegated to it by the board of directors, or the managing director (or chief executive) acting for the board.

Finally, like politics, business is the art of the possible. A company should produce only what it can sell and it can sell only what it can persuade its customers to buy. Survival is achieved by extracting *profit* from the market, in most instances. Therefore, the process of determining what the company will produce and how this production will be converted into profit must come from the marketing side of the business. It is, usually, the only one able, with some precision, to measure the total demand of each selected market, how this is shared between competitors and different customer categories or regions and how market consumption can be influenced. The marketing function is therefore an important one and must lead the others *in time*.

This does not mean that all future managing directors will be ex-marketing people. It means that until Marketing has studied and analysed its markets, customer needs and total demand for each product or service, confident forecasts cannot be made of the nature and volume of the company's business, i.e. how much of each product can be sold to selected markets or customers. Until this is done, manufacturing, financial and personnel departments cannot know what expectations will be placed on them and thus the contributions they will have to make in achieving the company's business targets. Marketing is thus the lead function but all the major activities of management (marketing, manufacturing, finance, personnel and technical) are of co-equal importance. It is vital, therefore, that there is full and continual co-operation between all these departments.

1.2 THE MEANING AND AIMS OF MARKETING

Marketing involves the systematic application of entrepreneurship to the almost constantly changing conditions of the present age. It is concerned with the rational and logical use of people, materials, plant, money and other resources to ensure profit, survival and growth over the longest possible period. It is not interested – except in some very rare instances – in a one-year, 'flash-in-the-pan' basis. To achieve this the company must assess objectively every factor important to its business so that decisions are based on judgement, which is in turn based on as much knowledge as it is possible, or practical, to obtain. The application of 'hunchplay' is almost doomed to ultimate failure especially as business becomes more complex and competitive and every business decision becomes more far-reaching in its effect.

(a) Theory and aims

The theory of good marketing is that it should comprehend what is known, make a scientific assessment of what is likely to happen in the future and then evolve a set of guides for action which will lead to improved managerial performance. Marketing is unlikely ever to be able to advance to the stage when it can eliminate all risks and uncertainties. It can reduce the margin of error and the incidence of risk.

The aims of good marketing require the observance of the following five basic rules.

(i) It must provide a means of classifying, assessing and integrating information relevant to a business. The mere accumulation of facts is not enough.

(ii) It must provide a sound base for thinking about and studying business problems, providing a method of approach which helps to draw correct conclusions which form a basis for action.

(iii) It must be able to explain, predict and control the process it employs and it requires not only an interpretation of facts but an appreciation of their interrelationships.

(iv) It must employ sufficient analytical methods to help solve its problems, existing methods being based on economics, statistics, sociology and psychology, wherever possible with the aid of a computer. Operational research and the behavioural sciences also make useful contributions to the planning and control of marketing operations.

(v) It should allow the derivation of a number of principles of marketing behaviour which are special to any particular business or technology.

Marketing as a management function aims to give direction and purpose to a company's activities. It does so through the collection and interpretation of information on the company's markets, products and competitors. It uses these facts to indicate what activities should be undertaken or how operations should be modified to meet changing circumstances in the selected product-market activities. Marketing, in conjunction with its sister departments, decides the products to be offered and the total marketing effort that can be placed behind the products. Marketing also aims to monitor the results of the selling and promotional activities to see how they match targeted performance. Adjustments to the operations can be made when results vary too much from plans. In all this Marketing seeks to make the whole company and its management *outward-looking*.

1.3 SOME COMMON MISCONCEPTIONS

There have been many misconceptions of what marketing is all about and some of them have survived, surprisingly, into the present day. To many people marketing is still 'market research' or 'advertising'. These two are parts of the total marketing function. Others hold the view that it is 'a rather expensive way of selling' without really knowing how this is so. Marketing improperly applied can lead to greater costs, whereas it is meant to provide improved profit, so in that sense it can be an expensive way of selling. Yet others have a pathetic belief in the cure-all magical powers of this newfangled thing called 'marketing'. Apart from the fact that marketing activities or techniques are not new, this last view may be a result of the still fashionable belief that because a thing is apparently 'new' it must be better than the 'old' one it replaces.

Unfortunately, just changing all titles beginning with 'sales' to those beginning with 'marketing' achieves nothing so long as the mental approach to the business and the methods of doing that business remain unchanged. Just changing titles and hoping all will come right may prove a death-wish for the company. Marketing involves a good deal of hard work, the application of common sense matched to knowledge, the use of certain special skills (explained later in this book) and a constant, total awareness of the market environment in which the company is operating. As stated, improperly applied marketing will just drain off existing profit, not add to it.

There is one further, dangerous misconception arising from the statement that the art of marketing is the art of producing what a market wants. Strict application of this idea can cause trouble. It could lead to additional capital expenditure which the company may not really be able to afford. Or the return obtained may be insufficient to sustain the overall profitability of the company. Worse still, the profitability of these new assets may not compensate for losses arising from some existing assets which may then be under-utilised or made idle. If these idle assets cannot be sold or turned into cash for investment in other profitable operations they will remain as a further drain on the company's profitability.

Since most companies already have substantial investments in plant and facilities, the marketing concept has to be modified. These companies should establish what products they are best able to make and, from market research information, they can persuade customers to buy. The cost of this 'persuasion' should not be excessive. In other words, these products must earn the profits targeted for them. Marketing then becomes the art of doing what is possible to obtain optimum profit at minimum cost.

Further, earlier books have tended to over-emphasise the importance of the marketing function. They implied the omnipotence of marketing or that marketing *is* (the whole of) management. Such attitudes are of course far from the truth. Successful management requires the right proportion, mix and balance of all the necessary management activities. No one function is really supreme. Therefore nothing in this book should be read as implying the omnipotence of marketing as a management activity. Interdepartmental co-operation is the key to sustained success in management.

1.4 WHY MARKETING CAN FAIL

There are many reasons why marketing can fail to achieve its purpose of improving profitability, sales, market shares and reputation. Bad management can strike here just as in any other area of an enterprise. This may be due to inefficiency, incompetence, sloth or any of the many human failings people are heir to even today. These difficulties may only be remedied by changing the personnel. However, there are other reasons for marketing's failure, and with careful training staff can be shown how not to make these mistakes.

First, there may be total ignorance of what marketing is, what techniques are available and the things they can and *cannot* do or achieve. In this case, the interdependence and interrelationships of the various techniques will not be known either. For example, there is little point in conducting any marketing research (see Table 1.1) if the company is in no position to be able to use the gathered information, or the cost of the research will be much more than any financial benefit which would accrue to the company as a result of obtaining the research data. For example the increased sales or profit gained may not justify the expenditure on the research.

Second, marketing techniques may be used blindly without any thought being given to their relevance to the business in question. For example, a company making construction products all of which are sold against official tenders of one sort or another, announced well in advance of the buying decision, has little need for full-scale marketing research or advertising. Research may be better restricted to analyses of the tenders coming forward so that the company can decide which tenders or products would give its factory the most profitable mix of business. It could then make useful decisions on the prices and deliveries it could offer for the items it wanted. Perhaps the company could load the prices for the unprofitable products or those it would have difficulty in making. This would either help the company to avoid getting orders for the items it did not want, or if it got the orders the profit margins would be big enough to compensate for problems that might be met in manufacture. The advertising might best be limited to corporate advertisements which highlight the name and reputation of the company and the products it made best. Such advertisements would keep the company in the minds of the people who issued the tenders, ensuring that the company received all the tenders it wanted.

Next there is the *ad hoc* use of marketing techniques. The most commonly abused are the marketing research activities. Some companies tend to pursue these occasionally – when they think about them or have some money to spare. The once-off marketing research study can be a waste of time and money, especially as the information obtained can be obsolescent in three months or so. It is better to have a planned programme for marketing research, relevant to the marketing objectives and plans of the company, at various appropriate times of a trading year. These studies should then be continued over subsequent years (how this is done is explained in Chapter 4) to keep the information up to date. However, as mentioned earlier, if the company cannot use the information there is usually little point in doing the research.

Finally there is failure to realise the importance, relevance and cost involved in the use of a technique. For example advertising is a costly venture these days. If it does not help to assist or enhance the selling activities, it could be a waste of resources. There is no point in doing any promotional work (advertising and sales promotions) if the goods are not in stock at depots and points of sale (e.g. shops). Potential customers whose interest is aroused by the promotional campaign will only be frustrated when they find they are unable to obtain the items from the shops. The consumers might even turn against the company and not buy other products it makes.

Nor is there any point in planning to develop new products if the company does not have the plant and skills to make them or if the sales force does not have the knowledge and ability to sell them. Distribution may also be a problem if, for example, the new products have to be distributed in bulk nationally when hitherto only small quantities to a few selected areas had to be handled.

In every example mentioned in this section, failure to achieve satisfactory levels of operation can prove very costly. It could even lead to cash-flow and liquidity problems of such magnitude that the company may be forced to close down! As with everything else in life, the application of sound common sense is needed in the use of marketing techniques. Blindly stumbling along, aping other companies or following fads of the moment, without appreciating what they really have done or why, usually spells disaster, no matter how one looks at it.

1.5 DEFINITIONS AND PRACTICAL IMPLICATIONS

There have been, and still are, several definitions of marketing. Most of them leave something to be desired, as it is difficult to define succinctly a multi-faceted activity like marketing with its rather complex involvement with both the external and the internal environments of the business in which it is involved. The external aspects cover customers or markets, economic conditions in countries, regions, industries and the trading world at large, competitors and their activities. There are also government controls and regulations of fiscal (especially taxation) matters affecting business and industry and consumer or customer purchasing power, import/export controls and political decisions, e.g. on state ownership of key industries and how mixed (state and privately owned enterprises) a country's economy should be. There are also political decisions which discourage or ban trade with some countries because of disagreement with their political or other systems. Many of these factors are outside the control of the firm. Internal factors cover the resources and capabilities of the company, the degree or nature of innovation required in different technical areas, technological development and trends, the role, nature and extent of sales and promotional activities required, the cost-price relationship and the way price changes and levels affect demand for the enterprise's products or services. As this book will indicate later, the interrelationships between all these are also complex.

(a) Definitions

The definition of the British Institute of Marketing is as follows: 'Marketing is the management process responsible for identifying, anticipating and satisfying customer requirements profitably.'

The American Marketing Association's definition is: 'The performance of business activities that direct the flow of goods and services from producer to customer or user'.

Most definitions encapsulate what is a surprisingly wide range of activities. For example:

(i) marketing begins *before* the production process when it researches into the design, styling and performance of the product or service that is needed and then on the potential demand that could exist and the market share the company could strive for;

(ii) then it plays a major role in pricing the products or services and the trade or customer discount structure that should be followed;

(iii) next, because it is not only a question of satisfying demand but also of creating or directing it, a large number of promotional decisions (advertising and sales promotion) have to be made; these cover the selection of media to be used, the size, frequency and content of the advertisements, the nature and duration of the sales promotion activities, not to forget the cost of all these and the actual expenditure budgets that will be possible;

(iv) then there are the physical distribution aspects of marketing, especially the depot/inventory questions and the transportation of the finished goods not only at the point of manufacture but also throughout the distribution network;

(v) in addition there are all the selling possibilities to be considered, from the appointment of agents or distributors to any franchising arrangements that may be advisable and any personal selling to be undertaken by the company itself; often dealers and customers alike may have to be educated on the products or services involved, what they can achieve for customers, their sales and profit-earning potentials for distributors and users and for technical products, the various technological factors that should be considered, etc.

(vi) and finally, how all this will be financed; estimates on the return that would be achieved and the after-sales services needed should be considered before the marketing plans can be agreed and launched.

(b) Practical implications

The complex practical implications arising from all these considerations are the subject of the chapters that follow. The scope of marketing will become clearer as the reader progresses through this book. It is because of the impossibility of encapsulating all this into a single concise definition that the following description is preferred to any definition. They represent the eight key points about marketing.

(i) Marketing is a philosophy that believes that a business and its decisions should be governed by its markets or customers rather than by its production or technical facilities.
(ii) It is an orderly, systematic process of business planning, execution and control.
(iii) It requires an improved form of commercial organisation.
(iv) It employs improved methods and systems based on scientific laws drawn from economics, statistics, finance and the behavioural sciences.
(v) It involves a system of commercial intelligence (i.e. relevant information on markets, competitors etc.).
(vi) It places strong emphasis on innovation.
(vii) It is a method for achieving dynamic business strategy.
(viii) It is a form of management by objectives.

All of these have a common purpose – to serve the customers and meet their needs with products or services designed for that purpose. Points (vi) and (vii) are important at all times but are particularly so in times of static or declining demand, or when competition is intensifying. It is only through striving to be innovative and so having a dynamic marketing strategy that a company can survive in such difficult conditions. Without these, a company can be driven to the wall by more aggressive and innovative competitors. It is also true that many of these points apply to other areas of management, which only helps to prove the integrative nature of management and the need for complete co-operation between the different departments.

(c) Marketing is applicable to all enterprises
The significant point that new students of marketing should grasp is that the basic concept of marketing is essential to all types of business. It is not only essential for the manufacture and selling of consumer products but also of industrial products, service industries, state enterprises and even non-profit-making activities. It is undoubtedly vital for all those involved in international marketing, whether just selling abroad items made in the home country or involving multinational operations through wholly owned subsidiaries, partly owned operations and joint ventures or partnerships. It is even necessary for public utilities. The basic marketing operations have to be modified in various ways to suit them to some of the enterprises mentioned above. The **adaptations** have to take into **account**

the special characteristics of such operations but the basic tenets of marketing are not really altered. These points will be discussed in subsequent sections and chapters.

1.6 BASIC MARKETING TECHNIQUES

The techniques normally considered the responsibility of the Marketing Department are listed in Table 1.1. Brief descriptions are given as they are, of course, discussed more fully in the book. However it is worth noting one or two points here.

Some executives are very careless in the way they refer to some of these activities. For example they use the phrase 'marketing research' when they mean 'market research' and *vice versa.* 'Market research' refers to studies of markets while 'marketing research' is the title given to all the researches – excluding technical or engineering studies – which are needed for marketing purposes. It may also be used (e.g. 'we need marketing research') if the executive means that (almost) every facet of the marketing operation needs study. Something may be going wrong or the company may be planning a major change in its operations. Also the phrase 'promotional activity' may be used when only 'advertising' or 'sales promotion' is meant. If 'promotional activity' is mentioned strictly it means all three techniques listed under this heading in Table 1.1. The use of the single word 'promotions' strictly refers only to 'sales promotions'!

1.7 THE MARKETING MIX

Marketing practitioners and academics alike agree that the phrase 'marketing mix' includes all activities involved in moving goods and services from producers to consumers, whether the latter are individuals or corporations. These activities give careful and detailed attention to the 'four Ps'. As Table 1.1 shows, a very large number of such activities exist. However, for most companies, only some of these are relevant and necessary to their business. The art in marketing is to select the most relevant and essential for an operation within the capabilities and cost limitations that apply. The selected items then become the company's marketing mix for their business.

All the functions in the total marketing mix are variable so that the emphasis that management places on any element it is using will change according to circumstances in the company and its markets. For example in difficult trading times the company may find it necessary to conduct more market, demand or consumer research since it needs accurate information on these matters to counter competition more effectively. It cannot afford to make mistakes. In boom times, when companies can sell

(*continued on page 15*)

Table 1.1 **basic marketing technique**

A MARKETING RESEARCH

(i) *Economic research*: study of the economy of a country, region, industry or market – usually concerned with broad studies to establish the basic but key economic and related aspects. The data obtained is, however, quite detailed since these researches are intended to give a good understanding of what is happening in the economy under study.

(ii) *Market research*: a more detailed study of a market, however defined, to identify total demand or volume of business available in the market – usually for all products or services under consideration – how this is declining, growing or changing, the competitors active in the market and their market shares, ruling market prices, factors affecting the market and trends and developments. Usually a more detailed study of a sector of the economy than (i) above, looking in greater depth at key market factors.

(iii) *Demand studies*: a very detailed study in depth of the demand for specified products and services to get a clearer or up-to-date picture of what is happening to demand for the products in question. May also be indicated as necessary by the results obtained from (ii) above which may not be detailed enough for definitive marketing planning, etc.

(iv) *Consumer studies*: detailed study of the buying behaviour, habits, patterns, etc., of specified groups of consumers or customers (see also 'Market Segmentation', Section 6.4) to establish 'consumer profiles', i.e. the critical factors which determine customers' propensity to buy a product or service, what they buy, why they buy it, what use they make of the product, the prices they pay or are prepared to pay, what they buy from competitors, why they buy from them etc.

(v) *Competitor research*: much more detailed study in depth of competitors, what they are doing, what products etc. they are offering, how and why they are successful etc. (i.e. to establish the 'competitor profile'). This is needed if sufficient information is not obtained from (ii), (iii) and (iv) above or if these studies are not needed or are not possible.

(vi) *Product research*: attempts to discover what products or services are required, or being bought by a market, industry, area or type of customer, the specification and performance expected by customers and the price they indicate they would pay for a stated specification. Tries to establish the technical features required including expected life of the product, after-sales or maintained services expected, etc. Helps to decide what the product range of the company should be.

(vii) *Sales research*: study of the pattern and nature of sales for specified products in selected market areas to identify the true sales pattern, how this is changing, etc. Used if critical developments are suspected or when the necessary detailed information is not available via (ii), (iii), (iv) or (v) especially if attempts to obtain this detailed sales information would make these other four studies too long or complicated. Also used to determine how successful the company's sales **operations** are and what modifications or changes are indicated

Table 1.1 (*contd*)

because of changes in customer needs, competition or technological developments.

(viii) *Distribution research*: helps to identify the physical distribution required to counter competition effectively or to give customers a better service. Also checks if the methods being used are achieving these aims within permitted costs. Also helps to show how distribution may be modified to keep costs under control, where to locate depots, the size of depots, size of inventories, method of transportation to be used, whether to own or lease depots, the type of agents to be used, etc.

(ix) *Promotional research*: helps to determine the promotional activities required, the nature and timing of them, etc., and the costs involved. Can cover all the promotional activities or just advertising and sales promotions. Also helps to determine how successful current promotional activities are proving and what changes to them are necessary. Helps with decisions on media selection, nature and timing of promotions and all cost and timing aspects.

(x) *Effectiveness of research*: determines how effective research methods are, whether the best use is being made of developments in research methods, what changes are necessary in the marketing research techniques being used, cost and time factors, etc.

(xi) *Other studies*: it is also necessary sometimes to check on the effectiveness and appropriateness of the packaging and merchandising methods being used, what changes, etc., are necessary. Sometimes *separate pricing studies* are necessary to indicate if present pricing strategies and policies are effective, whether changes are needed to match market developments, how price elastic or price sensitive markets are, etc.

B PROMOTIONAL ACTIVITIES

(i) *Advertising*: described as 'a paid form of promotional activity by an identified sponsor'. Involves media selection and decisions on the size, type or nature of the advertisement, the copy and number of colours to be used, the frequency of the advertisements, etc. All these influence the 'impact' of an advertising campaign.

(ii) *Sales promotions*: special activities, usually conducted over a limited period of time, to boost sales during peak sales periods, to support ailing product or to help launch new products. Activities include: special price reduction, free offers, banded packs, coupons, free gifts and point-of-sale displays with special posters, banners, show cards, etc. For industrial products: catalogues, technical leaflets, trade-in terms, etc., can be used here. Also exhibitions, seminars and conferences are now seen as part of the work of sales promotion.

(iii) *Public relations*: includes press relations, and seeks to keep public and press correctly informed of the company's activities, achievements and future intentions. Usually open days, special lunches and dinners, free editorial in appropriate media are employed. Exhibitions and conferences can also play roles in PR.

Table 1.1 (*contd*)

C PRODUCT MANAGEMENT: involves everything to do with the planning and management of the product (or service) side of a company. The work may be divided into:

(i) *Managing existing products*: maintaining profitability, sales and market shares for successful products; seeking out new customers and applications, especially any markets that may have been overlooked; keeping a watch on prices and costs, etc.

(ii) *Product modification*: when technological or other market conditions change it may be necessary to modify the specification, style or nature of the product or service to prolong its useful, profitable life. In competitive times, modifications may be needed to avoid cost and hence price increases or to reduce them. May be necessary also if the original concept or specification for the product or service proves to be wrong or is not being accepted by customers.

(iii) *Product rationalisation*: technical and market changes may be such as to make it impossible to modify a product, or the cost of modification may be too high in relation to the benefits (profit) which would be obtained. Competitors' new products will also make the company's products obsolete and all products and services eventually reach the end of their profitable life. In these instances, the products concerned have to be removed from the company's product range.

(iv) *New product development*: this is necessary if the company's long-term survival is to be assured and to take over from rationalised products. Also needed when major technological changes have taken place or are forecast and when a company wishes to expand its activities into other areas (technical or market). Involves the search for, assessment, planning and launching of new product/service ideas. When a company intends to move into an entirely new activity involving new technology it is often called *diversification*.

(v) *Pricing and profit management*: involves decisions on the pricing strategy, policy and plans to be followed and monitoring sales and profit results obtained with recommendations on any changes that are necessary. In profit planning, Marketing works with Manufacturing and Finance in agreeing what the company's profit targets should be and any subsequent changes dependent on results obtained (see also Chapter 5).

D MARKET MANAGEMENT: concerned with everything to do with the planning and management of the market side of a company's business activities. Again, this can be divided as follows.

(i) *Managing existing, successful markets*: making sure that operations continue successfully in the selected markets (or market segments) in which the company operates; keeping track of developments concerning customer needs, the effect of changing technology and competition, etc.; ensuring that the marketing activities are achieving optimal results etc.

(ii) *Modifying markets*: the original selection of markets, or more correctly market segments, may not have proved successful; may be necessary

Table 1.1 (*contd*)

to change the market mix by selecting a different category of customer in any given area or segment; or as the company develops, other categories of customer within a market segment can be added to the operations.

(iii) *Market rationalisation*: like products, markets have a finite life; they cease to be profitable or the company cannot exploit them profitably any more. Other factors may make it advisable for the company to withdraw from certain market segments and, usually, put the resources to more profitable use. Market rationalisation is then necessary.

(iv) *New market development*: again, if a company wishes to survive and develop in the long term, new market development is necessary, especially if market rationalisation has been essential. Involves the search for and assessment of possible new markets and the planning and launching of marketing operations into them. (Note also *diversification* in C (iv) above.)

E   SALES MANAGEMENT: responsible for all aspects of the sales activities of the company. Work involves:

 (i) Planning the size, nature and extent of the personal selling operation and the size, location and qualifications of the field sales force.

 (ii) Selecting the administrative and other methods to be used and the size and nature (also the qualifications) of the sales office staff.

(iii) Recruitment, remuneration and training of the members of the sales department, especially the sales force.

(iv) Devising a suitable monitoring service and information system to keep track of results v. plans and so recommending any alterations that may be necessary.

F   PHYSICAL DISTRIBUTION MANAGEMENT: responsible for all activities to do with physical distribution. This includes:

 (i) *Depots*: number, size, location, whether owned or leased;

 (ii) *Inventories and inventory control*: size, maximum and minimum levels, reordering levels, cost of etc.

(iii) *Channels of distribution* to be used: agents, distributors, franchises, etc., and terms of agreements;

(iv) *Transportation*: whether to use own fleet, have annual contracts with suitable transport organisation, or use casual hiring as needed; whether to use road, rail, sea or air transport, etc.

 (v) *Administration*: all administrative matters concerned with above; cost and cost control, insurance, control paperwork, etc.

G   OTHER ACTIVITIES: such as listed below, if and when the company's marketing operations require:

 (i) *Merchandising*

 (ii) *Packaging*

(iii) *Telephone selling*

(iv) *Systems selling*

 (v) *Commando marketing activities*, etc.

which will be discussed more fully later.

all they can make, such precision in information gathering may not be necessary and may represent unnecessary expenditure on research. If the company is selling all it can make, knowing that it could sell more may not be immediately important though it could point the way to short-term development.

Or should the company need more extensive or intensive advertising it may have to raise prices or reduce costs to make the additional funds for this available. If a new technological development makes a substantial or critical portion of its products obsolescent, the company may have to intensify its work in product modification and new product development. Where competition is intense it may be necessary to step up the personal selling activity. In the two last examples mentioned, it may be necessary to cut back on some other marketing activity in order to make available the additional funds needed.

In the case of marketing intangibles such as services (e.g. banking, investment services, tourism or travel facilities) some of the functions shown in Table 1.1 may be only of secondary importance or may not be used at all. There is no universal agreement on how much emphasis should be placed on different marketing activities. In the end a company must thoroughly analyse its own business (markets, products, competition, customers etc.), get to know what is important for success and then select its own 'mix' of marketing activities. By trial and error and careful monitoring of results it will learn, eventually, which 'marketing mix' produces the best, or optimal, results for it, in the long term as well as the short term (see also Section 9.1).

(a) Marketing strategy and policy

The widely held definitions of *strategy* and *policy* draw on the military analogy of *strategy* and *tactics*. Thus, as Professor Igor Ansoff states (*Corporate Strategy*, 8th ed. (Pelican, 1979) p. 105 *et seq*.): 'policy is a contingent decision whereas strategy is a rule for making decisions'. He goes on to state that while implementation of policy can be delegated to middle and lower management levels, implementation of strategy cannot as this will require last minute judgement by top executives (directors etc.). It is this commonly held concept that is followed in this book.

However, strategy can be further sub-classified into *grand or mixed strategy*, a decision rule setting the broad parameters of an operation, business or judgement that has to be made and *pure strategy*, a move or series of moves (e.g. product development programmes) needed to achieve the grand strategy (cf. Ansoff). Grand strategy then is equivalent to the preferred term 'strategy' and pure strategy is equivalent to 'policy'. It is perhaps because of the confusion that can arise if these sub-classifications were used that common practice stays with the original definitions.

Strategy establishes the long-term intentions (objectives and targets) while *policy* specifies the short-term action programmes that will be followed to achieve the strategy. Policies will be altered to counter changes in market factors (economic, competitive, technological political and suchlike) but strategy is usually only altered when some major change has occurred in the business environment or the company is changing course (i.e. moving into a new technology and thus markets and diversifying strongly to ensure the company's survival). *Marketing strategy* is primarily concerned with optimising profit and return on investment, not maximising sales. If there is any conflict between the first two objectives and the third, the first two should normally take precedence. In so doing the critical factor of market shares will come right, as will sales volume. In practice the *marketing policy* followed and hence the marketing mix selected will be a compromise between what is ideal and what is practical. The latter is determined by the constraints of minimum costs and the talents and assets available to the company, of which the most critical is usually money (funds).

In arriving at the best strategy and policy possible, executives must use thorough, scientifically based assessments and judgements of their present and forecasted future. The planning is research based, not the consequence solely of intuition or hunchplay, though these two should not be spurned completely. When information and data are scarce or non-existent, intelligent use of intuition and hunches based on experience, knowledge and past performance in related areas may be the only methods available. In all cases, however, executives must not be too introspective. They must think through their own situations to those of customer and competitor. They must appreciate the marketing strategies and mixes of their major competitors and the managerial concepts and criteria which motivate customers and competitors.

As readers will appreciate now – or later – many variables influence the decisions taken on marketing strategy and policy. They may, however, be classified under five headings or groupings.

(i) *Product strategy and policy*: involve decisions on product range and mix, rationalisation, modification and new product development; these in turn require consideration of product life-cycles, warranties and guarantees and, especially for consumer goods, packaging design, branding and trademarks. The work entails not only consideration of the physical product but also the satisfaction of customer needs.

(ii) *Market strategy and policy*: involves decisions on all aspects of the market mix, market segmentation, new market development and the relationship of these points with the product strategy and policy.

(iii) *Pricing strategy and policy*: involves one of the most difficult decision areas for executives and covers the prices and discounts to be operated, trade terms etc. These are themselves conditioned by cost aspects, the prices that are justified for the specification, performance and other properties of the products or services and selling methods that will be used. The overall aim here is to ensure that the company achieves its *profit targets* and objectives.

(iv) *Promotional strategy and policy*: involves decisions on the personal selling, advertising, sales promotions and PR activities to be followed. While these must be so co-ordinated as to optimise the company's communication with the selected markets and customers, they must also be integrated with all the other marketing activities and hence strategies and policies.

(v) *Physical distribution strategy and policy*: involves all decisions to do with the distribution of the product or service, especially the selection of the marketing channels and methods of distribution to be used.

All five of the above form another way of referring to the marketing mix.

(b) Product-market strategy and policy

As mentioned in the preceding subsection, decisions on product and market strategy and policy are closely interrelated. Some maintain this inter-relationship is irrevocable. In practice it seeks to exploit the concept, unique talents and orientation identified for the company. The company attempts to develop in an integrated form its products and markets. The form that the integration takes will depend on a clear definition and understanding of the company's business and skills.

This approach accepts that greater profit should accrue if products and markets are considered to be indivisible. This needs the sound base provided by correctly set objectives for profit, return on assets, market standing and shares and annual rates of growth for each of these factors. Of course, if any of these are poorly or incorrectly done, the benefits of working to a product-market strategy rather than non-related market and product strategies will not be realised.

All the points above will be discussed in more detail in the chapters that follow. In conclusion it is worth stating that marketing decisions cannot be made in a vacuum or in isolation from each other. It is dangerous to experiment with single variables while assuming that everything else is constant. While the mechanics of writing a book and the limitations of the human brain make it necessary for the subjects of markets and products to be considered in turn, it must be realised that decisions based on these studies must be made in the integrated or interrelated manner that has been stated above.

(c) Development of marketing philosophies

However, it is worth making a brief sketch here of how and why business and economic developments since the Industrial Revolution in the late 1700s made it necessary for company executives to consider the use of marketing in all businesses. In very early times everyone existed in a subsistence economy. The individual family units grew sufficient crops for their own needs. They were, in today's terms, very small smallholders, cultivating meagre plots of land. If they grew more than they needed they would barter the surplus, before the general advent or acceptance of money, for the things they could not grow or make themselves. When money began to be used they would sell their surplus, negotiating prices individually, and use the cash to buy whatever else they needed. As the feudal system developed in Europe, the greater part of the land was owned by the barons and the sovereign. The ordinary people, serfs, worked the land for their masters. Either they were permitted to work small plots in return for military service with their baron, or the bulk of the crop went to the owner of the estate and the peasants were permitted to keep a small amount for their own existence, or they worked just for their keep. The wealth of the country resided with the barons, and the ordinary population, much smaller than in modern times, had no wealth and no real purchasing power.

With the advent of the Industrial Revolution the old system changed, gradually at first and then ever more rapidly as industrialisation progressed. Many more goods, in ever-increasing variety, were produced. People who worked in the factories were paid for their labour and this gave them some purchasing power. As their wages increased so did their ability to purchase an ever-widening choice of goods. As mass production developed and as the population increased, the purchasing power of consumers and the ever-widening choice open to them increased. Demand for all products and the competition between them intensified. As production techniques improved, especially in more recent decades as automation increased, the direct labour content in manufacturing was reduced and the cost savings this achieved was passed on in the form of lower prices. This trend was intensified as automation and other improved techniques led to greater output. The increased earnings of the work-force allowed more people to afford the necessities of life and eventually a life-style in which the psychological needs (e.g. travel, leisure activities, entertainment and numerous services) gained in importance. The need for the more efficient distribution of this ever-widening range of goods and services became apparent.

However, in the earlier days when markets were many and mainly unsatisfied (i.e. demand exceeded supply), products and services enjoyed a seller's market. Businesses were production-orientated. Markets were many, goods were scarce and quite often made to order. The need to 'sell' anything was minimal. As industrial activity intensified throughout the world, markets became less plentiful and goods less scarce. They were made more and more for stock to gain the benefits of large batch or continuous mass production. These stocks had to be sold and the emphasis changed to a 'sales orientation'. As competition increased the need to improve distribution and to use advertising, sales promotion and more effective personal selling led to the need to identify markets, potential customers and their needs, the price they would pay and so on. Thus evolved what we know today as 'marketing'.

As stated, it was the consumer goods area that first identified the need for marketing. However, by the 1950s in most developed countries and some developing ones, unexploited markets for industrial products were less numerous and goods were usually in plentiful supply. The basic problem was to find customers for a company's products. Further, consumers, whether domestic or industrial, became more discriminating and demanding in what they were prepared to buy. In a buyer's market the customer is a force to be reckoned with and has to be prompted, either as an individual consumer or as an institutional or professional buyer in industry, to become a purchaser of any item, whether consumer goods or industrial products.

From the Second World War, countries like Britain who had led the Industrial Revolution found themselves facing even greater competition from newly industrialised nations. The latter invariably had the advantage of cheap labour, sometimes also cheap raw materials and the establishment of new industrial plant. By contrast, many established industrial countries had old plant and steeply rising labour costs. By the 1970s competition in every business activity, including industrial products, had become very severe. The world-wide recession or slump at the end of the 1970s, triggered by huge increases in the price of essential raw materials, especially oil, and fuelled by very substantial wage increases, intensified all the problems. The *ad hoc* manufacture and selling of industrial products, made to the satisfaction of the manufacturer without regard to customer needs, is no longer possible. Whether they like it or not, executives of industrial products companies must accept their need for marketing activities if they are to survive.

1.8 MARKETING AND THE SMALLER COMPANY

Executives in smaller companies may understandably wonder how the concepts mentioned above can be applied in their case without incurring heavy costs. They may be influenced in their thoughts by knowledge of the substantial marketing operations, large expenditure budgets and marketing departments of major industrial groups such as Ford Motor Co.,

General Motors, Shell Oil Co., Exxon/Esso Oil Co., Procter & Gamble, Unilever, British Petroleum, GEC Ltd, ITT, to mention just a few. They may feel that the marketing approach is beyond their means.

In reality, while the marketing activities of such companies are substantial, measured in terms of their total business or turnover, marketing operations are not excessive and costs represent a small percentage of total operating costs and are held within these reasonable bounds. Their marketing departments, while seemingly large to most people in terms of the number of people working in them are only as large as their very complex activities (many products involving several technologies and markets or user industries) require. A large marketing department is only required by a large business.

For smaller companies, the size of the marketing operation must be scaled down to match the needs of the business. Small companies, especially if they are not trying to sell their goods to the mass or national consumer market, will have no need for extensive and costly market or consumer research or demand studies. Its advertising activities can be very limited and selective. It may not need to use sales promotions at all, except to produce catalogues or leaflets on its products and if a special, small new product is in hand, send a few free samples to important customers to try out and report back on their usefulness and so on. The sales force too could be small and carefully selected and dispersed throughout its limited markets. As mentioned in Section 1.7 the art of successful marketing lies in the ability to identify and select only those techniques which are relevant and essential to a business. That is, companies should use only those techniques which improve the profitability of their business and help it to survive and develop over the long term as well as the short term.

The more specialised services could be bought, as needed, from the many sound organisations that now exist to provide these services. This avoids the need to add to overhead costs by trying to have appropriate specialists on the staff. It allows companies to select the specialists who have a good reputation for doing the work needed and who therefore have the experience, skills and knowledge to do it well. (In fact many large companies are now using such outside experts and saving on their own marketing overhead costs.) For example, market research facilities can be bought from appropriate market research consultants. The cost of the work can be charged to pre-taxed income. Even a £50 million group with six companies avoided heavy fixed costs by using research consultants and having just one person at head office to control and supervise all marketing research work.

To apply marketing successfully to a small company, the executives must first develop the frame of mind mentioned earlier in this chapter. This leads them to identify customers and their needs - including potential customers – so that the opportunities open to the company in their selected markets can be perceived. The potential and capabilities of the company can then be matched more precisely to these opportunities.

The executives must recognise that it is of little avail to hanker after a particular market or group of customers if the company's facilities just do not allow it to operate profitably in that area. Nor should they make a superb product for which there is little or no demand. With objective assessments of the markets they could tackle and the total demand involved, they could make appropriate sales plans to capture the market shares they require. They will of course have assessed the strength and skills of the competition they would face. Their marketing and sales plans should of course match their production capacity and cost capabilities. They will then be able to sell their products at prices which will provide the best profit possible.

In estimating market demand the executives may have called in marketing research consultants to help them. If the company is very small, they might also have used other management consultants to set up the necessary organisation, information and control systems, especially accounting systems, records and methods. Once all the donkey work has been done, even the smallest company should be able to keep things running well. Recourse to consultants should only be necessary again if some major change takes place in the market or if the company wishes to change its course or 'business orientation', methods or 'systems'.

Marketing techniques are as relevant to small operations as to large ones. Failure to recognise this will hinder the growth and continued well-being of the small company and may lead to liquidation. The application of these techniques does not necessarily require a major change of staff or organisation. It requires, principally, a change of mind leading to a more objective review of the company, its products, markets and customers. This is particularly important for large and small companies in difficult trading times.

1.9 MARKETING INDUSTRIAL PRODUCTS

Marketing techniques were originally developed for use with consumer goods sold to consumer markets. Probably because of this there was considerable resistance to the use of marketing for industrial products. Even now, several decades later, resistance to the use of marketing techniques in some companies manufacturing industrial products can be encountered. In these cases they hold to the belief that their products or technology or their customers' technical requirements make their business 'unique' in some way and this uniqueness 'saves' them from having to be involved in marketing. The implication is that there is something 'not quite gentlemanly' in the activities normally ascribed to marketing. 'What the consumer goods boys get up to does not concern those of us in the manufacture of industrial products and plant.' All the words in quotes above have featured frequently in arguments against the use of marketing. How wrong the last quote is, in more ways than one, will become clear in the text of this book.

At first glance, there would seem to be many differences involved in the marketing of industrial products, that is, marketing goods and services to industrial users rather than the individual consumer or the consumer markets. However, the marketing principles involved remain the same and so do the basic techniques. The observable difference lies in the blend of marketing mix used. For example, with consumer goods, greater emphasis has to be placed on the persuasion of the individual consumer to buy the goods. That is, greater use is made of advertising, sales promotion, merchandising, distribution and personal selling.

With industrial products and especially technical plant and equipment, emphasis is placed on the technical aspects and performance of the products, the economic contribution they make to the business of the companies buying them and in direct selling. The last usually involves sales people with the appropriate technical training and experience, negotiating contracts, often of substantial value, with other highly skilled professionals who make the buying decisions in the client companies. Whereas a 'consumer sale' to an individual may be small in volume (one or two items) and value, 'industrial sales' are of substantial volume or quantities and are of much greater value. (However, where consumer goods are sold to supermarkets and major chains of stores or shops, sales may involve large contracts of considerable value. In these cases the marketing and selling operations resemble those for industrial goods.) None the less there are some special differences or characteristics of industrial products markets which need to be taken into account and which call for some modification of basic marketing techniques. These are discussed in the sections that follow.

First, though, there is need for a clear statement of what is meant by consumer goods and industrial products marketing. Consumer goods are all those items sold to the ultimate user for personal or household use, usually without further processing (other than the cooking of foodstuffs). Excluding the wholesaling function (where items are bought in quantity) purchases are made in small quantities, sometimes on impulse or by force of habit. The exceptions are consumer durables (cars, washing machines, cookers and other household appliances, television sets and so on) where careful thought is given to cost or price and the suitability of the item for the purpose in mind. This is particularly so during hard economic times. Convenience and emotional factors usually govern decisions on consumer purchases. As almost everyone in a country requires them, nationwide distribution and sales are involved though the use of 'market segmentation' (see Section 6.4) helps to limit the problems encountered here. Generally the distribution and stockholding arrangements are substantial and complex. Channels of distribution (see Chapter 8) are long. Personal tastes and preferences dominate and there are a large number of potential customers.

Industrial products and services are sold to business and institutional buyers including agriculture, central and local government bodies, state or nationalised industries and public utilities for use in some form, in the conduct of their business. In this category are included raw materials, fabricated materials, components, other semi-manufacturers, capital goods, machinery, building supplies, consumables (items used in manufacturing processes such as greases, oils, cleaning materials etc.) and industrial services (e.g. repair, maintenance etc.). However, some basically consumer goods may also be purchased by industry. For example a small table may be bought not only by consumers and commercial organisations such as offices, schools, canteens, but also by industrial companies. While for the first-mentioned organisations marketing will follow the pattern used in consumer markets, where the tables are bought by industry or on bulk contract, the marketing methods can be similar to those used for normal industrial sales. In such cases it is the method of purchase (individual, small-volume sales v. large-volume contract sales) which determines the method of marketing used. Now let us consider the special characteristics of industrial markets.

(a) Derived demand

The demand for industrial products is said to be derived in nature since it depends on the demand for the end-product or service to which it makes some contribution. Because one product may be sold to different industries this derived demand will have many facets. Further, while most manufacturing companies buy a product for the economic contribution it makes to their business (e.g. saves them from having to invest capital and labour in making the product themselves, enhances the saleability of their own end-product, etc.) others may buy for social or political reasons. For example a local authority may build a new school and 'buy' all the items needed for this and to equip it. It is however primarily concerned with the social aspect of enhancing the educational facilities in its area. The central government may build a new motorway. In this case it is concerned with economic, social and political considerations. The first should help to improve the infrastructure of the economy by contributing better communications and hence distribution facilities. The social aspects may lie in the removal of traffic congestion from the area. The political aspects include the enhancement of the reputation and so on of the ruling party in the eyes of the electorate.

Consider also the case of the manufacturer of a plasticiser needed for the manufacture of some plastics. The plastics may be used by many users. One may use it in the manufacture of a circuit unit that fits into a computer or television set. The ultimate users of the computer or television set may have no idea what plasticiser has been used in the plastic making up the components of the finished article – and they may not care! Yet on the success of the plasticiser in use may depend the correct functioning of the plastic on which the circuit is mounted and hence the circuit itself and the computer or television set using the latter. It could be helpful for the plasticiser manufacturer to be able to discuss matters with the ultimate users. However, it can be appreciated that this is not possible, the lines of communication are too long and anyway the final user is not very aware about the plasticiser, its properties and performance.

In addition a high stable demand for the end-product, in this case the computer or television set, does not necessarily mean there will be a corresponding demand for the plasticiser. The plastics manufacturer may decide, for technical reasons, to use something else or the manufacturing process may change. In other cases, if government policies restrict consumer or user demand (accidentally or deliberately!), manufacturers of these goods may reduce the size and frequency of their orders for the raw materials, components or capital equipment they need for their business. In some instances, replacement or renewal of capital equipment may be deferred. Thus, if the plant was due for replacement say every seven years, but orders were deferred for say three years, the replacement period or life of the plant would be extended by nearly fifty per cent. This would have a serious effect on total demand for the equipment, reducing it substantially. Thus demand for any individual item may become unstable or at least difficult to predict.

(b) Value and frequency of orders

The purchasing officers with manufacturing companies are highly trained professionals, often with degrees in economics and other appropriate subjects. They are aware that buying items at the most advantageous terms requires them to place substantial orders at the right times. The size of the order depends on the economic situations at the time but it means, almost invariably, that individual orders are of substantial quantity and value. Further they know they must keep the inventory (stocks) of bought-in items to certain specified levels. To exceed them is costly for the company. Falling below minimum levels might disrupt production. So they have to match the timing of their orders with their company's production plans and level of inventories at the time. This means that orders will be carefully timed and with the need to buy as economically as possible will occur less frequently than impulse buying by individual consumers.

The sum total of these and other factors means not only that orders for industrial products, and especially capital equipment, are of greater value and occur at less frequent times than orders for consumer goods but also that forecasting demand and the pattern of sales (how sales will occur during a year) can be more difficult. The first point also makes each order for industrial products more important to the sellers. Miss an order and there may be a long wait for the next. In bad economic times this can adversely affect the cash flow and liquidity of the selling organisation. It is this fear of losing an order that may be one of the main reasons why prices for industrial products tend to approach the lowest possible level. (Intensifying competition is another. Pricing aspects are discussed more fully in Chapter 5.)

(c) Market definition

Theoretically it is easier to define markets for industrial products than consumer goods. In the latter case, everyone in a country is a potential customer and finding who are the real customers can be a major market research and statistical exercise. In the former case, industrial customers for any given product are much more limited in number. Further, as industries tend to group themselves in fairly easily identified geographical areas, usually near the major sources of supply for their essential materials, it is not too difficult to decide the geographical location of potential markets. (In recent decades in Britain the movement of companies to development areas and so on has led to industries being more widely spread than before but it is still easy to identify their general geographical locations.)

However, most industrial products are sold to users in several industries. Deciding which industries are potential users of a product or how and why some are using the product calls for considerable knowledge of a wide range of technologies. Market research and demand forecasting, if they are to be well done, call for considerable knowledge on the part of marketing executives and their manufacturing department colleagues. In addition, since a larger proportion of total demand resides in the hands of a limited number of firms, one wrong answer (deliberate or accidental) in the course of a demand study can produce disproportionately misleading or incorrect results. So defining a market may seem easy but in fact there are many pit-falls for the inexperienced and unwary.

(d) Technical factors

Obviously technical factors predominate in the marketing of industrial products. Potential users require considerable and detailed information on the specification, performance, expected life, quality and reliability of the product. They will also need information on maintenance needs and especially the assurance that between maintenance times the product will function properly. Also maintenance should not be too frequently needed. Thus while price is still an important consideration, it concedes precedence to technical factors.

Since the technical aspects and performance of an industrial product are of chief importance, potential customers will not normally respond to the type of advertising and selling used for consumer goods. They are not persuaded by general blandishments containing vague statements and claims which cannot be proved or disproved conclusively. They are interested in hard facts. Direct personal selling, involving detailed discussion of important technical aspects, is required instead. The more technical the product, the longer will the negotiations take. Where the new equipment has to be tested and approved (as with oil refining plant) the negotiations may take years.

(e) Buying motives

Impulse buying of consumer goods is said to be based on irrational motives. Decisions which are influenced by personal tastes, preferences, likes, dislikes and prejudices, not supported by fact or reality, are irrational decisions. On the other hand, since buying decisions for industrial products are based on technology, performance and hard economic facts, they are said to be rational. In fact when there is more than one product available, all of which could do the job in mind equally well and at competitive costs, the final buying decisions as to which product to buy could be based on irrational considerations. The group, or purchasing officer, making the final decisions may prefer one supplier over another. This may be because years previously the preferred company had helped out the buying organisation, when the latter was in difficulties. The fact that the supplier may not be in a position to do so again may not be realised. A buying decision exercising this preference is irrational. Or the purchasing officer may prefer one salesman to another for no real reason. Then if the former decides to place the order with the person he prefers that decision is also irrational. (If the two or more products under study are *not* equal as regards key economic, cost, technical and performance details, a decision not to take the best available product could be judged to be irrational.)

Buying motives can be classified under two headings.

(i) *Company patronage motives*: these vary for different categories of products but all are the result of cost-benefit considerations in relation to the efficiency and profitability of the buyer's own operations.

(ii) *Product patronage motives*: these vary with the class or type of buyer, but again cost-benefit considerations feature.

Figure 1.1 lists the principle motives involved under these headings for different categories of industrial products.

Fig 1.1 *buying motives for industrial products*

PRODUCT GP / MOTIVE GP	CAPITAL EQUIPMENT	RAW MATERIALS COMPONENTS & SUPPLIES
COMPANY PATRONAGE MOTIVES	performance after-sales service past experience of sellers general reliability of sellers credit facilities price	quality delivery reliability ease of access to supplier (communications & physical distribution), price & terms ability of seller to meet any emergency performance
PRODUCT PATRONAGE MOTIVES	economy of operation and productivity reliability – related to eqpt, the company and its services durability and labour-saving aspects of the equipment credit terms and facilities price	suitability reliability and uniformity of quality reliability of supplier, especially delivery degree to which the purchased item enhances the saleability of the end product price

Awareness of what are the primary motives and the order of priority assigned to them by major customers helps executives marketing industrial products to plan their operations with greater precision. Note that price often has a low priority. In the case of high technology products, technical factors, especially performance, reliability and output (where relevant) will usually be judged by potential buyers as being of supreme importance.

(f) Channels of distribution

In the case of consumer goods selling to a substantial part of a total, national market, the distribution system has to be an extensive one. Several of the many channels of distribution (see Chapter 8) may have to be used. The manufacturer is often at several removes from the ultimate customer and must depend on information obtained second, third and even fourth hand from the various 'middlemen' involved in the distribution network. Various forms of marketing research will be advisable from time to time to supplement and verify the information received in this remote way. (The sales force can also help here: see Chapter 7.)

In contrast, the channels of distribution for industrial products can be less complicated. While the general purpose industrial products of low unit price, no great technical content, used by almost everyone (e.g. hand tools, screws, nails, paints etc.) often require almost as widespread and complicated a network as consumer goods, the more technical a product the more direct is the distribution. In these cases delivery is often direct from the manufacturer to the customer. However, in recent years as distribution costs increased more use has been made of area agents and other distributors and even franchisees (see Chapter 8). The high technology product continues to be sold, distributed and serviced by the manufacturer. Agents cannot normally be expected to have the necessary expertise and to afford the high overheads that would be involved. In the case of overseas markets, if the manufacturer does not have its own or jointly owned subsidiary in them, whether this is a marketing, assembly and marketing, or manufacturing and marketing facility, then the use of overseas agents is unavoidable. These agents must, however, have the necessary technical skills and experience, as well as the contacts, to handle the business efficiently and profitably for everyone (see Chapter 9).

(g) Buying decisions

With consumer goods the buying decision is often taken by the individual consumer. Where goods are bought in bulk on contract by wholesalers, supermarkets and other chains, the buying decision may be taken by a professional 'buyer' or a group of executives responsible for the purchasing decisions. With low-cost, non-technical industrial products used widely, the same may apply. However with technical products the buying decisions will depend on a group of executives as well as the purchasing officer. The greater the cost of the product, the greater its importance to the potential buyer's business, and the more technical the product is, the larger will be the number of executives involved in the purchasing decision. The technical departments as well as manufacturing, perhaps even at director level, will want a say in the decision. So will the financial director. For decisions concerning vital or substantial plant the chief executive might also be involved. The purchasing officer may then be primarily concerned with carrying out the decision of the group.

The greater the technical content of a product the longer will be the time required to arrive at a buying decision. The development of a new product from its original idea will also take longer, the more so if there are several tricky technological points to be handled. Finally, the replacement of a technical product may not depend solely or entirely on the life of the product. All the associated economic factors will have effect, either in hastening or retarding the replacement of the original item. It should be clear that there are obvious dangers for suppliers who do not maintain close contact with their customers.

(h) Why the marketing of industrial products can fail

Marketing operations for industrial products can fail for the same reasons as those for consumer goods (see Section 1.4). In addition failure can arise if the basic marketing techniques are used in their original form, designed for consumer goods and not adapted to the special circumstances of the industrial product in question. Using consumer goods marketing methods *per se* is folly and will involve unnecessary expense. For example indulging in full-scale consumer studies and the full panoply of consumer advertising and sales promotions will incur heavy and unnecessary costs. As mentioned already, careful selection and modification of marketing techniques relevant to the task in hand is what is needed.

In addition the marketing plans may be badly done, lack precision and commitment without any firm statement of objectives and targets. Perhaps it is because executives in industrial products companies have not taken the trouble to study the subject carefully that the greatest misunderstanding about marketing arises. Thus they do not always appreciate what the various techniques are, what they can do and what they cannot achieve.

(Readers wishing to study this subject in greater detail should turn to specialist books on the subject or Chapter 8, Section 8.7 in one of the other books by this author: *Planning for Products and Markets* (Longman, 1972).)

1.10 SOME CASE ILLUSTRATIONS

The following brief case illustrations will show what accepting the marketing concept can mean in practice.

(a) Eastman Kodak

Eastman Kodak (of which Kodak Ltd is the British subsidiary) discovered in the 1950s that the popular hobby of photography did not appeal to everyone. A substantial proportion of the consumers in Western industrialised nations (in the United States of America it was said to be 50 per cent) were not taking any photographs at all. Market research showed that while most people wanted to record keystone events in their lives (e.g. the new baby and the baby's early years, other happy or important family events and so on) they found the technical knowledge needed to handle the cameras of the day and the various computations of settings involved, too much for them. Eighty per cent of the people researched in America were only interested in the contents of the pictures. A mere 20 per cent only showed any interest in the quality of the photography.

The cameras of the time, besides requiring somewhat complex manipulations of various settings, were cumbersome and not easy to load with film. Much film could be spoilt in the loading and unloading procedure, and if it was not properly loaded difficulties with winding on the film could be encountered, leading to partial or total double exposures and even the loss of the whole roll. Even the famed 'Brownie' was not trouble-free. Further, the bulk of the company's products were meant for the 20 per cent who were interested in quality photography.

Kodak began a long-range programme to simplify the technology and so expand its photography markets. It was realised that as design engineers and other specialists on their staff would encounter few problems in setting the cameras and threading the film through them, their ideas of product simplification would not match those of the potential user or customer. Task forces made up of a mixture of technical and non-technical staff members of the company were set up. They defined the types of products needed to make photography popular. Simplifying the loading and unloading procedure seemed the right place to start. The design of the drop-in cartridge which eliminated the two major problems of unloading and loading film rolls was a good starting-point.

Studies then began on a complete line of cameras that would appeal to the ordinary consumer. These included consumer studies. Emphasis was placed on reducing the number of settings needed and simplifying the procedures so that the user virtually had little more to do than aim the camera and take the snap. Prototype models were made and subjected to exhaustive laboratory tests. Several thousand were loaned to employees to see how the cameras performed in typical family conditions. The result was that decisions could be taken on the product range and market mix that would form the basis of the new operations. They were able to formalise and agree on their new product-market strategy and all the policies that flowed from it.

Thus the company had set out to give customers what they wanted. This not only increased sales and profits but also helped to make photography a fast-growing hobby, in America first, then Europe and eventually almost around the world through the Instamatic camera which was first marketed in 1963. Since then there has been a continuous stream of products designed to meet consumer needs. These ranged to the fully automatic Instamatic and other cameras and a cine-camera that used a cartridge film rather than the reversible film reel. Other developments included the flash cube that did away with individual flash bulbs and all the associated fumbling, to pocket Instamatics (including fully automatic versions) and a cartridge-loading single lens reflex camera. The company also maintains direct contact with the consumer through its customer service department. This department gets many thousands of letters a year from consumers and potential users.

(b) Two British pottery companies

Finally, consider the cases of two rival British pottery companies, founded in the nineteenth century and making near identical ranges of household crockery of all kinds. For obvious reasons they will be referred to as 'Company A' and 'Company B'. To simplify the cases only one part of their product range will be considered – egg-cups!

Company A produced a wide range of egg-cups, about five hundred items in china, porcelain and wood. There were various design but they were all in subdued colours and patterns then favoured by the British home market. The permutations totalled a staggering two thousand or so! The heights of the egg-cups ranged from three to six inches, the ones in wood being the tallest. All the internal diameters were the same, being about one and three-quarter inches, and this never varied. It was judged, in 1820, to be right for the average British egg, which corresponded to the average size of 'standard' eggs (now about the European Common Market – EEC – Size 3). It was a bit too small for the 'large' egg (EEC Sizes 1 and 2) and too large for the 'small' eggs (EEC Size 4 and smaller). It was certainly too big for the eggs laid by most overseas hens or pullets.

The company's product range had grown for various reasons. About 20 per cent of the range existed because the founder and his heirs just felt they would like to produce egg-cups in a particular colour or style. About another 20 per cent came into being because someone, somewhere, wanted such a design. They were incorporated into the company's range and remained even when demand for them had declined. In some instances the company had more than two years' of stock at the then current rate of sales. The majority of the remainder of relative recent vintage were produced initially for 'special offers' or 'free offers' for magazines, cereals and other food manufacturers. Although demand had been substantial during the initial period of the offer, it had declined and they were slow-moving lines. Stocks were building up on the shelves.

Company A's business for the first century of its existence was con-fined to the United Kingdom, but in the early 1900s sales began to British

Empire territories. They held an almost monopolistic position in these countries for some years although their egg-cups were far too large for the local eggs. The latter when placed in the cups could hardly be seen. Nevertheless the company took the view that their standard diameter could not be changed for these markets. 'Production problems' would arise it was claimed vaguely.

After the Second World War competition increased from other British companies and from Germany and Japan. These new competitors offered egg-cups of the right size and in the designs and colours favoured by these overseas markets. Within four years A's business had fallen from about 90 per cent of the total in these British territories to less than 50 per cent. In the late 1950s, after these countries had gained independence, the company's market shares fell to below 10 per cent. Despite this, Company A still spent a lot of time, effort and money trying to sell their existing egg-cups to these former 'British Raj' territories and their business had run at a loss since the late 1950s. *Company A was NOT a marketing-orientated company.*

Company B was formed in the late nineteenth century but developed to its present organisation by amalgamation with a number of smaller companies in the early 1930s. By the end of the Second World War it also had a range of 500 egg-cups in as many varieties as Company A and in the same standard size. In 1950 the new chief executive realised that market and other conditions were changing, national pride and preferences were ascendant and competition was increasing. He realised that traditional markets would not remain 'loyal' if they could obtain a better product at competitive prices from other suppliers.

He commissioned market research studies in the twelve overseas markets selected as being ones worth developing. The remaining thirty-eight (like Company A, this firm had dealt with about fifty overseas markets) were to be served via Agents on an order-by-order basis. The potential business of these thirty-eight markets was deemed to be too small to make them profitable by any other approach. Exclusive agencies were abolished, and in these markets the company made it known it would accept orders from anyone provided they met certain essential criteria that made them viable. For small orders additional handling charges would be levied. The money saved from this rationalisation of markets would be put behind the marketing effort in the parts of the world in which the company would operate in future.

A study was made, concurrently, of the company's product range. Each product was graded in terms of total sales, area of sales, costs incurred and profit earned. From this it was found that about 80 per cent of the company's profit was earned by about 20 per cent of its products. The remaining 20 per cent of profit was earned by about another 20 per cent of the products. The remainder (60 per cent) of the products were not really making any profit and most were making very substantial losses. At the same time manufacturing and finance executives were making an internal audit of the company to assess its capabilities. Ways of improving productivity and profitability were studied. These studies also confirmed that the initial selection of about twelve overseas markets was right since they took mainly the 40 per cent of the product range that was proving profitable. The market research studies, which covered the United Kingdom towards the end, also indicated what the potential profit was likely to be. They indicated what the competitive position would be and what size, shape, colour and designs of egg-cups were required by each market. The estimated sales potential was also recorded.

From all this Company B was able to estimate what market shares were possible, the profit that could be made and the product ranges to be offered for each of the selected markets. The resultant figures showed that the business could be made viable. The estimated targets were also in accord with the growth targets that had to be achieved over the next five years. The board considered the improvements in earnings per share and net worth would be acceptable to the company's shareholders. They would also help to attract the additional capital the company would eventually need to finance future expansion.

From the plans prepared from the findings of the market research and other studies the company was able to launch out on the major rationalisation of its business, similar studies having been made on the rest of its product range. They were not confined only to egg-cups. Unprofitable products and those not required were carefully phased out over a period of years. (Some unprofitable products had to be maintained for various reasons which are explained fully in Chapter 5.) Marketing activity were restricted mostly to the markets indicated as offering the best potential. Costs and prices were reviewed and altered to match market and other needs. The company grew and prospered and it managed to win business from its competitors. A much more dynamic, productive and profitable operation was achieved. In five years profit and return on assets had been doubled although sales volume had increased by only 50 per cent from pre-reorganisation days. *Company B was definitely a marketing-orientated company.*

It was interested in finding out what the markets wanted and then set out to try to satisfy these demands to the best of its ability and make the necessary profit. In a low-cost business with flexible production facilities, the company could be more selective about its markets and had a greater ability to match consumer needs without heavy capital expenditure. If heavy new investment had been necessary which it could not have afforded, some compromise solution would have had to be found.

The first compromise might have been to scale down its business much more by reducing its product-market mix considerably. (This is often referred to as 'contraction'.) In this it would have gone only for those egg-cups (and other products) offering the best profit and market potential in a limited number of markets. Or it could have tried to maintain its size and volume of business by seeking contracts from other, more general, crockery manufacturers. The worst compromise would have been to have gone into voluntary liquidation if the other possibilities had proved non-viable. To go into liquidation while the business is still profitable, or to sell out to another manufacturer, perhaps one who is diversifying from its own traditional, non-pottery business, ensures a better price and payout for shareholders.

1.11 VIGILANCE

Executives who keep themselves informed of changes and developments in their own business environment and that of customers should receive ample warning of the need for changes. They should not get caught as Company A in Section 1.10 did. With the availability of computers (large, mini- and micro-), collating the raw data and simulating possible outcomes is no longer the arduous and time-consuming task it was. The price for sustained success is eternal vigilance.

ASSIGNMENTS

1 Your company has decided to introduce the marketing concept into its business activities. You are assigned to carry out this work and are sent away on a three-week 'crash' course on marketing. On your return you are instructed to present a paper to the Board on the changes that would have to be introduced, the techniques that are relevant to the business and the basic approach that should be followed for (a) a division producing mass-market consumer goods and (b) another producing large batch production industrial products. Prepare such a paper.

2 You are a marketing consultant and have been called in by a company that has been using marketing for only four years. It makes consumer goods. Its promotional activities do not appear to be proving too successful. You are asked to advise on the promotional activities they should be using and discover the reasons why current efforts seem to be going wrong. What would be your advice?

3 As marketing manager you are far from happy at the sales and other results being obtained. Your director is equally unhappy and instructs you to produce a report highlighting what is going wrong and recommending corrective measures.

THE FIRM AND ITS

MARKETS

The marketing concept discussed in the last chapter emphasises the close, but often changing, relationship between the firm and the markets it seeks to serve. This applies to both the private and public sectors. The nature of the relationship depends on various market (or environmental) factors. Consideration must be given to the market economy, the society comprising the markets, the laws and ethics of society, the competitive situation, the social responsibilities of the business, human resources available, inflation and unemployment. The rates of change occurring in all these affect the volatile nature of the relationship. Further, when economic times are hard, attitudes change often unpredictably. Political factors accentuate the change in these relationships. The Western world has been savagely exposed to these truths in the late 1970s and it looks as if they will spill over into at least the first half of the 1980s. The key aspects are discussed in the sections that follow and are summarised in Section 2.9(a).

2.1 BUSINESS AND SOCIETY

From the Industrial Revolution to the end of the Second World War developments in industry, science, technology, transport and communications all appeared to support each other. They added to the general wealth of the world, or at least of the industralised nations. The net result also appeared to be beneficial to society at large. Even if the increased wealth was unevenly distributed and a minority remained at subsistence level, the majority, to differing degrees in different countries, achieved improving levels of wealth often undreamed of by earlier generations. The optimistic view was held that the intelligent application of human endeavour, knowledge and skills would maintain this growth in wealth and happiness. It seemed that all problems could be overcome. The expectations and quality of life seemed to improve in every decade, helped along by technological and other developments and discoveries. There was no reason why growth, in all its meanings, should not continue indefinitely.

The social developments stemming from the above demanded that growth and innovation should be continued. There was hope, if not belief, that continued progress would eventually eliminate the poverty and squalor that still remained. These views rested on the belief that business could provide a never-ending stream of goods and services. Improving educational standards would create new wealth through the creation of greater knowledge. This would solve economic and social problems and would lead to a better understanding of the human environment. Greater knowledge of human behaviour would extend these benefits to an ever-increasing number of the world's population. Competition would not only help to create this new wealth but would also direct it in the right direction and distribute it in a just pattern.

Since the Second World War these concepts have been seen to be somewhat naïve. Economic and technological growth and developments do not necessarily lead to an even spread of increasing wealth and well-being. Competition weeds out the inefficient firm, if slowly, especially if governments support inefficient enterprises 'in the national interest' by financial and other interventions. For the successful firms, growth can lead to the creation of very large organisations and this makes it difficult for lesser competitors to survive. Better education, growth, scientific and technological developments do not always lead to the solution of economic problems. They can also add to the pollution and destruction of the environment. Also, better education has shifted interest and desire away from materialistic ends to more psychological aims, so that personal values changed. As the 1970s showed, all these great developments can lead to greater social conflict. A study of economics will show how and why this is so. Students of marketing must appreciate the basic facts for they indicate that the original or traditional approach to their subject needs revision.

(a) Economic systems

Economics may be described, simply, as the social mechanism concerned with the many aspects associated with production and distribution. It is an important area for study since all societies, of affluent, developed and poor, developing nations, face a scarcity of important resources (money, skilled labour, raw materials, land, food). There are insufficient resources to satisfy all needs. The resources are finite while wants are infinite. This then is the basic economic problem facing all societies.

The executives in all enterprises have the task of making optimal use of scarce resources to satisfy the maximum number of consumer needs. Marketing is concerned with linking consumers to companies so that the latter can make correct decisions about the goods and services to be produced to satisfy customer needs, or wants. The firm as a whole has to decide what products or services should be produced, the quantities that should be made available, how they should be provided to maximise profitability and consumer satisfaction and how the output should be shared between the total number of markets (customers) that desire them.

Economics is also described as a 'social science'. The use of the word 'science' indicates that economists try to identify and measure scientifically the important relationships between the many factors at play in the economic system. However, these relationships are so complex that their exact nature cannot always be clearly identified. They also vary according to the economic conditions prevailing at any time and the nature of the business and markets concerned.

Controlled experiments are not always possible as in the physical sciences since economics involves people acting individually or in groups. While human behaviour can be generalised into various categories according to the backgrounds, expectations and status of different groups of people, such behaviour even within a group can vary considerably. The *science* of economics is, in many cases, the *art* of estimating correctly variable behaviour patterns. Further, these patterns have the habit of changing, sometimes for understandable reasons (e.g. inflation or deflation) but often for reasons more associated with changes of personal whim.

In practice, therefore, economic decisions cannot be free of subjective judgements and cannot depend only on objective appraisal of relevant facts. Often these 'facts' are unknown and their interrelationships still subject to much conjecture and argument. They rely quite often on personal views of intervening factors. An example of the last point is the size the public sector of an economy should be. Another is the degree of government intervention (or interference, depending on personal political outlook) there should be in a nation's business activity. In Britain a mixed economy (private and state enterprises) is usually considered to be best though by the 1980s a Conservative party government has put the emphasis on the private sector and seeks to reduce the size of the public sector. Socialist governments seek greater state involvement with more widespread nationalisation. India, on the other hand, gives strong emphasis to state-owned industrial activity, permitting private sector involvement usually only where the capital and skills required are beyond the nation's resources. Communist countries are totally committed to state ownership, though by the late 1970s there had been some minor relaxations in limited areas and more emphasis was placed on the need to make profit. Yugoslavia, Romania and to a lesser extent, China, are other examples that come to mind.

However, economists try to establish as objectively as possible the principles which under given conditions show how an economy should work. From this they try to predict the likely outcomes of specified policies. The inexactitude of the art is indicated, however, by the many instances when the outcomes do not match the predictions too closely. Decision-makers can thus be understood for brushing aside such theories, especially if the predictions are based too much on assumptions rather than accepted facts. They may also place different weights (importance) on the assumptions depending on the type and nature of their businesses and customers.

(i) *Free enterprise (private sector) economies*
This is where economic decisions are taken through the mechanism of the market-place, through the free operation of the forces of supply and demand. Two examples are the United States of America and Japan. Such economies may be more accurately described as 'capitalist' rather than 'free enterprise' when they are dominated by monopolistic organisations.

(ii) *Collectivist (public sector) economies*
Here all business activity is state owned or controlled. Decisions are taken collectively by the central government or its appointed agencies such as state planning committees. These are seen at their fullest extent in Communist countries such as the USSR, China and, in recent decades, Cuba. Many developing countries, especially in Africa, are tending to this path for political reasons or because resources are in very short supply. Scarcity is a very limiting factor and if the basic needs of the country are to be met in some balanced form, however imperfect, state control is unavoidable.

(iii) *The mixed economy*
As stated, this is the system of the moment in Britain and other countries of Western Europe and some in Asia and Africa. While government involvement is unavoidable in key activities (defence industries, public utilities and raw material producers such as coal-mining) activity is divided between private and state enterprises. The most successful country under this system is believed to be Sweden, which enjoys one of the highest standards of living. It is argued that a mixed economy gives a country the best of both worlds.

The above is a thumbnail sketch of a very big and complex subject. Like all such it is imperfect and subject to argument. Readers wishing to study this subject in greater depth should turn to a companion volume in this series, *Mastering Economics* by J. Harvey (Macmillan, 1982). Chapters 1 and 2 are of particular interest to marketing students.

(b) Business, society and the economy
The meaning of the term 'business enterprise' changes as the character and structure of the economy, its markets and the social expectations of the role of business change. The practical relationship between firms and their markets will then be modified. This fact must be appreciated by executives

since changes in corporate plans and operations will be necessary if the sustained success and survival of the company is to be ensured.

Society itself is an economic organisation. Firms play active roles in society by reacting to the opportunities and constraints facing them. Executives controlling successful enterprises see these as being determined by the character of the society in which they operate. Governments also respond to this character by their policies and actions. If they sense that society wants more government involvement in constraining business activity (often claimed to be 'for the common good') they will initiate suitable policies. If they think the majority require more free enterprise they will change their policies, if sometimes reluctantly. If business flags for any reason and this is seen as a threat to national prosperity, governments are compelled to remove or alleviate the obstacles facing the business community. Generally governments, according to their political dogma, will adopt policies they believe will create an environment in which business could flourish. The fact that these policies may often have the reverse effect may be due to misreading of the economic and social conditions or lack of knowledge of the relationships actually at play. Sometimes, too, it may be due to the government being blinded by the extremes of its own political dogma.

Executives must formulate their company's policies bearing these points in mind. All have bearing on the correct business strategies that should be applied. They must be aware of the role their business plays in society. This seems obvious in cold print. In practice it is much more difficult to implement because of imperfect knowledge of all these factors. The assumptions that may then be necessary are difficult to perceive accurately.

(c) Social responsibilities of business

In the last decade or so there has been growing awareness that businesses of all sorts have various social responsibilities they cannot ignore. These range from codes of conduct to the ethics of what they do, efficient utilisation of scarce resources, pollution and destruction of the environment and fair trading. While these may be ignored in the short term, in the long term public opinion and action could prove very harmful to the firm's prosperity and survival. The growing unease in this area will one day play a major role in modifying the business policies of firms.

At the moment little impact on policy formulation is evident. Strangely, the little evidence that is available arises from large international or multinational corporations. This is perhaps because the latter have to take account of the political attitudes in the host countries, especially those providing vital raw materials. The best example of recent times is the change in policies which the major oil corporations have had to make as a result of political and price pressures from OPEC countries.

One reason why the social responsibilities of business have received scant attention is the lack of interest of senior executives. Another inhibiting factor has been the growing acceptance of concepts proposed by Professor Milton Friedman. The kernel of these concepts is: 'the social responsibility of business is to increase its profits so long as it stays within the rules of the game, which is to say engages in open and free competition without fraud or deception'. But who sets the rules? If they are set by executives who ignore the points mentioned in the opening sentences of this subsection, or who are ignorant of them, what then of the future for society and the world at large?

Further, who decides where the community's interests lie? What constitutes social progress and responsibility? The larger firms become, the more immune they are to calls for the protection of society and the many disadvantaged people. It is hoped that as the debates continue a consensus will emerge, even if this is prompted by self-interest, that will appreciate what damage can be done to the environment and society by unbridled drives for profit. It is hoped that this realisation will not be too late in coming, before humanity launches itself on a path of no return leading to the destruction of the environment.

2.2 BUSINESS AND COMPETITION

Executives cannot ignore the competitive situation. They risk running into increasing difficulties and court disaster if they do. Yet many executives tend to pursue their own personal goals and these seldom coincide with profit optimisation. Competition occurs at all operational levels of business and in all functional areas. Two companies manufacturing the same type of product will compete in terms of design or formulation or specification, quality, sales, advertising, delivery, merchandising, packaging and price. However, while price is too often considered the prime competitive weapon, non-price competition can be more important. This is very true for products where quality, appearance and taste are considered important criteria by customers. Note from Figure 1.1 the low rating of price for industrial products where the dominant criteria are usually technical points.

Competition is both *intra-industry* (i.e. between firms in the same industry) and *inter-industry* (between companies in different industries). In present-day conditions, as competition increased nationally and internationally, labour and raw material costs rose steeply and companies diversified into new activities and technologies prompted by major technological advances, inter-industry competition has intensified. As standards of living and consumers' ideas on the quality of life improved so both forms of competition increased.

Competition is not now restricted to similar or near-substitute products. For example exotic holidays in distant lands now compete with other household purchases. The purchase of a better house competes, for a time, with the purchase of household appliances or a new car. Providing the children with a better education, which usually means expensive, private schooling, may compete with all other purchases if it takes all the family's discretionary income. These are just a few examples but they suffice to stress that business survival and profits in a free market or capitalist economy are not guaranteed by an economic system based on the survival of the fittest.

(a) Competition and marketing

To people not in business competition may be just a word. To those in marketing it represents a matter of business life or death. It is a basic life-style of free market economies and has many dimensions (economic, legal, ethical, psychological and political (see Sections 2.9(a) and 6.8). It is more intense in a consumer-based economy than in the planned and controlled environment of Communist countries.

Competition emphasises changing profit opportunities and stresses the need for greater innovation, especially in relation to the differential advantages in a firm's markets. It enhances the primacy of objectives, planning and innovation on a continuous basis so that a firm's offerings to its markets can be adjusted to match the changing competitive situation. It should stimulate the development of new products and services, new applications and markets and technological advances. In these situations promotional activities, personal selling, merchandising, packaging and price are all competitive weapons to be used by any firm.

In thinking of competition, executives often think only of the past and they may have mathematical models based on past experience. Little attention may be given to developments and trends taking place. Thus their decisions may not be relevant to the situations evolving around their business. The trouble is that competition, especially price competition for consumer goods, is often obscured. It is obscured by the use of varying pack sizes, discounts, service variations, special offers and the availability of various brands with minor variations in formulation or specification. The buyer's decisions must therefore encompass a large variety of factors.

2.3 THEORY OF BUSINESS STRATEGY AND POLICY

Deciding what business strategy and policy to follow involves executives in a detailed study of all the above points. Unfortunately while senior management does this, middle and junior executives are usually preoccupied with their own tiny bit of the operation. They fail to view the activities of their firm as a corporate whole. They tend not to give any thought either to the wider implications for society of what they do. While the development of *corporate planning* (see Chapter 3) has helped to overcome this, it is still not being used as widely as it should be. Further, business strategy and policy formulation is no longer the preserve of economists. Sociologists and social psychologists have positive contributions to make to this work.

(a) Human aspects

It has been fashionable for a long time, and continues to be so today, to believe that the main concern of executives is to balance the divergent interests of the different groups comprising the firm. They seek to balance the competitive claims of shareholders, financiers, customers and employees. Because resources are scarce the solution appears to lie in increasing the size of the firm's business as quickly as possible. They believe that this leads to unity of purpose (to grow and prosper as quickly as possible) and that it is in the self-interest of all groups to assist the board to achieve the objectives of growth and higher profits.

Unfortunately employees frequently behave in ways which indicate they have only qualified acceptance of this simple concept. They resist managerial control, withdraw their labour, disrupt output, indulge in absenteeism, give less than a fair return for their earnings and impose their own protective devices such as demarcations and restrictive practices. The affluent society, rather than healing these conflicts, has heightened them, especially when labour seeks to maintain wage differentials.

It is only in recent years that the importance of human aspects of firms has been realised. Various attempts have been made to lessen conflict, reduce absenteeism and improve labour productivity. The significance of good human relations and better management of human resources are better appreciated even if the early attempts have been frustrated by the intransigence of workers, management and governments.

(b) Conflict

Conflict seems to be an integral feature of business organisations. The search for improved harmony has advanced various theories on human motivation and how these can be used for the general good and that of the firm. They include 'job enrichment', 'job satisfaction' and better 'job design'. In recent years attempts have been made to promote 'industrial democracy' and 'worker participation' without an equally full exploration of their implications.

Participation can mean anything from autonomy on the job for individual workers to joint decision-making on an equal basis by work groups and management. Democracy can range from a vague consensus of opinion to the exercise of countervailing power against the unilateral authority of management. Difficulties arise because all these concepts underestimate the pluralistic nature of industrial organisations.

(c) Labour and manpower policies

It is obvious from the above that labour policies must acknowledge the varying personalities of the different groups of workers. Also redundancies cannot be considered as impersonally as the disposal of unwanted equipment. Unemployment creates social, political and psychological problems which increase the incidence of conflict in firms and society.

Labour policies are also conditioned by the *quality* of the labour available. How well trained and educated are the people? How suitable are they for the tasks in hand? How healthy and industrious are they? What is the mobility of labour? This last question covers both occupational mobility (the ability to move from job to job, e.g. an engineer becomes a college lecturer) and geographical mobility (willingness to move from one area to another). It is therefore not just the question of hiring anyone for a job but engaging the right person with the right skills and appropriate experience. These thoughts apply to all areas of management including marketing and especially the sales force, when labour policy has to be decided.

2.4 PUBLIC CONTROL

The significant development in Western economies in the latter half of the twentieth century has been the increasing involvement of governments in business activity. Public control, overt and covert, has increased. This is not only in terms of the proportion of GDP devoted to public sector activities but also in the additional responsibilities assumed by governments to regulate and influence businesses and consumers in the private sector. Such involvement extends to regulations and laws controlling working conditions, inter-firm competition, disclosure of corporate information and consumer protection. Executives appear to tolerate these restrictions but do not deny that they are extensive limitations of their activities.

Executives are faced with the need to be prepared to change traditional business policies to match current circumstances. This is akin to Marketing having to change objectives, strategies, policies and operations to match changes in customer needs and wants. They have to identify and adopt new performance criteria and roles for their firm and themselves. They have to consider the appropriateness of their existing and possible new concepts to present and future problems and needs.

2.5 OBJECTIVES OF THE FIRM

A firm is not an isolated economic unit. It must survive and thrive in the general economic system of the countries in which it operates. Therefore it must take note too of the objectives of government economic policies. In non-Communist countries this policy is dictated by the following objectives.

(i) Improve or at least maintain the standard of living, though hard economic conditions may demand a departure from this for the short term. For example, in trying to reduce inflation some deterioration in the standard of living is unavoidable. As soon as inflation is controlled reversion to this objective should have priority.

(ii) Maintain a sound balance of payments position, though again in inflationary times this may be difficult to do.

(iii) Maintain reasonably full employment so that all who wish to work may do so. Again with inflation this may not be possible. Some economists believe that in order to control modern inflation, the ideal of (over-?) full employment may have to be modified.

(iv) Achieve reasonable price stability. For an exporting country like Britain, too violent and frequent price fluctuations can be destructive to the economic well-being of the nation, especially the balance of payments position. Price increases linked to wage increases can produce 'cost-push' inflation (see Section 2.6).

These objectives permit a government three basic strategies although they tend to use a mixture of two or all of them!

(i) Follow policies designed to maximise the country's productive capacity.

(ii) Implement policies that change (increase or decrease) the degree of utilisation of existing capacity – for several reasons – by changing levels of demand and expenditure by industry and the individual consumer.

(iii) Devaluation.

(a) Company objectives

Decisions on corporate objectives and policies must take into account the points mentioned in the preceding sections. The nature of the business and how this is likely to change, or must change to take account of forecasts on the future of the business environment, must also be considered. It will be appreciated that most firms will have a diversity of objectives. While the planning process should strive for compatibility between these objectives, circumstances may place the emphasis on one objective at a given point in time and another objective at another period. Flexibility in decision-making is necessary. There must be willingness to switch priorities as economic and market factors dictate.

The aim should be to limit the number of objectives to those that are important and relevant to the long-term survival and prosperity of the firm. In general terms, these objectives are as follows.

(i) Survival for as long as possible.
(ii) Maintenance and increase of profits.
(iii) Improvement of market shares, provided this does not reach the 'point of diminishing return' (see Figure 2.1).
(iv) Achieve long-term growth and other developments.

Fig 2.1 *point of diminishing return and optimal market share*

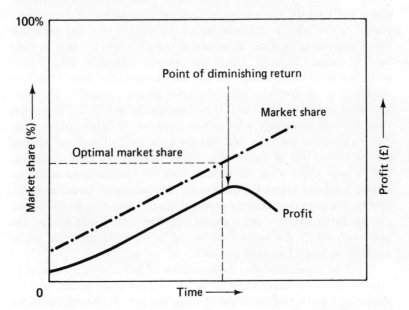

Survival is usually considered the most important, the ultimate objective. It can have different implications. For some companies standing still is not possible for various market and technological reasons. They must grow or die. For others, growth except at moderate rates may be too risky or overstretch their limited resources.

Growth is highly necessary in competitive economies. If a competitor is allowed to grow too big it will have increased its power and may be able to eliminate the static firm. Growth properly planned and controlled leads to stability of profits and sales volume. It can take many forms. It can mean expansion of the geographical market coverage and thus sales volume.

Or it can be in improvement in excellence (quality, technical aspects and so on). Growth can also be achieved by company acquisition or merger. The main danger is that growth can be pushed too far and cause the firm's resources to be over-stretched, often to breaking point.

Profitability is important. Without profits to cover contributions to future development and satisfy the needs of workers, shareholders and financiers, a company will die. Increasing profitability is thus a major aim of any business policy. Without it the other objectives cannot be achieved. Consideration must also be given to the *margin* by which revenue must exceed costs to allow for corporate taxes, current interest rates on borrowed capital and so on.

Increasing market shares and sales volume are also necessary. These ensure survival, growth and profitability. However, increased market shares and sales do not necessarily increase profitability. If the effort is pushed too far, each incremental increase in profit or sales may mean that the corresponding incremental increase in costs becomes too high, or more than the increase in profit. This is the 'point of diminishing return'. Total profit can be eroded. Further, if a firm has a large market share it becomes vulnerable to competition, especially from smaller companies. The latter with their lower overheads and other costs have little difficulty in nibbling away the odd percentage point or two from the big firm's market share. The big company can soon find that the total result of all these 'nibbles' can be critical loss of market share, thus business and competitiveness. This is most likely when the smaller firms can specialise and offer customers products tailored more exactly to customers' needs or wants. Finally, if a given market is not expected to offer long-term profitability it may be better to carry out a phased withdrawal from that market. The assets released by this could then be put to the development of a new market with better long-term prospects.

It will be appreciated that determination of business policy cannot be divorced from the many variables in the business environment. Nor can Marketing leave it to experts elsewhere in the firm. Marketing executives have an important role to play here. How they do it is detailed in the chapters that follow.

2.6 INFLATION

Inflation may be defined as a sustained upward pressure on prices resulting in a general rise in the level of prices and thus in the cost of living. The rate of inflation is the percentage increase in the general price level for a given period (year, month etc.). It is usual to differentiate between demand-pull (or 'demand') inflation and cost-push ('cost') inflation.

Demand inflation is the upward pressure on prices that results when aggregate demand is in excess of aggregate supply of goods and services and supply is inelastic. Suppliers in a free economy will then charge the highest prices they can for goods in short supply. This type of inflation can be caused by a consumption boom with a decreased willingness to save by consumers and a corresponding fall in investment demand. Or it can be due to increased government expenditure without restriction of consumer demand or by an export boom without curtailment of home demand.

Cost inflation occurs when pressure on prices is caused by increases in costs without corresponding growth in output. This can be due to lack of productive resources, (capital, plant and labour), excessive wage increases or unwillingness of the productive workers to work harder or longer hours. Increased wages is not the major culprit, however. Rises in prices of imported raw materials (as at the end of the 1970s with oil), increased cost of capital due to high interest rates and excessive drive for higher profits are other substantial contributory factors.

In fact in all cases of inflation both demand and cost elements are present. Like unemployment, inflation tends to feed on itself. If the community expects inflation to continue they will make allowances for it in their economic bargains. Individuals will strive for higher earnings. Firms will seek higher profit margins. This can be aggravated by incautious government actions ranging from increases in direct and indirect taxes to maintenance of artificially high exchange rates to bolster the currency. Hyperinflation is said to exist when inflation rates reach very high figures.

The bad effects of inflation are insidious. Even when the rate is low and is not expected it leads to a redistribution of wealth and income with no regard to social justice. High rates disrupt economic life leading to more bankruptcies and higher unemployment. If it gets out of hand (hyperinflation) there can be a breakdown of the whole economic system and it can even undermine a country's political system.

Marketing executives have a very real interest in what happens to inflation. The end result for them can be intensified competition as firms fight to maintain their sales volume from a smaller cake of total demand. Inflation can also put up their operating costs until it becomes doubtful if the firm can continue with some or all of their operations. Customers' willingness to buy can decline rapidly. Marketing executives, with their colleagues in other departments, must study the whole complex problem and deduce the implications for their firm's business.

2.7 UNEMPLOYMENT

Inflation usually causes higher unemployment. The spectacular inflation rate and subsequent high unemployment and rate of growth of it in

Britain in 1979 to 1981 is a case in point. However, there are other causes of unemployment.

First, unemployment will rise if there is a shortage of productive resources (money, plant etc.) which prevents the gainful employment of surplus labour. Second, unemployment rises when the structure of the economy is changed. This can be due either to deliberate government intervention as in Britain in 1979–1983 or major changes in technology or in the pattern of demand for products and services. Third, unstable and insufficient demand can be another cause.

The last is the most critical for developed countries. Unemployment leading to a drop in income of the unemployed will accentuate the drop in demand. More will become unemployed and so income, expenditure (or demand) and output will fall further. The thing tends to snowball. Whatever form it takes, unemployment wastes resources and, if it is sustained over the long term, leads to considerable human misery and suffering. Again, in their planning and actions, Marketing cannot ignore the subject of unemployment and its effects on the business environment.

2.8 DEMAND

Demand refers to the willingness *and ability* of consumers to buy products and services. Marketing executives are responsible for determining the demand for their goods and services under varying market and economic conditions. As stated, the multiple variables involved make this a difficult task. The size and nature of demand is affected by general economic conditions including inflation and unemployment, promotional activities and personal selling, product range and development, and technological and other environmental factors. Demand does not have an unalterable character and individual firms are not faced by an inflexible situation.

Indeed by the 1970s for most countries, the demand picture for most products and services had become very complex and considerably unstable. While most of the items above are generally controllable by the firm, there are others which are not. These include government and political actions, regulations and controls by foreign countries and major technological breakthroughs. There are also various situations that affect demand. These are as shown below.

(i) *Buyer rejection*
This occurs when buyers do not want the product regardless of the marketing strategy followed. Products and services must therefore be designed to match customer wants more precisely.

(ii) *Buyer dynamics*

This refers to the time when customers' needs and preferences change requiring the seller to modify or change its product range. This situation does offer new opportunities and sellers must perceive the shifts in customer wants.

(iii) *Buyer autonomy*

Especially in free market economies customers have reasonable freedom of choice. They are not so easy to manipulate as some executives believe, witness the many new products that have failed. Unless a product or service offers an advantage (real, or as imagined by customers) the potential buyer will not be sold. Again, a good understanding of product-market situations and customer attitudes are required.

(iv) *Buyer motives*

Many motives are at play and those relevant to industrial products have been listed in Figure 1.1. Those for consumer goods will be discussed later (Chapters 4 and 6). Identifying the motives that are paramount in any sales situation is not easy. Product-market strategy and policy must cater for both rational and irrational motives.

(v) *Buyers and demand*

Whilst most buyers, especially the individual consumer, enjoy purchasing a good, particularly one that is new to them, demand does not exist automatically. It is not 'something' that is there and sellers just go along and take their share. In modern competitive economies, demand has to be created, potential customers have to be made aware that they have an unsatisfied need. Once it has been created, demand has to be nurtured so that there is reasonable, profitable life for the products or services involved. The correct use of marketing techniques is necessary. Marketing executives must learn how to create and develop demand that is of real importance to potential customers, i.e. not pure 'gimmicks'. Other executives must also appreciate what Marketing is doing in this respect.

(a) Elastic and inelastic demand

The basic principles discussed here generally apply to all products and services. Perhaps only the specially produced, one-off product appears not to, but in fact the underlying principles still apply. However, demand for some products and services is more flexible than that for others. This fact must be taken into account in the pricing process (Chapter 5). Two basic situations are, however, possible, that of *inelastic* and *elastic demand* (see Figure 6.1).

Demand is said to be *inelastic* when it is comparatively insensitive to price changes. For example, if the price of a product is reduced by x per cent and demand does not change, or increases by less than x per cent, then it is said to be inelastic. Similarly if prices are raised by y per cent and demand remains the same or falls by less than y per cent, it is also said to be inelastic. On the other hand, if demand changes substantially as prices change then the demand is said to be *elastic*. In academic terms, these two descriptions refer to the incremental change in demand that takes place with proportionate incremental changes in price. Little or no change in the former indicates an inelastic market while big changes show that demand is elastic. There are several reasons why these conditions arise and these are covered in the later chapters.

In most practical situations both elements are usually present. Total demand for any product group can be elastic over some part of the price range and inelastic over others. There are many reasons ranging from the simple fact that some products may be more essential to customer needs than others, some may be used widely and thus required in bulk so that price reductions prompt buyers to take advantage and build reasonable stocks of them, to those where technological or other factors are of greater importance than price. Also there are products and services (e.g. electricity and water, petroleum products etc.) which customers cannot do without, so they just have to buy them even when prices rise. In these cases total usage over a year may be static anyway, so purchases may not increase even if prices are reduced. Storage may not be possible, or prove expensive, as with electricity and water, or it may be dangerous, as with petroleum products which are potential fire and explosion hazards. So in studying the nature of demand, executives should think in terms of *relevant portions* of total demand and not just total demand itself.

2.9 THE ECONOMIC ENVIRONMENT AND MARKETING

It is worth summarising why marketing executives must understand the effect the economic environment and its many variables have on a business operating in it. First, marketing executives are responsible for the successful conduct of their activities within the business system of the firm and its markets. This involves analyses and decisions that establish the strategy, policies and goals (or targets) for their operations. This affects also the development of a suitable organisation and its associated methods of operation, the attainment of the necessary resources to allow them to create successful marketing offerings (products and services) and effective control of the entire activity.

Second, in the analyses and identification of product-market opportunities they must take account of the interactions between the business system (firm) and the economic and other variables at play. These considerations must therefore also cover technological, social, political and legal factors. These cannot be done in isolation from each other or by ignoring the overriding economic aspects. This cannot be ignored, especially as the economic cycle is itself dynamic and can move from a state of recession or slump, through that of depression, recovery and boom. The economic variables change as the economy moves through this cycle. How they change will affect customers' willingness to buy products and services and thus the marketing operations needed to sustain business success.

(a) Market factors, demand, market mix and shares and product-market strategy

To end this chapter a few words on the relationships between market factors, total demand (see Section 6.1), market mix (Section 6.3(a)), market shares (Section 6.5) and product-market strategy (Section 5.1) would be useful.

The *economic* aspects of importance to marketing considerations include the general state of the economy and relevant industries, income levels (especially net discretionary incomes - or n.d.i. - for consumer markets), the income structure of the different customer categories (e.g. social groups etc.) and the turnover of firms, levels of employment, inflation and competitive activity. As these improve or grow, so normally should total demand for product and services. Indeed, once essential expenditures have been met, the increased balance of n.d.i. remaining may be spent on greater purchases of non-essentials and luxuries (e.g. expensive holidays, the second car, other durables etc.) or may be saved or invested. In the last two cases, demand for banking, investment and insurance services would be increased. When they decline (e.g. price increases exceed growth in earnings and n.d.i. is squeezed; unemployment increased and so on) total demand will fall as everyone is forced to buy less of all products and services. Or, as the earnings of one customer group rise so should their n.d.i. and their ability or willingness to spend more on essentials and non-essentials. The poorer a group becomes the less will they have to spend. Indeed their n.d.i. may approximate to nil when a drop in earnings is accompanied by high inflation and prices.

The *legal* aspect covers all the laws and regulations that control people's lives and the actions of business organisations. These can inhibit or enhance demand for products and services. They also can restrict or assist business activities, the products that can be sold, how they may be and so on, thus contributing to demand growth or decline. For example in the 1960s in Britain, regulations were enacted that made it an offence to drive a vehicle whose tyres had a depth of thread of less than one millimetre. These controls produce a boom in sales almost immediately and has had some effect on the volume of replacement sales. On the other hand, banning the use of cyclamate artifical sweeteners in edible products and drinks has seen demand for these almost wiped out. Demand for products using alternatives (e.g. Sorbitol) has increased. The various laws which influence business activity are listed in Table 7.9. The regulations seriously restricting the foreign exchange that may be used for travel purposes (holidays or business) or that may be remitted abroad by firms for any purpose, inhibit demand for all types of travel and other business activity. If no real limitations are enforced then demand for travel services, accommodation and so on could be much greater. Firms would make greater use of (and so increase demand for) international banking facilities.

On the *social* side, people's attitudes towards the standard of living and quality of life they should have, coupled with their earnings levels, influence total demand for several products and services. For example, in the 1950s and 1960s, the accent was on ownership of domestic appliances to ease the drudgery of housework. Demand for these goods was high. In the 1970s most households had the basic appliances and interest shifted to the ownership of deep-freezers. The family could buy their food in bulk, save money and have the convenience of a varied supply at hand. They could use what they wanted without having to undertake any shopping trips except at their usual times of a month. There was also a certain 'status' attached to ownership of a freezer. Sales increased. There was interest also in the more sophisticated cookers then on the market and with high incomes prevalent at the time, demand for these products also increased. Then in the late 1970s interest had developed in cultural subjects of all kinds (music, art, archaeology etc.). Demand for associated products (books, records, tapes and cultural holidays based on visits to concerts, museums, art galleries and archaeological sites) increased. As prices rose because of inflation, total demand eased to lower levels.

Linked to the above are ideas and concepts on correct *ethical* behaviour. Attitudes changed and as they did, so too did demand for different products and services. For example, nude bathing on public beaches was not acceptable. However, by the 1970s it is accepted in some countries so demand for holidays to these resorts increased.

Technological developments, including new raw materials or new ways of using established ones, also influence the level of demand for the end-products. If a new machine tool is produced that provides more efficient, better production or quality at no extra cost, or allows costs to be reduced leading to lower prices without loss of profit, the better quality and lower prices could increase sales and demand for the product. New ideas such as xerography can alter the entire pattern of needs and purchases by all who have reprographic requirements. The computer has led to many developments that stimulated demand not only for its own products (hardware and software) but for many other items also. The development of reinforced glass fibre material has pushed out many traditional ones (e.g. wood and mild steel) for many products. Because products in the new material were so much better, had low maintenance needs, better eye appeal perhaps and initially were cheaper and lighter, so easier to handle, demand for them grew. However as the price of the new material rose rapidly in recent years, demand has fallen off. The effects of inflation have taken their toll here too.

These are just a few examples to show how changes in market factors affect the level and nature of demand. The nature and intensity of *competition* also has effect. If competition is fierce, total demand may not be affected but the fight for market shares will be more intense. While competition is limited, the firms already in the business can strive for substantial market shares, and in the process could stimulate interest from customers and so the demand for the products involved. When total demand increases, firms may decide not to increase their market shares, being content with the extra volume the increase in total demand should bring them. If they have spare capacity, they could decide to step up their marketing to gain a larger market share. If the economy is depressed and total demand falls they may choose between fighting harder to maintain their share or accepting a smaller market share, thus contracting their business. In the latter case they may feel that they could defend their business more effectively against intensifying competition.

All this will require firms to rethink their decisions on their market mix (which markets should they exploit or leave?) and the products or services they will offer to them. Thus they will have to review their product-market strategies and policies. The existing ones may no longer be tenable or advisable. Review of their pricing policies would also be needed. These are just some of the interactions at play between the five subjects that form the heading of this subsection. There are others, but these are sufficient to show readers that in marketing a thorough examination of the implications of all major changes and their effects on interrelated aspects is vital for success and dynamic management.

For readers wishing to study the economic aspects in greater depth, recourse to Jack Harvey's book, *Mastering Economics*, is recommended. For marketing students particular attention is drawn to chapters 1 to 6.

2.10 THE FUTURE

While it is difficult to forecast more than five years ahead, especially in the early 1980s, certain signs are clear. First, with the demise of labour-intensive traditional industries and their replacement by high technology ones using limited amounts of skilled labour, high unemployment is likely to persist. Any government's ability to provide jobs by stimulating the economy will be limited.

Second, international competition will increase in intensity. The revolution in global transportation and the fact that the new technologies will allow, say, Asian labour to assemble and export high technology products, will increase competition in developed countries. The need for Western economies to export more will increase pressures for protectionism in trade. All these factors will provide new challenges to marketing and management. They must seek higher *added value*, rather than increased volume, by optimising price and reducing costs and go for specialised world markets. They must seek out micro-economic opportunities and there may be many of them in future years.

ASSIGNMENTS

1 You have been instructed by your company's Board to review the firm's marketing operations in the light of changing economic circumstances and rising unemployment and inflation. Prepare such a report showing how economic and other market factors can affect marketing strategy and policy to be followed.

2 In addition to (1) above you are asked susbsequently to show how elastic and inelastic demand could further affect the marketing policies that would otherwise be suitable.

3 Your company is considering the creation of a new, small department to look after the social responsibility aspects of its business. You are short-listed to head this department. Prepare a short paper showing what you see to be the main areas of work for it.

4 With the economic situation in your major markets deteriorating, you anticipate that competition will become more severe. Prepare a memorandum to your Marketing Director showing how you think business will be affected if competition is ignored and what steps should be taken to counteract intensifying competition.

MARKETING'S ROLE
IN MANAGEMENT

Sustained success in management demands continuous co-operation, of a high order, between all the departments of a firm, acknowledging the inter- and intra-dependence of all managerial decisions and action. No one management discipline is omnipotent. All are co-equals though sometimes, according to the nature and needs of a business, one activity might have to be the leader. The discontinuities of modern business environment have forced many executives to acknowledge these realities. It has also been necessary to abandon the previous concept that each discipline of management should be contained – or cocooned? – in its own watertight compartment, into which others trespass at their peril. It is appreciated now that every discipline must be totally involved in, and committed to, corporate activity.

Figure 3.1 outlines the principal disciplines and departments in manufacturing enterprises. For service industries, some departments are not required (for example, possibly engineering and research and development departments) and others (for example, manufacturing or production divisions) may appear in a different guise. In the latter case, if the firm were a tour operator, providing packaged tours of various kinds, the people responsible for making advance selection and booking of accommodation, transportation and other services, would be the equivalent of manufacturing industry's production department. They 'produce' the 'goods' (packaged holidays) offered to the consumer.

It will be useful to outline briefly in this chapter where Marketing fits into, or co-operates with, all the other activities of the firm as outlined in Figure 3.1. It is not an isolated activity that can stand aloof from the other departments of the firm.

Fig 3.1 *the major functional divisions of management*

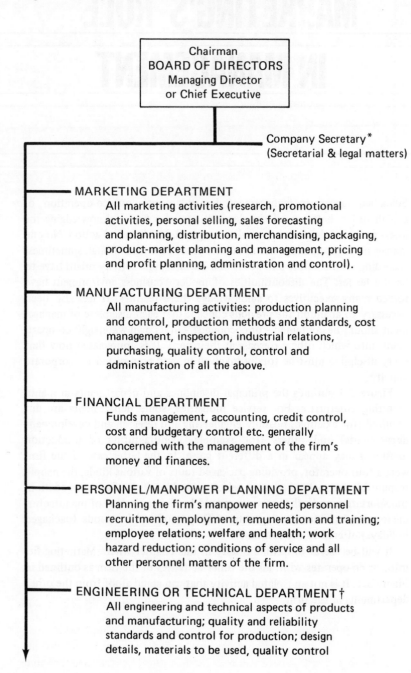

Chairman
BOARD OF DIRECTORS
Managing Director
or Chief Executive

Company Secretary*
(Secretarial & legal matters)

MARKETING DEPARTMENT
All marketing activities (research, promotional
activities, personal selling, sales forecasting
and planning, distribution, merchandising, packaging,
product-market planning and management, pricing
and profit planning, administration and control).

MANUFACTURING DEPARTMENT
All manufacturing activities: production planning
and control, production methods and standards, cost
management, inspection, industrial relations,
purchasing, quality control, control and
administration of all the above.

FINANCIAL DEPARTMENT
Funds management, accounting, credit control,
cost and budgetary control etc. generally
concerned with the management of the firm's
money and finances.

PERSONNEL/MANPOWER PLANNING DEPARTMENT
Planning the firm's manpower needs; personnel
recruitment, employment, remuneration and training;
employee relations; welfare and health; work
hazard reduction; conditions of service and all
other personnel matters of the firm.

ENGINEERING OR TECHNICAL DEPARTMENT†
All engineering and technical aspects of products
and manufacturing; quality and reliability
standards and control for production; design
details, materials to be used, quality control

on bought-in materials; preparation of product
specifications for manufacturing from 'customer
specification' of products received from marketing.

RESEARCH AND DEVELOPMENT (R & D) DEPARTMENT †
Carries out fundamental and applied research;
product and process development and improvement;
obtains technical data relevant to the business;
testing of products (prototype and established),
for performance, quality verification etc.; studies
on plant development and improvement.

PHYSICAL DISTRIBUTION DEPARTMENT ‡
Manages and controls all movement of bought-in
items, manufactured products and stocks of
work-in-progress and finished goods, into,
through and out of the factories to the
middlemen and ultimate customer; depots and
depot management; inventories and inventory
control; transportation methods; channels of
distribution; and all administrative matters
associated with their work.

*   Sometimes one of the top executives in
    Financial Department; deals with Company
    Secretarial and Legal matters.

†   If not a department of MANUFACTURING

‡   If not a department of MARKETING

3.1 MARKETING AND CORPORATE PLANNING

It is logical to begin with corporate planning, which is not so much a
management technique but a complete way of running a business. It
involves detailed study of all facets of the business to obtain a clear idea
of what is being achieved so that this can be compared with general and
detailed forecasts of future developments and how they will affect the
firm. The future implications of every decision are evaluated before their
implementation. In the process the company defines clearly what it has
to achieve and will set standards of performance against specified time

horizons. These standards will be used to measure results. The time horizons extend into the future and are not limited just to the annual budget period.

Continual study is made of the firm's business environment, current and possible future ones, so that changes and trends can be spotted sufficiently in advance for the firm to make correct decisions. However, the uncertainties existing in any business environment, especially the way the numerous variables involved interact and change, make it impossible for corporate planning to *guarantee* results. However, it does help the firm to avoid major mistakes and to take remedial action quickly when errors or problems occur. It helps to reduce the risks taken and, in most instances, increases the profitability of the company. It aids in the more purposeful and correct planning for future growth and development and maintains a high level of competitiveness.

Since all executives, at some time or another, are involved in the work of corporate planning, it improves the communication process, motivates executives more effectively and eases the initiation of change in a business system. In the process of planning everyone becomes adequately briefed on everyone else's activities and plans, at least as they affect the former's own responsibilities. Being better informed, the executive team works more effectively. Also the control system needed for corporate planning improves this aspect of management, reducing the waste of resources (time, money, materials and effort) and makes sure resources are provided when needed. Since the corporate planning model is based on realistic interpretations of what is happening in the business environment, the resultant proposals are more readily accepted and implemented by executives.

Figure 3.2 shows the relative time relationships between management disciplines while Figure 3.3 summarises the basic work involved in corporate planning. Of course, in practice, the manufacturing department does not wait for Marketing to complete its planning before it (Manufacturing) begins its work and so on. The planning goes on concurrently with executives of all departments in regular consultation with each other. For example, product managers will have discussions with production and quality controllers and appropriate financial colleagues to arrive at consensus decisions. However, Manufacturing, Finance and Personnel cannot finalise their own ideas until Marketing has nominated what it proposes to do regarding the product-market mix and associated activities in the period covered by the corporate plan under formulation.

Further, if X represents the time when the new plan must start, so the corporate planning work must start some few months before X. This explains the position of Corporate Planning in Figure 3.2. This figure illustrates only the time relativity between the different management disciplines and stresses that every facet is involved at some time or other. Engineering, R and D, technical and general management activities are

Fig 3.2 *relative time relationship during the planning period*

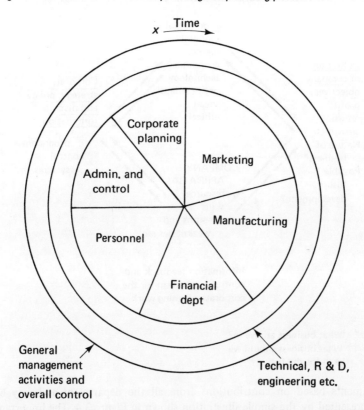

shown as concentric rings around the major disciplines to emphasise that the latters' decisions and operations are also affected by the former (four) activities.

(a) The corporate plan and planner

Initially, company planning was concerned with problems associated with the determination of the facilities and financial resources that a firm needed. Now, with intensive competition and especially in tough economic conditions, attention must also be given to the markets which should be served and the products offered to them. This means that consideration must also be give to associated areas of marketing such as prices, product quality, market and consumer profiles, distribution, merchandising, packaging and promotions; in fact the entire marketing operation. Thus Marketing is very much involved in the planning and decision-making work of the corporate plan. All the other disciplines of the firm are similarly involved in this exercise. The corporate plan is made up of different

Fig 3.3 *basic work in corporate planning*

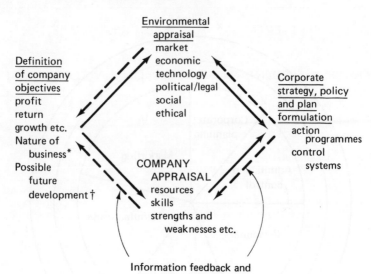

* 'What business are we in?'
† 'What business should we
   be in for the future?'

elements based on contributions from all the department and may be represented by the simple illustration shown in Figure 3.4. The important thing to remember is that these contributions and decisions are reached through mutual inter-departmental agreement.

The company executive responsible for corporate planning decisions is the managing director or chief executive. This responsibility cannot be abrogated. However, it is usual for the considerable work involved to be delegated to another senior member of the organisation, the *corporate planner,* who is responsible for the work to the chief executive. The planner is not a line executive in that he or she does not make decisions, give orders to lay down or determine objectives. The executive studies the wider economic environment, paying particular attention to changes or anticipated developments in areas of importance to the firm. These include ones relevant to the company's present and future interest. The latter will include consideration of possible long-term developments and growth planned for the firm. From the results of this work the corporate planner can advise, indicate and recommend courses of action to the line executives, from the different operating divisions or departments, forming the planning group. This allows the executives to arrive at more correct

Fig 3.4 *simple illustration of the elements of a corporate plan*

MARKETING ELEMENT	MANUFACTURING ELEMENT
FINANCIAL ELEMENT	PERSONNEL/MANPOWER ELEMENT
ADMINISTRATION ELEMENT	CONTROL METHODS ETC.
Board requirements	Corporate Planners' forecasts

Note: The layout should not be read to mean that any one 'element' is more important than the others. The 'Board requirements' and 'Corporate Planner's forecasts' are shown since the first set the initial, preliminary targets for the planning work. The second makes vital contributions to the forecasting work on which the decisions are based (see also text, Section 3.1(b)).

decisions than otherwise. However, the decisions and the implementation of the agreed plans remain the responsibility of the line executives or functional managers.

The corporate planner is responsible for indicating when plans are not being properly implemented or are going off course. This advice will usually be supported by further recommendations on the corrective action needed. Quite often the planner will also act as an arbitrator when executives from different departments are in some conflict and cannot reach agreement on decisions or actions. Besides having the appropriate training and experience, the planner must be an imaginative, creative person able to grasp quickly the meaning of business trends and understand how all changes in the business environment are likely to affect the firm's business. He or she must obviously possess tact and have rapport with the chief executive and colleagues from all the other departments of the company, for without these qualities success in the corporate planning work will not be easily achieved.

(b) The corporate planning process
Figure 3.5 outlines this process and Figure 3.6 summarises Marke involvement. The work usually begins with the board reviewing the progress, the future needs of the company, its shareholders an interested groups and what is believed to be happening in the environment. From this they will be able to indicate the provisic tives and targets for the forthcoming planning period. Line ex the meantime have been conducting a detailed analysis of their c

(continue

62

Fig 3.5 *the corporate planning process*

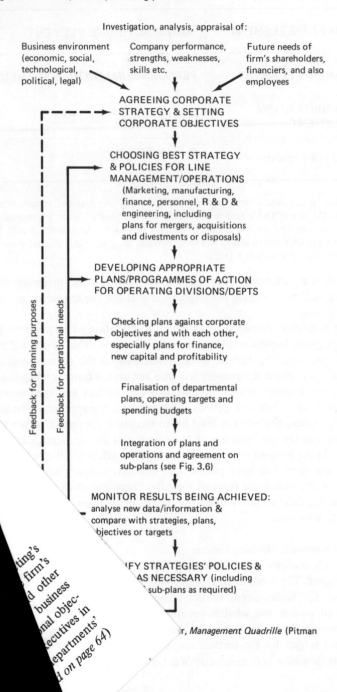

Investigation, analysis, appraisal of:

Business environment (economic, social, technological, political, legal)

Company performance, strengths, weaknesses, skills etc.

Future needs of firm's shareholders, financiers, and also employees

AGREEING CORPORATE STRATEGY & SETTING CORPORATE OBJECTIVES

CHOOSING BEST STRATEGY & POLICIES FOR LINE MANAGEMENT/OPERATIONS
(Marketing, manufacturing, finance, personnel, R & D & engineering, including plans for mergers, acquisitions and divestments or disposals)

DEVELOPING APPROPRIATE PLANS/PROGRAMMES OF ACTION FOR OPERATING DIVISIONS/DEPTS

Checking plans against corporate objectives and with each other, especially plans for finance, new capital and profitability

Finalisation of departmental plans, operating targets and spending budgets

Integration of plans and operations and agreement on sub-plans (see Fig. 3.6)

MONITOR RESULTS BEING ACHIEVED: analyse new data/information & compare with strategies, plans, objectives or targets

...IFY STRATEGIES' POLICIES & ... AS NECESSARY (including ... sub-plans as required)

Feedback for planning purposes

Feedback for operational needs

..r, *Management Quadrille* (Pitman

ting's
firm's
d other
business
nal objec-
ecutives in
epartments'
d on page 64)

Fig 3.6 *the marketing process and corporate planning*

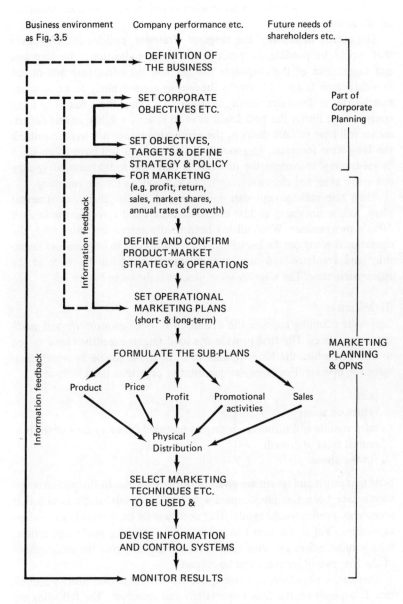

Investigation, analysis, appraisal of:

Business environment as Fig. 3.5 — Company performance etc. — Future needs of shareholders etc.

DEFINITION OF THE BUSINESS

SET CORPORATE OBJECTIVES ETC.

SET OBJECTIVES, TARGETS & DEFINE STRATEGY & POLICY FOR MARKETING (e.g. profit, return, sales, market shares, annual rates of growth)

DEFINE AND CONFIRM PRODUCT-MARKET STRATEGY & OPERATIONS

SET OPERATIONAL MARKETING PLANS (short- & long-term)

FORMULATE THE SUB-PLANS

Product — Price — Profit — Promotional activities — Sales

Physical Distribution

SELECT MARKETING TECHNIQUES ETC. TO BE USED &

DEVISE INFORMATION AND CONTROL SYSTEMS

MONITOR RESULTS

Part of Corporate Planning

MARKETING PLANNING & OPNS

Information feedback

Source: Adapted from Douglas Foster, *Planning for Products and Markets* (Longman, 1972).

activities, the successes and failures. Guided by the board's indicated requirements, line departments, collectively and individually, study the situation to determine what each of them can do in the future, given the *status quo*. They will also indicate what could be done if more resources are made available.

The aim is to identify the range of strategies, policies and objectives that would be possible. In practice the board indications, the forecasts and suggestions of the corporate planner and the initial forecasts of the line departments agreed between themselves are not likely to be an exact match. This is illustrated simply in Figure 3.7. Thus there has to be some compromise. Either the board will have to lower its sights, or line departments will have to raise theirs or the corporate planner will have to rethink the long-term forecasts. In general all three groups will have to do some 'horse-trading' to narrow the differences that exist so that ultimately they can arrive at agreed objectives, strategies and policies for the company.

Then line management can go ahead and finalise their departmental plans, still maintaining regular communications and agreement with each other's programmes. When all has been finally agreed and integrated, the operational plans can be launched. The results need to be monitored carefully and regulated and any amendments required can be made at the appropriate time. The stage-by-stage process is shown in Figure 3.5.

(i) *Objectives*

Corporate planning requires the definition of both *quantitative* and *qualitative* objectives. The first provide the hard targets executives have agreed to aim for, while the latter remind them of the rationale by which they agreed to operate. For example, quantitative objectives must include:

profit
return on assets
sales volume and turnover $\left.\right\}$ targets specified for every year of the plan
annual rates of growth
for the above

Note that profit and return are given priority over sales. In the past managements have been too preoccupied with 'making a sale' and assumed that acceptable profits would result. This need not be so, especially in modern conditions. Yet if the firm concentrates on optimising profit and return, sales volume, prices and thus sales turnover resulting from the achievement of the first two objectives must be correct.

Qualitative objectives are descriptive and can range over many possibilities. It depends on the firm's operations and resources. The following are just a few examples of qualitative objectives used by this author in past years:

Fig 3.7 *corporate planning: conflict of views*

(a) initially

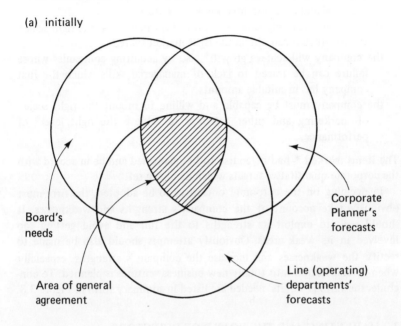

Board's needs

Corporate Planner's forecasts

Line (operating) departments' forecasts

Area of general agreement

(b) compromise position

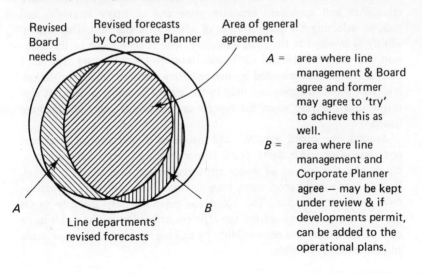

Revised Board needs

Revised forecasts by Corporate Planner

Area of general agreement

Line departments' revised forecasts

A = area where line management & Board agree and former may agree to 'try' to achieve this as well.

B = area where line management and Corporate Planner agree — may be kept under review & if developments permit, can be added to the operational plans.

the company will only enter operations to which it can make positive and vital contributions to ensure success (e.g. management skills, technical and other essential know-how etc.);

the company will only consider a project it can enter at the right scale* and in which it can obtain the right market share;*

the company will achieve growth* also by acquiring companies whose failure can be traced to lack of managerial skills which the first company has in suitable amounts;

the company must be capable and willing to mount the right scale* of marketing and other activities to achieve the right level* of performance.

The items marked * had of course to be quantified and be in accord with the corporate quantitative targets which had been set.

In deciding on the corporate objectives to be adopted, the firm must obviously take account of the company's strengths and weaknesses. It should seek to exploit its strengths to the full and avoid getting too involved in its weak areas. Obviously attempts should also be made to rectify the weaknesses and increase the company's strengths, especially when diversification into totally new business ventures is planned. To conclude, the various 'audits' needed are listed in summary form in Figure 3.8.

3.2 MARKETING AND THE BOARD OF DIRECTORS

The detailed activities of a board vary from company to company. The legal requirements of each country are also different. However, in general, boards of directors have the following responsibilities. First, the board establishes and approves corporate plans and all major strategies and policies, selecting the general areas of activity for the firm. This responsibility is invested in the chief executive, who is answerable to the chairman and other members of the board. Decisions taken here are dependent on the information provided by the operating divisions, including Marketing. This should happen not only in the annual planning period but also throughout the year when the reports on the results being obtained are issued.

Second, the board approves and maintains overall control of annual operating plans and budgets. Third, it approves and controls capital expenditure and the use of all assets entrusted to the firm by its investors. Fourth, it selects the most senior managers and fixes their terms of employment and remuneration. The board has collective responsibility to its shareholders and investors for the efficient utilisation of the assets in its care. It discharges this responsibility by making the company as profitable and successful as possible.

Fig 3.8 *'audits' for planning purpose*

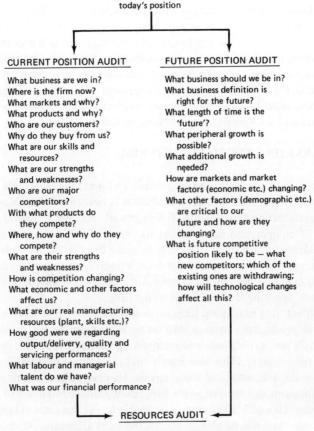

today's position

CURRENT POSITION AUDIT

What business are we in?
Where is the firm now?
What markets and why?
What products and why?
Who are our customers?
Why do they buy from us?
What are our skills and
    resources?
What are our strengths
    and weaknesses?
Who are our major
    competitors?
With what products do
    they compete?
Where, how and why do they
    compete?
What are their strengths
    and weaknesses?
How is competition changing?
What economic and other factors
    affect us?
What are our real manufacturing
    resources (plant, skills etc.)?
How good were we regarding
    output/delivery, quality and
    servicing performances?
What labour and managerial
    talent do we have?
What was our financial performance?

FUTURE POSITION AUDIT

What business should we be in?
What business definition is
    right for the future?
What length of time is the
    'future'?
What peripheral growth is
    possible?
What additional growth is
    needed?
How are markets and market
    factors (economic etc.) changing?
What other factors (demographic etc.)
    are critical to our
    future and how are they
    changing?
What is future competitive
    position likely to be — what
    new competitors; which of the
    existing ones are withdrawing;
    how will technological changes
    affect all this?

RESOURCES AUDIT

What are our financial resources? Adequate for the future?
What additional finance will be needed for the future?
What will be its cost? Thus what return has to be achieved?
How will our present plant & skills meet future needs?
What additional plant and skills of all kinds will be needed?
How can these be developed? How much must be obtained
    from outside the firm? What is the likely cost?
How good has the firm been in utilising all resources?
What improvements in utilisation are needed/or possible?
What manpower training and management development needed?
How good have been the firm's cost and credit control systems?
What improvements needed?
What cost reduction programmes would be advisable?
What is our present labour/management needs? What increase
    will be necessary for the future?

FUTURE CORPORATE ACTIVITIES & OBJECTIVES

In practice the board, collectively and individually, must show interest in and commitment to the objectives, plans and operations of the firm. The individual directors charged with specific responsibilities must involve themselves in them and advise and assist their executives to the full without interfering with their day-to-day actions, except when things are going wrong or seem to be outside the responsibility and capability of executives. The directors must seek a balance between control and supervision of and interest in the work, providing encouragement to the firm's employees. Thus there must be close and continual contact and co-operation between the board and the operating departments, including Marketing.

3.3 MARKETING AND MANUFACTURING

If a firm is to be successful and is to remain so for as long as possible, close, continual co-operation and communication is needed between Marketing and Manufacturing departments. The degree of success will depend on the degree of co-operation achieved. At its worst, if the executives are not really talking to each other (they may be going through the motions but in practice refusing to understand the other's point of view and needs) then the firm could be heading for disaster. Unfortunately the seeds of conflict lie in their opposing responsibilities to the firm.

Manufacturing must keep its plant loaded to satisfactory levels to meet cost and productivity targets. Marketing is responsible for earning the company's profit, obtaining and maintaining market shares with products of the right quality. This also means that the volume of sales should be right for the attainment of these targets. However, Manufacturing, in its overenthusiasm to keep unit costs low, could produce too much of one or more products and Marketing may be unable to sell this extra volume. The market may just not be able to absorb the extra quantities for economic, competitive or other reasons. Marketing is then stuck with unsold stocks and considerable effort (time and money too) may have to be expended to clear them. Any nominal benefit of lower unit production costs will be lost in the additional marketing costs that would be incurred. This problem still arises too frequently.

Then the quality standards expected by customers can lead to further conflict with the cost constraints and profit requirements for the product. For example a manufacturer of electric blankets, aware of the hesitancy, if not fear of many users of the latent hazards that could arise in the use of this product, will want to offer blankets with all the latest safety devices. It will also have to achieve a certain percentage mark-up on ex-works prices to satisfy the firm's profit or return targets. Manufacturing, having certain unit cost targets to meet, will argue that fitting all these devices would increase manufacturing costs beyond acceptable limits. The resultant sale prices could then be too high to compete with prices ruling in the market. This last point could inhibit sales despite all the safety attractions. The need for all these devices might hold up production and increase costs further because of the extra development work that would be needed. The availability of the product would also be delayed and could let competitors establish a strong position in the market. Some compromise is needed, and this cannot be reached unless there is total co-operation and communication between the two departments involved.

Thus it will be appreciated that co-operation is needed on the product range to be produced (quantities, timing of the output), inventory levels and the modification, rationalisation and new product development that will be required over specified periods of time. Then there are the questions of quality standards, performance, reliability and the maintenance or service that customers expect. Further, there are the subjects of unit sale prices and costs that have to be agreed. Thus marketing executives, especially marketing, sales, physical distribution and product managers, will have to maintain close liaison with production planners and controllers, quality controllers, R and D experts, technical and engineering executives. As the material content of the products can also be important, purchasing executives will be involved in discussions from time to time. Marketing executives responsible for the promotional activities will also be included in appropriate discussions. Without all this, the manufacturing programme cannot be matched to the marketing operations and successful marketing cannot be assured.

A sound basis for co-operation will be established if both departments appreciate the other's tasks, objectives and problems and work closely to find mutually acceptable solutions. Compromise on both sides is necessary. For example, Marketing should not demand unreasonable delivery times, nor the achievement of specifications and quality outside the possibilities imposed by plant limitations and cost constraints. Nor should Manufacturing insist on plant locations and sizes which may suit its needs but impose unreasonable problems on Marketing. Strictly, plants or factories should be located close to major markets. However, if the road and other transportation facilities pose problems, for example the road network may be inadequate so that traffic bottlenecks occur, other locations may prove to be better. On the other hand if production requires easy access to large sources of power supply (e.g. large amounts of cheap electricity is needed for aluminium production, so ideally access to hydroelectricity is required) the factories may have to be some distance from the major markets.

Then the size of the plants must be considered by both departments. If a very large factory is needed to keep unit costs down but this creates delivery and sales problems which Marketing cannot resolve except at high costs, further compromise is needed. Further, the technical excellence or standards need to be agreed. There is little point in Manufacturing producing superb products which nevertheless are too expensive for customers or are not required. There is no benefit to be gained, for example, by producing say ships which will last a hundred years if the rate of change in technology on cargo transportation and handling is resulting in change of customer needs say every twenty-five years. Co-operation on product design is thus also vital. These are just a few illustrations. In practice Marketing and Manufacturing must co-operate in every sector of their activities.

3.4 MARKETING AND FINANCIAL DEPARTMENT

Financial executives have interests also in the points discussed in the preceding section and so close co-operation between Finance, Marketing and Manufacturing departments is needed. The executives in the Finance Department (of whatever name used) are accountable for the efficient management of the company's money. This responsibility covers not just money but all investments in plant, equipment, buildings and other facilities. For example, financial executives will wish to verify that the decisions reached on costs and prices will in fact lead to the attainment of the firm's plans regarding profits. They will play a strong role in profit planning (see Chapter 5) and in monitoring the results achieved by Marketing.

Then there are the questions of cost control, cost reduction programmes (to improve funds utilisation), credit control, the settlement of the company's invoices and payment of its bills. While Marketing should not be used as the firm's debt collectors, it must ensure that the company does not become heavily involved in too many bad debts, or the risk of them. Marketing's involvement here must not be such as to endanger its long-term prospects. Similarly, while the credit control system is a necessary safeguard and Marketing must see that it adheres to it, credit controls should not be so severe as to inhibit business, especially future prospects. For example, it might be academically correct to limit credit terms to small, relevantly insignificant customers. Yet small customers can develop, sometimes unexpectedly and quickly, into major customers. Often they will not forget the tight constraints placed on them and may then favour competitors who were more liberal with their credit in earlier years. Nor should financial control systems be imposed on the firm so rigidly that they hinder the operations and development of Marketing and Manufacturing, especially long-term possibilities and the growth of the company as a whole.

(a) Budgetary control
The nature of control in business is often misunderstood. It is frequently

associated with restrictions or restraints. Yet control systems are intended to guide the business activities of a firm to correct judgement, decisions and actions in the attainment of agreed corporate and associated departmental objectives and targets. In every area involving expense of any kind, control of expenditure is needed if things are not to get out of hand. However, these budgetary controls should be realistic and be arrived at through discussions between Finance, Marketing and other operating departments. The systems agreed should also indicate when remedial action is required, when operations are veering off course.

Properly done, budgetary control sytems, linked with close co-operation between all departments, will allow the Finance Department to achieve its three basic aims without unduly restricting the activities of colleagues. These aims may be summarised as:

(i) keep the business solvent with sufficient liquidity for the firm's needs and purpose;
(ii) provide the firm with the finance necessary to sustain operations and achieve the developments that have been planned;
(iii) provide the means whereby the firm can satisfy, at optimum levels, the economic and other needs of customers and all those who work for or are associated with the company.

These aims cannot be achieved if there is little or no co-operation between Finance, Marketing, Manufacturing and the other departments. In fact financial strategy formulation plays a vital role in the shaping of the firm's other strategies and policies. Financial executives cannot arrive at a sound financial strategy in isolation from other colleagues.

(b) Project appraisal

Capital investment decisions are amongst the most difficult to make for any firm. When capital is scarce and has been made expensive by rising inflation and thus costs, the difficulties are increased. Further, investments may often be difficult to alter when once made and are sometimes irreversible. For example a hotel group's decision to invest in a new hotel requires considerable capital, and once built the hotel is not easy to change to other usage. Sound investment decisions and project appraisal can only be achieved through detailed consideration by all operating departments, especially Marketing.

The process is very similar to that followed for all planning decisions. All relevant facts have to be gathered and studied in depth. The consequences of the alternative decisions possible must also be considered both for the short and long term. The market situation, including all the market and other factors that might affect it, must be studied. The commercial risks involved cannot be ignored also. So here too close co-operation is needed between all the firm's departments, especially those that will be affected by the final decision. The four major departments, Marketing, Manufacturing, Finance and Personnel, will therefore contribute to this task of project appraisal.

3.5 MARKETING AND THE PERSONNEL DEPARTMENT

All firms are social organisations comprised of individuals striving, hopefully, to help the company realise its plans and achieve agreed targets. The prosperity of a firm depends on the efforts of the human beings it employs. Without the right amounts of shop-floor and managerial personnel, with the requisite skills and capabilities, a firm cannot hope to perform satisfactorily, especially over the long term. Personnel executives in Britain were, for far too long, subjected to too low a status in a firm. They have now achieved their rightful place in the management process, as the experts on all aspects of personnel matters including manpower planning for the future. Colleagues in the other departments cannot ignore them with impunity when decisions on personnel matters have to be made. Marketing, particularly dependent on getting the right personalities in jobs requiring persuasive abilities (i.e. sales, distribution, promotions and marketing research) have special need for their help. A high degree of co-operation between Marketing and Personnel is necessary.

The work of this department may be summarised briefly as follows.

(i) *Employment*: selection, recruitment, remuneration and terms of employment of shop-floor and managerial labour (though senior executives are the responsibility of the board – see Section 3.2).

(ii) *Training and education*: training and development of all employees to keep them abreast of developments in their specialisms and to prepare them for promotion; selection of colleges and courses for the general education and development of key employees; etc.

(iii) *Labour relations*: including joint negotiations with trade unions and management; labour utilisation and improvement of this; job evaluations; wage rates; etc.

(iv) *Health and safety*: the health and safety of the employees; reduction of hazards involved in the firms activities and associated social aspects (social club, canteen, nursery centres etc.).

(v) *Research*: to ensure that personnel activities are in accord with advancing knowledge on selection, training, remuneration and manpower planning.

In carrying out its responsibilities, Personnel implements the agreed personnel policies of the firm and makes recommendations when these should be changed. It also operates as the company's experts in the behavioural sciences, interpreting the behaviour of individuals and groups within the organisation. The department advises colleagues on the implications of such behaviour for the achievement of departmental and company goals. Thus again, close and regular consultation with colleagues from other departments, including Marketing, is essential for more effective management.

3.6 COMMUNICATIONS

Given the need for extensive co-operation between all departments, it is worth considering briefly the subject of communications within a firm. Good communication systems are vital if co-operation is to be successful. This is considered to be particularly vital when Personnel are devising job descriptions and specifications for other departments. Misunderstanding here can lead to mistakes in recruitment with very unfortunate results for the employees recruited and the firm as a whole.

Too often a firm's failure can be traced to bad communications and the resultant misunderstandings. Effective communications is not a propaganda exercise but the art of correctly informing and persuading others. It is not a flood of directives from seniors to juniors that inundate, irritate and frustrate the recipients. It should be a multi-channel flow of ideas between all levels of the enterprise, as necessary. Also executives should not only talk or write; they should be prepared to read and listen to the other's point of view. Listening to the other fellow, rather than just pretending to listen, is essential to good, effective communications.

The communications system must also be selective. Information sent to an executive should be relevant to that executive's task and responsibilities. At some time or other, in an imperfect world, this can mean that someone will not get the information needed. The answer is not to create a complex system but to build an atmosphere of co-operation that allows the executive to retrieve quickly the missing piece of information.

The other basic ground rules for good communications can be summarised as follows. First, the purpose of the communication should be clear and the message itself should possess clarity and not be open to misunderstanding. Next, the background of the recipient should be appreciated so that the form of the message is correct. People, according to their education, experience and training, use words differently. Key words should therefore be used in the context the recipient will use. Checking the proposed message with a colleague, especially one with a similar background to the recipient, can help to avoid misinterpretations. Finally, a follow-up to check that the communication has been understood correctly and the right action has been taken helps to overcome communication problems.

(a) Barriers to communication

The nature of the human animal must also be rememberd. Each one can be egotistical, self-centred and selfish, interested only in its own well-being and progress. There may be also an inflated opinion of its own abilities and powers. No one is entirely free of these traits. Thus from time to time the executive can be secretive or uncommunicative. These failings may also be due to lack of intelligence, simple ignorance of the subject discussed, overwork or some other character defect. All these have to be taken into account.

People's individual nature, character and behaviour patterns vary widely. A few will receive a message as it was intended. Some, probably a greater number, will resist or resent the import of the communication, resulting in total misunderstanding. This may be due to some remote but deep-seated prejudice. Then there are others who because of some deep prejudice just will not accept any message however it is put. Further, the size of the firm can increase the distortion factor. The greater the number of layers of supervision or management, or its geographical or physical spread, the longer will be the lines of communication. This will increase the possibilities for misunderstanding. The inter-staff relationships are also more complex and, given the greater time lag involved, communication problems can increase. Finally, the difference in corporate and social status will also determine the variance between points of view on the subject being communicated.

(b) Resistance to change

Communication problems can increase when a firm plans any change in either its organisation and methods or in its business strategies because some executives will resist such change to varying degrees. This is regardless of the essentiality of the need to make changes. This resistance to anything new is a natural phenomenon of the human being. All are guilty of it at some time or another. Humans cling desperately to the known or familiar and are apprehensive of anything new.

In business, change can have three effects. The first is the behavioural aspect of change in that it causes employees to change their method of work in some way. Second is what is called the social effect. The established relationships between individuals alter as their method of work changes. Finally, there is the psychological effect; the reactions of each individual to the relevance of the changes in work, personal prospects and the assumed needs of the company. How bad the third effect is depends on the scale of the other two effects.

Resistance to change may not be due so much to the change itself being opposed but rather the way the change is brought about and what the individuals imagine the real effects will be, especially for themselves.

The change may be just a signal for resistance which, in the absence of a common cause, may have been smouldering just below the surface for some time. Therefore executives have to anticipate resistance to any change and estimate its possibility intensity. They must try to avoid the building up of dissatisfaction on other fronts which may well up when any change, even those irrelevant to the cause of the dissatisfaction, is introduced.

The factors affecting an individual's reaction to change are usually as shown below. They have complex interactions with each other. As listed they are not necessarily in the right order for everyone.

  (i) the extent of feelings of insecurity;
 (ii) the extent of trust in the management, unions and work groups;
(iii) the manner in which the change is introduced and implemented;
(iv) the predisposed feelings about change of any kind;
 (v) the view of immediate historical events relevant to the change and sometimes, those not relevant;
(vi) specific apprehensions (or expectations) about each particular change;
(vii) the prevailing cultural beliefs and norms which might be in conflict with the change and which may, in part, be a result of background, education, upbringing and experience.

Resistance to change may be reduced or overcome if the following principles are kept in mind.

  (i) change is more acceptable to people who have participated in planning for it rather than to those who have had it imposed on them;
 (ii) change is more acceptable when it is not seen as a threat but rather as an opportunity for greater endeavour and advancement;
(iii) change is more acceptable to those who are not affected by it than those who are; the latter will attempt to defend the system apparently under attack;
(iv) change is acceptable to those who are new on the job;
 (v) change is more acceptable when an organisation has been trained to accept change as a normal development and a continuing necessity in present-day circumstances;
(vi) finally, changes are more readily accepted after partial changes have been successfully implemented, i.e. change should be planned to take place in steps which are easily understood and accepted by those involved.

In other words, change is accepted when it is understood and when the executives involved have played a part in planning and implementing it.

All this must also be taken into account when planning a sound, effective communication system. (For those readers wishing to understand more about the integrated approach to management implied by the contents of this chapter, it is suggested that they read this author's book, *Management Quadrille* (London: Pitman, 1980).)

3.7 FUTURE MANAGEMENT

Three recent developments may alter management procedures. First, mini- and micro-computers could mean that some executive and office administration tasks may be performed from the executives' homes using a small computer linked to the company's main computer. Salespersons could work mainly from their homes. Executives would travel to their offices less frequently. Second, wages and salaries are getting more expensive so the payment of fees on receipt of good quality work may prove advantageous. Third, employees wish to be regarded as assets not just cost elements. They want to be less vulnerable to changing market forces. Thus by the turn of the century, management structures, attitudes and procedures may have undergone fundamental changes from present ones.

ASSIGNMENTS

1 You have just been promoted to be marketing manager. The company's Corporate Planner has asked you to submit a memorandum on the role that you see your department playing in the corporate planning work. What are your views on this and which corporate objectives do you see as most relevant to Marketing?

2 In the course of the planning meetings you are asked to outline the possible areas of conflict between Marketing and Corporate Planning and Marketing and the other 'line departments' and how these could be minimised. Prepare a paper on this.

3 In your company the level of co-operation between the major departments has not been good. You are asked to prepare a paper showing the areas where co-operation between departments is vital for sustained corporate success and what would occur if this co-operation is not maintained at a high level continuously. Also show what an effective communications system can do to enhance this co-operation.

4 The company has been encountering considerable resistance to changes in its operations and methods. You intend to discuss this at the next board meeting, identifying the main reasons for this and the ways the problem could be overcome. Prepare a memorandum for this meeting.

MARKETING

INFORMATION

The considerable amount of data and information that flows from marketing research (see Table 1.1) allows executives to identify product-market opportunities. It leads also to a better understanding of the marketing processes that are used and permits more efficient and effective control of the marketing operations. The work involved provides the basis for strategy and policy planning and formulation and for decision-making purposes. The 'flow' itself should be two-way between the firm and its markets or customers. Otherwise the many questions that have to be answered in the planning process cannot be dealt with satisfactorily. The key questions were indicated under 'Marketing Research' in Table 1.1.

However, it is worth repeating that what actually takes place in a market is conditioned by many factors or variables, internal and external to the firm, which are notoriously unstable in themselves and their inter-relationships with one another. This is particularly so where human behaviour aspects, responses to product or service offerings and marketing activities, are concerned. Thus while this data and information flow helps to reduce uncertainty and risk, it cannot be precise in all details.

Since they are used indiscriminately, it may help the reader to define what should be meant when the words 'data', 'information' and 'intelligence' are used in this context. In its most correct sense, 'data' comprise statistical facts presented in some specific format.

'Information' is descriptive and explains the rationale of what is happening and gives direction to, or indicates the purpose of, the associated data. Without it, the marketing problem that has to be solved cannot be fully understood and the associated data may be of little value. Thus 'data' is said to be 'passive' while 'information' is 'active' in that it allows correct decisions and actions to be taken. The collection, interpretation or analysis and utilisation of data and information provide a firm with the marketing 'intelligence' service it needs.

Marketing research itself can be defined as 'the systematic and objective search for and analysis of (data and) information relevant to the identification and solution of any problem in the field of marketing'. Note the use of the word 'systematic', which stresses the need for careful planning of the research in all its stages. This requires a clear and concise statement of the objective of the exercise, the techniques to be used, the information that is required and the analytical techniques that will be employed. The word 'objective' stresses the need for impartiality, that is, seeking the facts without colouring due to already held views and opinions. Many practitioners hold that research intended to prove a prior opinion may be wasteful, though there will be occasions when research may be used to verify whether a belief, long held, is true or imaginary.

4.1 MARKETING INTELLIGENCE SYSTEMS

Marketing intelligence systems are concerned with the analysis and interpretation of data and information, not mere data collection. It is concerned with problem prevention as well as problem-solving tasks. It must indicate what changes in present circumstances mean for the future and how a firm may influence its product-market destiny. It should induce innovative and risk-acceptance possibilities. Through anticipations of future possibilities, it guides present actions which in turn shape the firm's future. It is concerned not only with the immediate or short-term aspects but also with intermediate and long-term possibilities.

The ideal marketing intelligence system has thus to perform four inter-related functions. First, it should pinpoint marketing problems. Second, it should collect all available data and information relevant to these problems. Third, through the analysis of the intelligence, it should determine what changes may be necessary to overcome the anticipated problems. Fourth, it must suggest ways in which these changes can be implemented. However, it is unreasonable to assume that any system can obtain all the information it needs. Time and budgetary limitations are the main constraints but some information or data may just not be available. Nor does everyone have perfect analytical ability. The real significance of some intelligence may be overlooked or misinterpreted.

These disadvantages are ever-present and arrangements should be made that allow the system to react quickly when such 'errors' are discovered. The system should also be designed to keep out the irrelevant intelligence even though this may not be easily perceived. It should act as the nerve centre of the firm, providing information and intelligence for each level of management as quickly as is relevant to executives' needs and their ability to use the information effectively. By continually monitoring a firm's markets and its own progress, the system can indicate when operations are deviating from plans and recommend corrective action. For example, if increased competition is making the company miss its sales, profit and return on assets targets, the system should indicate how competition is proving more effective and thus the alterations the firm should make to its own activities.

4.2 TYPES OF MARKETING INFORMATION AND INTELLIGENCE

Marketing information and intelligence have to suggest possible answers to a number of questions. Some important ones are listed in Table 4.1 for easy reference. In trying to cover such a wide spectrum of study, it helps to recognise the five natures of sources of information and intelligence. These are described briefly below.

(a) Internal information

This is obtained from all the firm's own records of its activities, past results and forecasts. Every department has a useful contribution to make here. Given a good reporting system, information is easily available on sales, sales costs and profit; production capacity, volumes; inventories; distribution and delivery; pricing; promotional expenditure; cash flows and other financial matters (e.g. cost control exercises, credit control); manpower and personnel matters including labour availability, turnover and utilisation. Often internal records provide the best and only sources of such vital data. With the general availability of computers, computer time and, more recently, inexpensive mini-computers, there should be no barrier to the effective use of this information. It provides not only the historical base information for forecasting but is useful in achieving more effective control of ongoing operations. For example airlines are able to discover what the seat availability is for specific flights at any time. Manufacturers can get instant status reports on sales to date, prices operating, inventory positions, current market shares and even estimates on the profit being earned. Banks can get instant printouts on the status of deposits and withdrawals at each branch, the amount and type of loans made and so on.

(b) Environmental (external) information

This allows analyses and assessments of the competition, technology and economics affecting the firm's business environment and the effect social, political and legal factors are having on it. These represent both opportunities and constraints on the company's activities.

(c) Position intelligence

This indicates the firm's current position in its industry and markets and is evolved from (a) and (b) above. Opinions can be formulated about the

Table 4.1   key questions to be resolved by marketing information

Markets
What is the total market potential?
How is this changing? What factors causing change?
What market shares are possible?
Who are the competitors? How, where, why, when do they compete?
What can be done to counter this competition?
What distribution should be used? What channels?
What inventory levels are needed? Where and when?

Products
What products do customers want?
Are there any unsatisfied needs?
How do our products compare with competitors re quality, performance,
    reliability, maintenance etc.?
How relevant is our product mix for the future?
What changes in the product mix are indicated? When?
How are technological, economic and other market factors affecting this?
How relevant is our after-sales services of all kinds?
What changes in services are indicated?
How do our costs and prices compare with competitors?
Is there price elasticity or price sensitivity?
How should we alter our costs and prices?

Other
How effective are our marketing operations?
In particular, how effective are the promotional and personal selling
    activities?
How effective and accurate are the marketing research and intelligence
    systems?
What modifications are indicated for the future?
How effective are our reporting and control systems?
What changes are necessary for future developments?
                    etc., etc.

In reality these questions should be answered for all markets, home and overseas!

effectiveness of the selling activity, advertising, marketing costs, the relative
profitability of product lines and estimated return on assets.

(d) Projective intelligence

This is evolved from the three sources listed above. They help in the
evaluation and development of possible future marketing strategies,
policies, constraints and variables projected into some specified future
time period.

(e) Decision intelligence

Records the firm's decisions on present and future strategies, policies,
plans and control methods. It establishes the pattern for future marketing

commitments and records and rationale for the decisions taken. Thus at any future date executives can refer back to this intelligence to remind themselves how and why these decisions were taken. Then it forms the springboard for further future planning and decisions.

4.3 TYPES OF DATA

Data (and information) is also sub-classified into two groups.

(a) Primary data

This is generated by original research designed to answer specific questions. It covers facts which are not known and have not previously been published. For example an hotel group may wish to know the nationalities of its guests and the purpose of their stay (business, holiday, other personal reasons). Or a manufacturer may wish to establish if there is any pending change in customers' requirements (e.g. in the formulation of the products bought, its quality or life, price and so on). For firms using marketing research regularly, the primary data from one study may become the secondary data for another.

The research for primary data should be tailored to the needs of the firm commissioning the study. Thus it has the advantage of *specificity*, being tailored to situations currently confronting the firm. Another advantage is that of *practicality* in that this data deals with real situations, to a greater or lesser degree. The disadvantage is that its collection is always costly in time and money. It may take some time to construct the framework of the research as well as to carry it out and this time may not be available, especially if the research is badly timed (left too late for example). Then the firm may not have made sufficient allowance in the budget for all the work to be done. Hence the need for careful forward planning of marketing research.

Another point to be remembered is that accepted 'experts' have to be contacted when primary data is sought. Apart from the fact that these people may be difficult to contact, human nature being what it is, the experts' view will tend to reflect their own 'expert opinions' and their reputations. This may inject incorrect bias into the data. Experts are however useful in indicating others who could make helpful comments. If the latter are not 'experts', or seen as such, their comments may be less biased and based more on the reality of the subject concerned. Thus there is need to check the veracity of the sources used in research for primary data.

Observational methods can also be used when studies of customer responses, customer movements and sales techniques are required. They should give a more objective picture of behaviour than reliance on respondents' accounts of how they behave, thus reducing response bias. However, this assumes that researchers are accurate and diligent observers and that the act of observing does not alter the behaviour of those being observed. Further, the method reveals little about respondents' state of mind or their buying motives. Thus motivational research may be needed (see Section 4.4(c)).

Another weakness of the observational method is that there is little control of the environment or behaviour being observed. It cannot give conclusive proof of the cause-and-effect relationships in marketing. It may be necessary, therefore, to employ *experimental methods*. These involve the injection of selected stimuli and systematically varying them in a controlled environment and observing the results. They are useful in testing hypotheses on behaviour when a particular marketing stimulus is applied. For example how will customers respond to new packaging or point-of-sale material? What response will occur with price changes? How will customers react to changes in product formulation? What promotional activity would be most effective? And so on. Experimental methods are normally associated with *test marketing*, where these ideas can be tried out in segments of the market that are known to be a reasonable cross-sectional representation of the total market. The results could then be deduced to be generally applicable to the total market. The experimental method is useful where the necessary information cannot be obtained by normal research of opinions, observations of behaviour or study of secondary data.

(b) Secondary data

Secondary data is information that is already available or published by official statistics and other government publications, research organisations, university and major banking reports, competitors' and customers' publications, trade associations and the firm's own records (see Section 4.2(a)). A firm's primary data from a previous study can become the secondary data for a future research programme. The stock of secondary data available has increased over the years but, like experts' views, is only as good as the compilers. Further, the method of compilation varies from country to country. This applies particularly to official statistics so it is advisable to leave their interpretation to executives experienced in deciphering national statistics, usually nationals of the countries concerned. Care is also needed to note that the extent and value of official statistics vary from nation to nation. For example the United States of America, through its Department of Commerce and the libraries of its embassies, can provide comprehensive information if the enquirer's needs are clearly defined in the former's terms. In many developing countries, understandably, official statistics may be unavailable or valueless. Again, the researcher should check the veracity of the sources used.

Secondary data has the advantage over primary data that it is less costly to obtain. It is cheaper to visit a library, embassy or government department to study relevant documents than to mount a full-scale field research. Executives tend, therefore, to consider what published data is available before they design the research project. Care is needed, however, to ensure that cost saving does not overrule the need for objectivity nor forget the objective of the research. Over-emphasis on keeping costs low can inject bias into the results if the research is not as detailed or selective as is dictated by the problem being investigated. In addition, secondary data is anyway easier to obtain, in most cases, than primary data and some information may only be obtainable from secondary sources.

Besides the danger of injecting *cost-bias*, mentioned above, there is the disadvantage that much secondary data is of *limited applicability*. Rarely does this data fit the firm's exact intelligence requirements. By its nature also, it is *obsolescent* if not *obsolete*. Once gathered, data and information have short relevance since market and other factors are in states of continuous change. This is particularly true in times of great innovation or economic recession. Customers' incomes, attitudes, circumstances and requirements are not static but alter in various ways. Incomes and profit increase and decrease. Technical requirements are overtaken by technological change. Permitted activities are altered by political, legal and social changes. There is also the question of *limited credibility* in that doubts may exist about the validity of this data. There is thus need to consider many points before placing too much reliance on secondary data. For example, studies of an industry's expenditure on promotional activities would not be homogeneous if the number and nature (size etc.) of the firms studied varied in every study or if, for example, the definition of promotional costs was also changed frequently.

(c) Sources of information

The range of sources available varies from country to country and for different industries. Some mention has been made of the more general sources in the text of the two preceding sub-sections, (a) and (b). For easy reference, the more general sources are listed in Table 4.2. They are not in any order of significance and the source that would be used will depend on the subject under study.

(d) Value of information

While the value of any piece of information will vary from company to company and the situation to be resolved, the value of information, in general terms, depends also on the following:

the degree of uncertainity prevailing about the possible outcomes of the alternative course of action open to the firm;

the economic and other consequences of making an incorrect decision (e.g. unknown to the decision-maker at the time, not taking the action that would in fact give the 'best' outcome);

the degree by which the information, if obtained, is expected to reduce the initial uncertainty.

The greater the initial uncertainty, the larger are the consequences of making a wrong decision. Further, the greater the amount by which the information is expected to reduce uncertainty the more valuable the information appears to become to executives.

Thus, if the cost of obtaining the information is greater than the value of it, consideration should be given to whether its collection would be worthwhile. Generally the answer may be not to gather such information but there are many instances when it may be advisable to go ahead. For example the value may not be totally quantifiable in money terms; the information may not eliminate uncertainty or guarantee increased earnings or profit but it could project knowledge that at a future date may be useful or needed. This consideration helps when a choice has to be made between the packages of information that should be gathered and there is a limited budget making the collection of all of them impossible.

How the value of information is estimated is a complex subject embracing Bayesian Theory, decision trees and other classical approaches of marketing research statisticians. They are outside the scope of this book and those wishing to go into this subject in more detail should turn to the many specialist books on it. However, the marketing and research strategies selected should specify the information that should be obtained. This should be consistent with the research budget provided. The budget in turn should be consistent with the objectives and targets that have been agreed for the entire marketing operation.

(e) Data collection

Data (and in fact all intelligence) is normally gathered on both a continuous and *ad hoc* basis. 'Continuous data collection' is all that intelligence (sales results, market shares, costs and prices, competitive activity, other regularly published information etc.) which is collected regularly in some standardised way. This material includes the 'meat' of regular company reports on its operations and results. It forms some 90 per cent of the data and information on which marketing and management information systems rely.

'*Ad hoc* data collection' refers to the additional data and information that has to be obtained from time to time, when the continuous system

Table 4.2 **some major sources of data and information**

Customers	current; potential; in present markets and ones to be developed in short and long term.
Distributors	including agents, franchisees where used, i.e. all in the firm's distribution network (present and potential future), at home and overseas.
Competitors	home and overseas; from the latter will come greater co-operation and could lead to licensing, with mutual benefits.
Research organisation	in firm's own industry and those of current and potential customers; especially 'experts' in subject under study.
Trade associations	in firm's own industry and those of current and potential customers; especially 'experts' in subject under study.
Government departments	including quasi-governmental bodies (e.g. various commodities marketing boards, British Standards Institution, British Tourist Authority, National Economic Development Office); embassies (libraries and commercial attaches at home and abroad); State (nationalised) industries boards.
Publications	trade, government, corporations and major banks, company reports; specialist magazines; newspapers; technical and scientific papers.
Official statistics	
Others	e.g. directories, stock exchange reports, universities, professional and learned societies, chambers of commerce, international bodies (e.g. United Nations, International Labour Office); registers such as *Kompass*.
The firm	all internal departments and divisions.

cannot provide the intelligence. This may be due to changing circumstances in the company's business, its market environment and so on and is the intelligence normally obtained via marketing research studies. These changes create new or modified needs for a company and so some aspects of this *ad hoc* collection may then be incorporated, in some modified form, into the regular 'continuous collection' system. They can also replace or modify some parts of the continuous collection system. So the whole data collection process itself needs to be reviewed and revised regularly to keep it up to date with the company's business needs.

4.4 TYPES OF STUDIES

The various research studies possible under the title 'Marketing Research' were set out briefly in Table 1.1. Some further comments are advisable here. Figure 4.1 sets out the various environmental factors which need consideration from time to time.

Fig 4.1 *factors affecting the business environment*

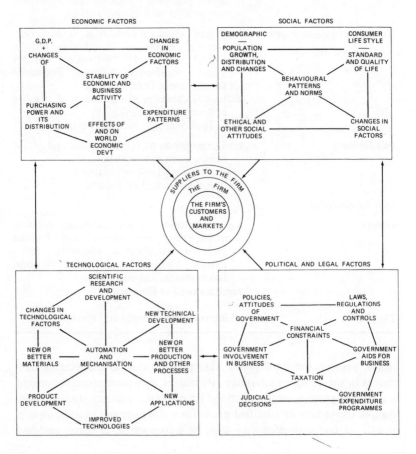

(a) Market research

Besides the purposes mentioned in Table 1.1 these studies can also be used to indicate how total markets segment into smaller, specific groups of present and potential buyers having homogeneous or common character- istics as buyers (see Section 6.4). The market potential revealed by this research also helps define sales territories and quotas and indicates if any changes have taken place in retailing practice. Market research will also show if major retailing has moved away from town centres to planned urban centres close to customers' homes. It can also indicate where or when test marketing and store audits are possible or necessary.

Market research may also be done by means of *consumer panels*, though this is often used as a supplementary aid to normal market research methods. Panels consist of a careful sample of customers, selected to represent the normal cross-section of a market or market segment or some other special requirement. Their views and reactions are tested against changes in a product, proposed new products, price changes and so on. It is maintained that the composition of a panel should be changed though at infrequent intervals, so that it does not become set in its ways and represent only the panel's views and not be representative of the market they are meant to represent. If changed too frequently, the results from the changing panels will not be comparable. The jargon is that the results will no longer be statistically significant.

It follows that *trade panels*, comprising a cross-section of the trades or industries being served, or the distributors, can be similarly used for industrial products and consumer durables as well as consumer goods. Panels are also used to test reactions to advertising programmes and changes thereof. This last type of panel is usually operated by independent agencies such as advertising agencies or the appropriate media (TV company, news- paper). Consumer and trade panels, the former often called 'consumer purchase panel' may be operated by the firm or an agency, jointly or separately.

The typical panel furnishes information at regular, prescribed intervals on specified points. Usually they have to complete forms prepared for this purpose. Or the information can be recorded in 'diaries' which are mailed back to the controlling organisation at set times. The usual information sought covers levels of sales, changes in the sales pattern, shifts in market composition, trends in competitor prices and appeals, brand loyalty and brand switching (for industrial products where used, changes in manu- facturer preference). They can also be used to indicate when and why heavy purchases result, indicate when innovative buyers arise, especially with new products and the basic characteristics of buyers. Trade panels provide information on inventory buildup or depletion, response and takeoffs by the different component members of the channel of distribution being used and customer reactions as seen by the distributor or trade member. While consumer and trade panels for consumer goods are now generally accepted in most developed nations, their use for bulk produced industrial products has still to be accepted as a normal and useful aid to the whole marketing process.

(i) *Potential*

Potential refers strictly to the *capacity* of markets to consume or purchase sellers' offerings. *Opportunity* is also used in this context but is an estimate, really, of the absolute or relative number of units that a market or market segment has capacity to buy or use in a specified period. Recent practice differentiates between *market* potential and *sales* potential.

Market potential refers to the capacity of the various segments of a market to buy or use the offerings from all sellers. It should refer to specific offerings in a specified geographical, technical or industry market and period of time. Sales potential is then a measure of the *share* of market potential for an individual seller. Potential may be estimated by macro-methods (e.g. use of industry sales indices) or micro-methods (e.g. market surveys, census of production and so on). The latter is obviously more costly than the former and in practice most estimates of potential use a mix of the two methods. Micro-methods are used when absolute measures of potential are needed and there is insufficient industry data or official statistics prove not to be particularly relevant or usable.

(b) Demand studies

When evaluating marketing opportunities, a company will usually have to estimate what the market demand for a product, in fact all the products in its product mix, is likely to be over a specified future period. However, estimating market demand is not as simple as it sounds. Consider one definition, given by Philip Kotler in his book *Marketing Management, Analysis, Planning and Control* (Prentice-Hall.): 'Market demand for a *product class* is the *total volume* which would be *bought* by a defined *customer group* in a *defined time period* under defined *environmental conditions* and *marketing effort*.'

It is seen that there are *eight variables* that affect market demand. First, the class of product has to be clearly defined. For example the manufacturer of basic cleaning fluids must decide whether its products are applicable to the home detergent market, which itself has many product classes (e.g. for washing clothes, crockery, floors), whether the end product is liquid or powder, or whether the products will be important ingredients of liquid cleaners for industrial or commercial use. The opportunities for a successful penetration of all these potential markets vary and the potential itself is affected by economic, technological and other environmental factors. For example a government may decide, rightly or not, that a particular product is hazardous for household use (as happened with 'biological' washing powders in some areas). They may ban or place restrictions on its use, thus altering its market potential.

Second, there is the question of how total volume is measured. This can be by physical volume (units etc.), monetary units or both. It may also be expressed in relative terms, for example, the demand in a particular segment may be expressed as x per cent of the total market. Physical volume is useful if the product is reasonably homogeneous as historical sales are not distorted by any change in the value of the money units used. But if homogeneity is changing or lacking, volume measurements can be misleading.

Third, what is 'bought' has to be defined. Is it the volume ordered, shipped, paid for, received or consumed? The figures vary according to the basis used and it is important not to change the basis from year to year otherwise the volume estimated in any year will not be comparable with historical figures. Fourth, demand can be measured for the total market or any segment or customer group comprising the total. What is required by the whole transport industry and say an airline will be very different.

Fifth, the location of the market must be clear. Is the demand being measured for a country, a region or an area or an industry in a given country or region? Sixth, demand must be estimated for specified time periods, whether this is the next trading year or the next x years. Seventh, the environmental factors applicable to all the above, especially the specified time period, must be known and their effect on demand estimated. Finally, the marketing effort proposed will help to determine what demand is likely to arise. This involves estimating market reaction to price, the degree of price elasticity likely to be encountered, response to promotional and distribution effort.

(c) Consumer studies

Consumer studies for consumer goods and services markets and customer studies for industrial products, as stated in Table 1.1, are intended to define the 'profile' of customers, in particular their behaviour as buyers and how they are motivated in making their buying decisions. For industrial products the positions have been summarised in Section 1.9 (e) and Figure 1.1. Further comments regarding consumer and services markets are advisable here.

(i) *Buyer behaviour*

Understanding buyer behaviour is a perplexing but essential task especially in current market and economic conditions. Difficulties arise because of the heterogeneity of the different buying or customer groups and the individuals comprising a group. Behavioural studies have therefore to identify the attitudes, opinions, desires and reactions to marketing offerings at different periods of time. This means that variables such as price, product features, corporate image and promotional activities, including personal selling, affect buyers. The economic, sociological and psychological aspects have to be studied.

These studies try to establish how customers identify a need for a product or service, the pre-purchase activity they follow (e.g. seeking information on the proposed purchase, watching advertisements, talking to friends and so on), the use they plan to make of the purchase item and their post-purchase feelings (e.g. are they satisfied, partly satisfied or dissatisfied with their acquisition). All will help to establish the usefulness of products on offer while the use that customers would make of any item helps to decide the total quantities and pack sizes that should be considered. For example will users' purchases be limited or occasional or frequent and do they prefer buying small quantities or large? Their pre-purchase activity can also indicate what cues have to be put their way by the marketing effort in order to get customers to proceed to the 'right' decision or response, the purchase of the firm's products.

Demand refers to consumers' willingness and ability to buy and buyer behaviour indicates how willingness can be enhanced, thus leading to the making of a sale. Behavioural studies indicate how marketing operations can be planned to affect or shape demand by causing changes in buyer preferences and reactions. They also help to bring products and services more into line with customer needs. They assist when decisions on product modification, rationalisation and new product development have to be taken and not just with decisions concerning promotional, personal selling, pricing and distribution matters. With industrial products, internal influences within the buying organisation, as shown in Figure 1.1, are also dominant.

(ii) *Motivational research*

This has been described as the measurement of attitudes and preferences which can be shown to affect consumption of a product or service, using indirect questioning techniques borrowed from the behavioural sciences. It helps to identify what customers want, why they want it and the images of products, brand names and companies. Findings from it have been successfully applied to the design and specification of modified and new products, packaging, advertising, sales promotions, selection of retail or point-of-sale outlets and pricing decisions.

Through the application of psychological and psycho-analytical methods and interviews in considerable depth, the research tries to determine why customers behave as they do. Yet intelligence on motives is not easily obtained. The respondent may not know why he or she behaves in a certain way and might not want to admit to it! Ridicule, insecurity and social disapproval may all be inhibitors. Consumers may not be able to express reactions in clear language and terms, nor be consciously aware they do react in a specified way. Further, motives may change before the intelligence gathered can be used and they certainly change in time as various circumstances also change. Finally, it may be difficult to obtain intelligence about stimuli below the level of consciousness and hence the resultant motivation. The intelligence can also be difficult to translate into correct action.

In behavioural and motivational studies, the research has to establish how far basic needs are being met and how much purchasing decisions depend on the desire for status, self-actualisation and esteem. It must try to establish how behaviour as a result of motivation affect individual's perception of the posed problem or product offering. It must also indicate how attitudes change and how the learning process changes behaviour as a result of knowledge and experience.

To summarise, the main factors influencing human behaviour and character are listed below.

Primary factors
Family background and life-style
Social background and reference group to which person belongs
Education and work groups
Race or nationality and religion (if any)
Secondary factors
Profession or work status
Income
Social status in community
Social and other aspirations or expectations
External personalised factors
Information and knowledge on the subject requiring decision
Relevant (and sometimes irrelevant) experience
Fears, doubts, uncertainties on the decision to be made
Ignorance – the decision to be made is an entirely new one
Taboos and prejudices

Irrelevant experience refers to the fact that people will sometimes believe that what are facts totally irrelevant to their pending decision do have bearing or significance on the decision to be made. For example, knowledge and experience of holidays in Spain may be used incorrectly to arrive at decisions about a holiday in Southeast Asia. This mistake is likely to occur most frequently when the consumer is ignorant about the matter, as interpreted above.

(iii) *Reference groups*

This approach is an attempt to categorise and identify potential buyers into mutually exclusive groups whose responses to marketing effort display a high degree of homogeneity. That is, each member of the group has similar behaviour characteristics *as buyers*. Their other personality characteristics, which do not affect buying responses, could be quite diverse. Each group is said to have certain behavioural characteristics which are seen as the norms or standard of behaviour of the group. Establishing these characteristics for the different groups comprising a total market helps executives to select the most effective marketing operations for the groups that form the targets of their marketing activities. It helps also in the selection of these target groups.

Most consumers do in fact relate to a number of different reference groups. Their background, including their profession, job status, educational standards, social class and family, will give them a variety of behaviour patterns according to the buying decision involved. For example in Britain, an ex-public school boy (i.e. private, usually expensive, schools) will not normally have similar tastes for holidays and leisure pursuits of a boy who has been to a state school. (However, the development of comprehensive schools in the state sector is narrowing this gap.) A senior executive will have quite different needs, attitudes, desires and ability to purchase products and services from a junior just starting out in life. Again, an accountant in a senior position who has had tertiary (university) education usually has different needs, attitudes and so on from an engineer who has worked his way up from the shop-floor. Thus which reference group norms apply to particular potential buyers can vary according to the product or service and buying decision involved.

(iv) *Opinion leaders*

Every reference group has a few 'members' who are considered by others as being opinion leaders or trend-setters. Usually they are people who are more ready to make new purchases (i.e. buy new products) or who have greater knowledge and experience and are thus more self-assured and ready to experiment. A few may have had this reputation pinned to them when in fact their knowledge and experience may not be greater than the others or which may not be relevant to the decision in question. For example, some years ago in India, when attitudes towards family planning were being researched, in almost every village the oldest male member of the village, their leader, was allowed to be the opinion leader on this subject. Yet most knew nothing about it and were biased by their religious or other beliefs. The true opinion leader should have been a woman, whose experience and knowledge were most relevant to the subject.

These people's opinions are respected and often sought after. Because of their importance, their views have to be canvassed. They are also useful in helping to distribute advice and information. If they can be convinced that a particular marketing offering is worthwhile, their acceptance of it should mean that others in their group will also respond favourably.

However, it is not always easy to identify opinion leaders or early adopters of new ideas or presentations. They tend to be innovative in some areas but not others. For example, senior executives may normally dress conservatively but are ready to try unfamiliar foods. When their behaviour characteristics are known, more effective marketing communications (personal selling and promotional activities) can be planned. In particular their known media habits and attitudes to advertising can be used to increase the firm's marketing effectiveness.

4.5 PLANNING THE RESEARCH

As stated in the opening remarks to this chapter (fifth paragraph in particular) it is necessary for each research project to be carefully planned. Then the results of the study are likely to prove most relevant and useful to the problem that has to be resolved. In addition the whole marketing research programme should form an integral part of the entire marketing operation and be consistent with marketing and corporate objectives. It may prove just a waste of money for a firm to embark on any research just when the executives feel like it, especially if a grandiose research project is intended. For example, a few years ago, the chief executive of a company in the civil engineering business, making pre-stressed, reinforced concrete products in a limited range, wanted an extensive study done in *all* markets for *all* such products used in civil engineering structures (roads, railways, bridges, culverts, tunnels and so on). Even with the most careful planning, over one hundred questions would have been necessary. Some 80 per cent of the information requested had no relevance at all to the firm's current and future operations. It would just have been filed away. The cost of the study, in 1983 terms, would have been about £700,000. There was difficulty in persuading him that this would be just a waste. Only when he was told that the information would be obsolescent in three months and the work would have to be done four times a year if its value was to be maintained that he reluctantly agreed that the work should not be done. In fact studies from time to time on a much more limited area, costing about £10,000, would have been most relevant to current and future activities. These were initiated and helped the firm to improve its profitability substantially over several years.

(a) Designing a research project

There are several steps that have to be taken in the design of any project
and there is a logical sequence for them. These are set out in Table 4.3.
Table 4.4 indicates the questions that should be considered when designing any research. These points are relevant to all projects, consumer goods
and durables, industrial products and capital equipment, as well as services.
For industrial products and capital equipment the special characteristics of
these markets (see Section 1.9) must be taken into account and smaller
samples will be used (see Section 4.6). For services (for example tourism,
banking, insurance, transport) the procedures and approach are basically
the same as for consumer goods but any special characteristics must also
be considered (see Section 9.4).

In some cases, when it is not clear what problem the research must
resolve, for example the basic hypothesis may not be clear, it is advisable
to embark on short *exploratory studies*. They help to decide what the
brief for the main study should be. Specific research questions can then
be deduced. It is important in exploratory work that flexibility and
versatility are encouraged. This form of study may also be used to uncover
sources of secondary information, interview key people with good knowledge of the subject being explored and examine analogous situations.

Exploratory studies and full-scale research are also used to establish
the causal relationships between important variables, the reason why certain things that have to be forecast happen under certain stimuli. These
are referred to often as *causal studies*. Finally, the real-world environment
affects real-world events. The environment establishes the 'rules' that
describe the relationships between events. These are referred to as *deter-
ministic causations*.

(b) The research brief

Many research studies fail to satisfy the requirements of executives because
their purpose is not clearly defined. Also the executives who need the
information may not take the researchers into their confidence. Often the
researchers do not probe deeply enough into the objectives or purpose of
a study. It may well be that the problem to be solved is not as defined by
the executives. For example a product may not be selling well not because
there is something wrong with its formulation. It may be that the selling
or promotional support is wrong, or is being aimed at the wrong customers
or is wrongly timed. Production and distribution factors may also contribute to the problem. A thorough discussion of the subject should lead to a
better understanding of what the problem really is and thus more effective
research. Since the marketing problem may have nothing to do with anything being wrong in the marketing area, all departments of the firm should

Table 4.3 **basic steps in research design and work**

1 Isolate or identify the problem to be resolved, the purpose of the study, or the hypothesis to be tested.
2 Review relevant literature/published data (secondary data); discuss this with informed and interested people.
3 Design the study, making hypotheses specific to the situation or problem.
4 Design or adapt research methods and techniques necessary for the work; if necessary conduct pilot or exploratory studies to indicate when revision of methods and techniques needed.
5 Decide on nature, type and size of sample; select people to be interviewed.
6 Conduct the fieldwork – (primary) data collection and returns.
7 Process the data, coding responses if necessary.
8 Conduct statistical analyses; test for statistical significance.
9 Assemble results and test hypotheses.
10 Write up results, relating findings to other research and information where available, make interpretations and draw conclusions and recommendations.

Table 4.4 **key questions to consider when planning research**

1 What is the objective or purpose of the study? What must be known to meet the objective? What problems must be resolved? What variables must be measured? Can this be done? Is the required data/information available or obtainable?
2 What published (secondary) data/information is available?
    How current, relevant and reliable is it? What are the reputations and standing of the sources? How detailed is it? Any key points omitted? What further data/verification is needed?
3 What kind and size of sample should be drawn? Why? How? Are control groups needed? Who should be questioned? More than once?
4 What field studies for primary data/information are needed?
    What sources should be tapped? What is the extent of their knowledge, relevancy and reliability? How reliable are the 'experts'? What accuracy is expected of this data? What amount of raw data will result and how should/can this be processed? Is any scaling necessary?
5 What methods should be used?
    Postal questionnaires, telephoned interviews, personal interviews with/without prompting questionnaires? Use of panels? What should be the work-plan? What are the cost and time constraints? How do these affect the work-plan?
6 How should the total data/information be collated, analysed and presented?
7 Therefore, what should be specified in the brief for the research, in particular the terms of reference for it?

be involved in this critical preliminary discussion, before the brief can be prepared.

Further, it is essential for the researchers to have sympathetic understanding of the requirements of the sponsors of the study. It should be remembered also that the complexity of marketing problems contributes to the difficulty encountered in defining the purpose of a study. While ideally each study should look into one problem, cost and time constraints may force a study to investigate more than one problem at a time, thus aggravating the difficulties encountered in this work.

Then there is the data/information associated with variables that can change quickly or unexpectedly or are in a state of rapid change (for example declining demand due to a rapidly deteriorating national economy or rising unemployment). The information is perishable in that it can become obsolete in a short time. This problem arises especially with studies that cover long periods of time. In such cases it is vital that researchers make interim reports to their sponsors and this requirement is one which should be in the terms of reference in the brief.

The main items that should be in any brief for a marketing research study are listed in Table 4.5. The brief should mean the same thing to all interested parties and should not ask for irrelevant information. It should define the relevant populations (customers) to be sampled in existing markets, immediate potential markets and those intended for later development. It should indicate the order or priority of the required accuracy of the various analyses to be presented while indicating the required accuracy of the main results. It should not prejudge the selection of research techniques and procedures nor prejudice nor prejudge the results.

(c) Desk research

This refers to the detailed study that should be made by researchers 'at their desks', of all secondary data and information relevant to the project, before any field studies are contemplated. It is not only done when some specific research is to be undertaken. It should form a regular part of the information collection and analysis that form the normal ongoing work of any marketing information system, in order to keep the collected data and information as up-to-date as possible.

If desk research is to be done effectively, the research team must have a good knowledge of the sources of relevant secondary data. They should know also how reliable such sources are and the usual dependence that can be placed on the information provided by them. The researchers must be able to convert 'raw' data into intelligence relevant to the firm's marketing needs as well as any specific problems that may be under study. When published information is not satisfactory, complete or relevant enough to specific needs, ingenuity is needed in deducing the possible use and relevance of it and the subsequent field studies that would be needed to improve on or supplement this incomplete knowledge. Given the cost of field studies, which continue to rise, it is important for marketing executives to ensure that desk research is done as thoroughly and efficiently as possible. Too often it is treated scantily or superficially. As a result field studies have to be much more extensive than they could be otherwise.

Table 4.5   **main contents of a research brief**

---

1 *Objective of the research*
    (i) Purpose of the study or use to which results will be put.

2 *Terms of reference of study*: includes
    (i)   The data/information required;
   (ii) the customers/respondents to be interviewed;
  (iii) the size and nature of the sample to be used;
  (iv) the degree of accuracy required, or error permitted;
   (v) timing, including commencement and completion dates;
  (vi) permitted costs;
 (vii) if interim reports and thus flexibility in the research are needed.

3 *Methods to be used*
    (i)   Amount and nature of secondary data or information to be used;
   (ii) type of field studies to be employed;
  (iii) detailed breakdown of composition of sample;
  (iv) what follow-up interviews would be undertaken, when and under what circumstances;
   (v) how the data/information collected will be collated, analysed and presented.

4 *The report*
    (i)   Nature and contents;
   (ii) conclusions that would be drawn;
  (iii) method of presentation and circulation.

5 *Recommendations*
    (i)   Whether these will be made;
   (ii) probable nature and extent of them.

(d) Field studies

While desk studies will also cover analyses of data internal to the firm, field studies are concerned with external data. This may be done by observation, mailed questionnaires, telephoned interviews or personal (face-to-face) interviews. Group discussions, conferences and various panels can also be used. The method used will depend on the nature of the study, its complexity, accessibility of respondents and the non-availability of suitable published data/information.

(i) *Postal questionnaires*

The advantages and disadvantages of these are summarised in Table 4.6, but some additional comments are advisable. First, the relative cheapness of the method may be misleading since the response rate is usually lower than by other methods. For consumer goods surveys, the response rate can be less than 40 per cent. With industrial products, this author has experi-

Table 4.6 **postal questionnaires**

	ADVANTAGES:
Cheap distribution	Economical costs, but see *Disadvantages*. Widespread distribution of questionnaire is possible, useful when customers are widely dispersed geographically; within limits, costs not increased because respondents are widely dispersed.
Speed	Responses from entire sample obtained more quickly than if interviews necessary.
Anonymity	Respondents assured of remaining anonymous, provided forms are not 'keyed'.
Time	Gives respondents time to check data etc. with records, reports and for consultations with others; better accuracy possible.
Contact	Some important respondents, by definition, are difficult to contact personally; work and responsibilities require them to travel extensively etc.; they may not have time for interview but might be more willing to complete mailed questionnaire.
	DISADVANTAGES:
Questionnaire	Few respondents prepared to complete long questionnaire (some allergic to them anyway), so must be kept short; problems of design, selection of questions etc. (see Section 4.7).
Unstructured	No control over respondents actually completing the form; they can read whole thing first and so prejudice the answers given to individual questions.
Questions	Must be simple; no one present to answer queries on complex questions which put many respondents off anyway.
Observation	Researchers not present so cannot observe respondent's attitudes and background.
Response	Response rate is usually low. Initial answers cannot be probed at the time.

enced rates of 10 per cent and less. Where the total sample has to be heavily stratified (i.e. several groups or types of respondents make up the whole), low response may mean that so few replies are received from one or more sub-group that the data is statistically insignificant for those groups and perhaps the whole survey. Some or all of the disadvantages listed could also mean that follow-up questionnaires may have to be sent, or telephone interviews conducted, to clarify doubts and uncertainties that arise from the initial answers. This all adds to the total cost.

The point about anonymity is also doubted by some respondents, especially with industrial products surveys. They know that the questionnaires can be 'coded', that is have numbers or letters on them, or bits snipped out of the edges. These can indicate to the researcher who or what type of respondent has completed the form. Some people will not return the forms if they feel that true anonymity is not being maintained.

Finally, with industrial products surveys, experience shows that questionnaires posted on Mondays and Tuesdays tend to be seen by more executives. Those posted on Wednesdays are less likely to be redirected to the right executive while those posted on Thursdays are most likely to be destroyed! (In Britain this assumes that first class mail is used and delivery is made within twenty-four hours. If deliveries take longer then only the Monday/Tuesday mailings seem assured of some sort of response.)

(ii) Telephone interviews

Telephone interviews permit controlled contact on a personal level with a selected sample of respondents. It is a more expensive method than postal questionnaires, but much cheaper than personal interviews. The main advantages and disadvantages are summarised in Table 4.7. While postal questionnaires are best when limited straightforward information is needed or blanket coverage is acceptable (respondents are not identified specifically) telephone interviews can probe more deeply into important aspects. For industrial products surveys, this method has proved most effective in establishing who uses a product, the use made of it and the level and timing of purchases. However, the greater cost of this method inhibits the wide geographical coverage possible with postal questionnaires.

Telephone interviews are useful as a follow-up to other survey methods and for validating quantitative and qualitative information from other sources. If the intelligence obtained is not carefully recorded at the time of the call, accidental interviewer bias can result from later analysis. Finally, it can be difficult to identify the status of the respondent answering the call and, with industrial surveys, what the firm makes, its industrial classification and that of its main customers.

Table 4.7 **telephone interviews**

	ADVANTAGES:
Cost	Still cheaper than personal interviews but more expensive than mailing.
Time	Survey can be completed much more quickly than with personal interviews and give time saving over postal surveys.
Response	Very good response rates possible.
Contact	Important respondents can be contacted more easily, even if not available on first call, not so disruptive as with personal interviews where a wasted visit can increase total cost of survey.
Undemanding	Respondents view this method as less demanding of them, time-saving etc.
Follow-up	Complex, difficult answers can be probed immediately and difficult points can be explained to respondent at the time.
Inhibitions	Some respondents inhibited by face-to-face interviews; not so over the telephone. Usually feel free to respond without seeking authorisation of a superior.
Anonymity	Respondents can be assured on this.
	DISADVANTAGES:
Time	Costs make it necessary to keep calls as short as possible; limits amount of information that can be gathered.
Questions	Best kept to those that can be answered off the top of the head, i.e. instantly; no chance to consult others except if a second call is agreed. Not always possible to comprehend importance of answer immediately.
Observation	Not possible. Also personal rapport not always easy to establish.
Interruption	Call can be interrupted or terminated before all points covered.

(iii) *Personal interviews*

While this is the most expensive and time-consuming of the methods available, it offers many advantages. The amount of information obtained by a single interview can be considerable. Complex matters can be dealt with efficiently and the responses can be probed deeply. The structure or nature of the interview can be altered according to the responses being obtained and the interviewer can observe the attitude of respondents and the environment in which they live (consumer goods) or work (industrial products). If a questionnaire is used, complex questions can be explained. If respondents read ambiguity into any question, this too can be cleared up before the answer is given by the interviewer. The great flexibility of this method is perhaps its greatest advantage since field surveys can be adjusted quickly and cheaply, especially when the early answers indicate that some hypothesis of the survey may not be correct. Faults in method or approach can be spotted early enough to avoid having to redo the survey later. Finally, the respondents are more easily identified and, with industrial products, the activities of the responding firms can be more accurately gauged.

The main disadvantage is the cost. This requires the sample to be kept as small as possible. If too small, however, doubts may arise about the statistical validity of the results. Then, especially with industrial products research, the executives who must be interviewed may have difficulty in making the time available. Even when an appointment is granted, something urgent may arise which takes the respondent out of his or her office. The visit is wasted and all the problems of trying to arrange another will arise. Further, the interviewers must be skilled in the work involved. With industrial studies, often they must have more than superficial knowledge of the business and technology of the respondents and, frequently, of their major customers. Balancing these disadvantages is the fact that a very high rate of response is achieved, especially where respondents can be assured of anonymity.

The cost aspect means also that a wide geographical spread of the survey has to be avoided. This problem is partially overcome for consumer studies by conducting the survey in regions known to be reasonably representative of the nation as a whole. However, doubts exist whether all these zones really are 'typical' and the researchers can never be certain that changes taking place in them are occurring at the same rate nationally, or are indeed occurring elsewhere at all. For industrial products, where specific industries have to be studied, the locations of the firms in them are known. Also industries tend to collect in a few geographical regions for historical reasons or because important sources of supply or major markets are located nearby.

(iv) *Group surveys*

These, called *focus group surveys* in America and sometimes elsewhere, involve groups of eight to twelve persons called together for two or more hours to discuss specific points. The person in charge, a researcher, specifies the subject for discussion and suggests where the group discussion might begin. Thereafter the researcher's role is to stimulate interaction and discussion of the points involved without imposing his or her own views or directives on the group. That is, there should be no firm steering of the course the discussion takes except to keep it within the broad parameters of the subject. Otherwise the results – usually taped – will have interviewer bias and be useless. Initially used for consumer goods and durables markets, it has been found to be very useful for industrial studies, especially where complex or new technological and economic factors are involved.

This should not be confused with *panels*. Focus groups are called together for usually one, but occasionally two or more, meetings to discuss specified subjects. Panels comprise a larger number of people, usually representative of a market or market segment, are kept in existence for a substantial period of time and have to return reports at regular intervals on many marketing aspects relevant to their purpose. Composition of the panels is changed occasionally, especially if the composition of the groups they represent is known to have altered.

4.6 SAMPLING

In this book the word 'sampling' refers to the selection of groups of customers for the purpose of a marketing research study. It does not mean the alternative (American) interpretation: the free distribution of a product to obtain further sales. The main terms and their meanings are summarised in Table 4.8. Some further comments are made here.

Systematic sampling is a slight variation of simple random sampling. This method assumes that population elements are ordered in some way, for example in telephone or other directories. Thus if a population is known to be made up of N elements and a sample size of n is needed, the ratio of $N : n$ is calculated and rounded off to the nearest integer to arrive at the sampling interval. Thus if there were 800 members in a universe and a sample of 80 was required, the sampling interval would be 10. A random number is selected (between 1 and 10). If this were say 5, the sample elements would be 5, 15, 25, 35 etc. Thus the fifth, fifteenth, twenty-fifth (and so on) names on the population list would be interviewed.

The *sampling frame* is a list, file or other collection of all the units in the population under study. It is vital in sampling work since the form of it, or the lack, determines the whole structure of the research, especially the accuracy of the results. If it does not exist then it may mean the abandonment of ideas for a survey. Constructing a frame is a major job. For example it was a major task establishing the type and location of consumers who took both summer and winter package holidays. Without it, research on the profiles of such consumers was wasteful as many who did not take two holidays a year could not be eliminated from the sample. In industrial products, a similar problem arose with identification of firms in specified industries who used competitors' products.

Table 4.8   **sampling: terms and meaning**

Universe or population	All consumers (for consumer goods and durables) or all firms (for industrial goods and capital equipment) comprising a 'total market' or geographical region etc.
Sample	A subgroup of the 'universe'.
Sampling fraction	The proportion of the 'population' forming the sample, e.g. $\frac{1}{10}$ (one in ten units), $\frac{1}{100}$ (one in every 100 units).
Random or probability sample	Every unit of the 'universe' has a known or stated chance of selection. The different units of the 'universe' need not have an equal chance of being selected.
Non-random or purposive sample	Uncontrolled chance of selection or where choice of respondents is influenced by need to investigate a particular aspect of the market (e.g. number of calls made by a doctor and how much time is spent in promoting a new drug may give better measure of the chance of new drug being widely adopted by the medical profession).
Quota sample	Non-random sampling where the choice of respondents is left to interviewer; unlike random samples when interviewers are given names and addresses of persons to be interviewed and how to select respondent at each address or location. Recalls are necessary if selected respondent not available on first call. Substitutes rarely permitted.
Other samples	
Stratified	Sample where the various units or subgroups (i.e. 'strata') of the universe are selected in proportions that reflect the stratification of the universe, or certain other known characteristics.
Cluster	A sample where a group, location, or cluster of respondents are selected at random, rather than individual respondents: e.g. a random selection of blocks of homes rather than individual consumers; a sales district rather than individual sales people. Reduces the cost per interview but if the clusters have to be spread widely over a geographical market, cost of transporting the researchers could be increased.

Table 4.8 *(contd)*

Area	A form of cluster sampling where there is random sampling of geographical areas. Once selected the further sampling is restricted to the areas selected.
Fixed size	The total size of the sample is fixed and all interviews are done before data analysis begins. The sample tries to achieve balance between the cost and reliability of the study.
Sequential	Rules are established for an early stop to interviews, before all the projected respondents are seen or to conduct extra interviews to seek more information. The first is applied when data received becomes repetitive (e.g. as in industrial surveys). The latter when further clarification may be needed.
Multi-stage	This form of sampling involves random sampling of the sub-units of the universe. When the primary sample has been drawn it may be advisable to subdivide this into further random samples. For example, if the first sample is based on townships, further samples may be needed, drawn from residential blocks, etc.
Systematic sampling	See text under this heading.

4.7 QUESTIONNAIRE DESIGN

There are basically three forms of questionnaires:

structured,
semi-structured and
unstructured.

Structured questionnaires are those where all the answers fall into a pre-selected pattern reflected in the format and layout of the form. They give a rigid interpretation of the subject or questions. They are useful where simple, straightforward information is required and with postal surveys where the respondents have to complete the forms on their own. Where a complex situation exists, or where the interrelationships of the variables are complex, as with major industrial products, they are not of much use.

Semi-structured questionnaires have been described as a series of standard questions used by the interviewer with a set of operating instructions designed to cope with most response pattern situations. That is, the questions are designed to provide the basic or important answers but when an interviewer finds responses are varying from what was expected, certain freedom is given to the interviewer to ask alternative or supplementary questions. This permits flexibility in the research as does the use of open-ended and multiple-choice questions (explained a little later). With these questionnaires, interviewers are more in control of the interviews and there is ease of tabulation and recording of the responses. Subsequent analysis is also easier. The fact that part of the questionnaire is structured forces the research planners to consider deeply just what information is needed and how the questions would be best put to draw relevant information easily from the respondents. Open-ended questions with their usual verbal answers, though sometimes difficult to classify and analyse, add colour and meaning to the interpretation of the many statistics obtained by the rest of the interview.

Unstructured questionnaires are really just notes to the interviewer of the key points that should be investigated in depth. They are really interview guides and prompts. This approach is very useful where very complex technical and other factors are being investigated, especially when there is uncertainty about the underlying hypotheses. They are also very useful where free but very detailed discussion is sought of a major factor and the respondents should not be influenced or deflected by having to answer specific questions.

Usually this 'questionnaire' is used for only a limited number of interviews and often for pilot surveys to establish the correct basis for the major study. The free-flowing verbal answers are difficult to analyse and interpret. Worse, if the responses cannot be recorded at the time of the interview, the opinions have to be committed to memory and recalled later. The danger of incorrect interpretation of the responses is increased. Also no two interviews need be compatible; many are downright incompatible. If only a few interviews are conducted, doubts about the significance of the responses arise. Finally, if the interviewer is not very experienced in, and knowledgeable about, the subject, important questions may not be asked because the interview has wandered off the main objective of the exercise. The comments may seem important at the time but on later analysis may be found to be irrelevant to the subject.

(a) Design considerations

Table 4.9 lists some of the questions that have to be considered before a questionnaire can be designed. Frequently surveys and their questionnaires are not designed or planned at all. Executives get carried away by what seems to them to be an exciting activity. They do not realise that questionnaire design in particular is not an easy task. It calls for great skill, experi-

Table 4.9   **questionnaire design: questions to consider**

1	What is the purpose of the survey?
2	What pattern must the enquiry follow?
3	What purpose does it serve?
4	Which variables have to be measured?
5	What kind of sample must be drawn?
6	How large should the sample be?
7	Who will comprise the sample (men, women, housewives only, executives etc.)?
8	How frequently will respondents be interviewed?
9	What scaling will be necessary?
10	Must it identify or check seasonal and other fluctuations?
11	Is it a short, factual enquiry or a depth analysis or analytical study?
12	What order of questioning is needed? That is, how should the question sequences be built up?
13	What method of approach will be used to respondents?
14	What will be the main and auxiliary methods of data collection?
15	What order of questioning must be followed for each variable being surveyed?
16	Should pre-coded or free-response questions be used?

ence and understanding of human behaviour and motivation. Many marketing executives who have been tempted to go it alone discover the error of their ways only when they have implemented plans based on their faulty research and have paid the penalty. The work calls for not only a great deal of technical knowledge but also a prolonged and arduous intellectual exercise.

Surveys and their questionnaires must aim for precision, sound logic and efficiency in the work. Poorly designed, they fail to provide accurate answers. These lead to faulty conclusions, plans and actions. Much of the information provided could be irrelevant to the issues in hand. The work is thus wasteful of time and money.

(b) Questions

Basically there are three types of questions. First, there is the *dichotomous question* which is meant to provide a simple 'yes'/'no' answer. Alternatively, the respondents have to choose between only two clear-cut answers. Second, there is the *multiple-choice question*. Here respondents have to chose one answer from several indicated possibilities. Alternatively the interviewees are asked to rank each choice in some order of priority or rating. This is normally referred to as 'scaling'. The problem is how wide a choice should be given? If too many are suggested, respondents may have difficulty in choosing one answer and even in rating them. Also, with many choices, the total selection for any one of them might be so small as to give data that are statistically insignificant.

Finally there is the *open-ended question*. In this the question is put and respondents are left to answer verbally in any manner they choose. Although these are difficult to collate and analyse they allow respondents to express themselves freely (though some may find this difficult to do!). They permit a wider, deeper study of the points covered by them. They may be used to establish a hypothesis or when the choice of possible answers is not known, or unclear or there are in fact too many possible answers.

There is also the *'control' question*, which can be of any of the three basic types mentioned above. Its function is to verify the correctness of respondents' answers. If it is believed that in key areas misleading answers can be given for any of the reasons implied in Table 4.10, it is advisable to slip in a control question later in the questionnaire. These questions, using a different phraseology and thus possible answers, will provide responses which the analysts can check with the original questions for consistency. For example, in a survey of holiday habits attempting to measure the number of holidays taken a year, an original question may be 'How many holidays do you have each year? 1? 2? 3? (Tick as appropriate).' The interviewees may tick '2' or '3'. Later an open-ended questions could be used as follows: 'When do you take your holiday? . . .' If the reply to the second is just one month, say 'August' the interviewer knows the first response may be wrong (i.e. the status point in (8) in Table 4.10), or the second question could have been misunderstood. The interviewer should then query one or other of the answers exampled above.

It should also be remembered that the questions should orientate and stimulate respondents to co-operate correctly in the study. Further, because of the complexities of modern life and the interrelationships of the variables influencing the subject under consideration, many respondents may genuinely not know which answer to give. Provision should be made with all three types of questions for interviewees to give a 'Don't know' answer. This is as valid and useful an answer as any apparently more positive one.

4.8 BIAS

The reader will realise by now that there are many opportunities for unintentional and unwanted bias to be injected in any marketing research project. The more common causes are listed in Table 4.11. Such bias should be avoided, but if this is not possible the degree of bias present should be known and allowances made for it in the collation and analyses of the results of the survey.

In some instances bias is unavoidable or deliberately brought about. For example, if it is impossible for cost, time or other reasons to survey every group of customer who should be surveyed, some group or other will be

Table 4.10 **question formulation: points to remember**

1 *Avoid poor question construction by avoiding*
   (i) ambiguity,
   (ii) lack of mutual exclusiveness,
   (iii) lack of meaningfulness,
   in the questions.
2 *Follow a logical sequence in the questioning.*
3 *Keep questions as simple as possible.*
4 *Avoid complex words or phrases.*
5 *Avoid words which would be unfamiliar to respondents.*
6 *Avoid leading questions and emotionally loaded words which would appear to respondents as hinting at the answer required.*
7 *Avoid questions that the respondents' background, experience etc. does not equip them to answer correctly.*
8 *Do not use questions, or choice of answers, where one answer may appear to respondents to confer some status to them, or make them appear to have a higher standing than they do.* (The interviewees will tend to pick that answer whether it is true or not in their case.)
9 *With all questions provide a space where respondents can answer 'don't know'.* (If this is a genuine view, encourage them to select this answer rather than guess at an answer or give an incorrect one.)
10 *Avoid questions that tax the memory too much* (or which respondents do not wish to answer because they think it belittles them).
11 *Avoid too wide a choice of answers* (see text).
12 *Do not narrow the choice so that answers are not fully representative of the main possibilities.*

Table 4.11 **common causes of bias in research results**

1 Use of a faulty sampling frame.
2 Sample incorrectly drawn for the purpose.
3 Non-representative sample used.
4 Sample too large (so much data provided as to confuse or hide the true significance).
5 Sample too small and results may not be statistically significant.
6 Failure to cover some important market segment.
7 Non-response (either respondents not willing or able to answer, or selected respondent not at home or available for interview).
8 Unintentional interviewer bias (through researcher over-stressing a word or question).
9 Resulting from the questions posed (see Table 4.10).
10 Lack of precision or accuracy in the research.
11 Misinterpretation or incorrect analyses of responses.
12 Use of too many open-ended questions or too many choices with multiple-choice ones.
13 Unintentional incorrect response; no use made of control questions.
14 Ambiguity in questions or some other part of the research.
15 Unavoidable bias (see text).
16 Faulty processing of data/information.

excluded from the sample. These are usually groups that are not major customers or are not likely to be in the planning period for which the survey is being done. Or it is difficult to obtain information from one group. By ignoring these groups, assuming that the *status quo* will continue into the period concerned, the assumption is made that the results of the survey will not be affected significantly. This ignores the possibility of changes occurring in purchasing habits and so on and thus some unknown bias is being injected into the results.

Thus the realities of life today makes it difficult to arrive at a truly objective probability statement about the accuracy of the results of a survey. Provided this fact is known and allowance made for it in the resultant forecasting and planning, the dangers inherent in it can be minimised. The damage is done when the presence of major bias is realised too late, at the end of the day, when the firm has committed itself to various activities based on the faulty data/information. Marketing researchers must obviously be aware of the various ways in which unwanted bias can be injected into their work. They must strive to avoid these pitfalls. Where bias is unavoidable, the extent of it must be estimated and due allowances made in the results. Their colleagues should also be told fully what nature and degree of bias has been allowed for in research reports.

4.9 FORECASTING

Forecasting is not planning though all plans are based on a variety of forecasts. For example marketing plans will be based on forecasts of market potential, market shares, prices, competitive activity, effects of market factors on demand, demand studies for important products in the firm's product range, customer needs, distribution requirements, promotional activities and even the nature and scale of marketing research. Some newcomers to marketing complain that it seems to be all forecasting and planning. It isn't of course but the acts of forecasting and planning force executives to consider in depth all the important aspects of their activities leading, usually, to more profitable and efficient operations.

There are many forecasting methods available to executives (and the major ones will be discussed briefly later) but all of them deal with one or other of the many elements of uncertainty that exist in the business environment. The methods range from blind guesses through informed judgement based on experience and past results to more scientific approaches based on sound statistical and other theories. These last do not, however, obviate the need for executives involved in research to maintain a good sense of proportion based on their experiences.

For example they should appreciate what degree of accuracy is obtainable or appropriate for the task in hand and avoid going for the theoretical best. Striving too hard for the latter will increase costs, delay results and reduce the value of the planning. On the other hand, with environmental or market factors a high degree of accuracy in forecasting possible events is usually necessary. Finally, complexity is not necessarily beneficial. Simple methods can often be more cost-effective and should be preferred if they produce satisfactory results for the firm's needs.

(a) Statistical projections

These are based on the assumption that past performance can be a guide to the future. Such an assumption can be dangerous at times of great economic change or uncertainty. In 'normal' times, the correctness of it depends on the length of time for which the forecasts are made, the age of the products and the point they have reached in their life-cycles (see Chapter 5). These methods do, however, allow executives to see where *trends* may lead if no major changes in market factors occur. However, they are more accurate for short-term forecasts (say up to a year) than for longer ones.

(i) *Growth patterns*

This method takes the average annual rate of growth, calculated for a specified period of years, expresses the last year as an index of the earliest and works out the growth rate from compound interest tables. The expected change is expressed as a percentage of the previous growth rate and allowances can be made for any erratic changes in data.

(ii) *Moving averages*

This method is an attempt to eliminate cyclical or seasonal patterns from the data to indicate the underlying, smoothed trend. This method is rarely useful for long-term forecasts since one disadvantage is that it always falls short of the actual data available.

(iii) *Mathematical trends*

This group encompasses many methods and mathematical formulae for calculating a trend line in a time series. This line can then be projected to some future date. The line of 'best fit' may be calculated mathematically as it is not easy to place exactly, by eye, on a graph.

(iv) *Exponential smoothing*

This employs moving averages which are exponentially weighted so that more recent data is given greater weighting or importance. Past forecasting errors are taken into account in each successive forecast. This method is useful for short-term forecasts for inventory and production control purposes and sales forecasting. However, all four of these methods give little indication of changes in market and business environments and in the

(b) Marketing research

The methods here range from comparative studies to special surveys and experimental marketing. They assume that data gathered some weeks previously is still valid when the decisions based on these forecasts are taken, usually some time later. The inherent dangers should be obvious.

(i) *Leading indicators*

A leading indicator is some event which always precedes an event of another type and is seen as giving prior warning of a pending change. For example a change in a nation's economic activity can be deduced to have some effect on the economy of a specific market and hence demand for certain product groups. Or the rise and fall in the number of advertisements for executives for a specific industry may indicate how activity in them and hence demand for the products they use may be changing. This method is useful for short-term forecasts.

(ii) *Comparative studies*

Here the performance of a product similar to the one for which a forecast is required is used to indicate possibilities. For example the demand for a new product might well be deduced from studies of the progress of other similar products, especially with regard to prices and promotional activities. The market performances of competitive products also offer useful comparisons as does the performance of similar products in overseas markets, especially those having similar basic characteristics to Britain.

(iii) *Survey of buying intentions*

These surveys try to measure the buying intentions of both consumers (for consumer goods) and professional buyers in business and industry (for industrial and other products). They can be used for both existing and new products and goods. They provide a predictive index for forecasting future sales. With industrial products, where there are only a few customers, the data obtained can be reliable enough to use in its original state, i.e. not indexed.

(iv) *Experimental research*

This heading covers test marketing, advertising weighting experiments, experimentation with marketing methods and pricing. Their aim is to give information that can be used in forecasting, especially the probability of various levels of profitability being achieved with different decisions and actions. They can provide simple forecasts or information on causal relationships which can form the basis for more complex forms of forecasting. The main disadvantage is that all variables except the one being measured have to be assumed to be constant and this is not true in practice.

(v) *Other methods*

Under this heading are included marketing judgement, consumer usage and attitude surveys. The first is used when relevant data is not available but the firm has extensive knowledge and experience of its markets and their behaviour. The application of common sense then can give usable forecasts though a company can never be sure of the accuracy of them. Caution in the decision-making process is thus also advisable.

Consumer usage and attitude surveys help to determine probable demand and the factors that influence this. The forecasts are helpful when new products are contemplated. They can also form the basis for the formulation of appropriate marketing models.

(c) Analytical methods

There are three main methods under this heading:

(i) *Econometric models*

These are attempts to represent in mathematical terms the interdependent relationships between the variables affecting a particular activity. They can be used to forecast economic activity, prices, market and sales performance. There must be understanding of the causal relationships with the things being forecast. Thus a sales forecasting model must take into account all the distribution, inventory and promotional factors affecting sales or demand. The building of these models usually calls for considerable marketing and economic research.

(ii) *Input-output analysis*

This attempts to estimate the outputs of an industry or firm for different inputs of effort and other resources. Or how the output of one industry will affect the inputs from another. For example, if the motor industry is in recession, with considerable cutback of output, the inputs from the industries supplying it will be reduced. So demand for the latter's products will decline. An input-output model should indicate what this relationship is, but it is an expensive one to set up. Any additional benefit accruing because of improved demand forecasting will have to be judged carefully against the cost of building the model.

(iii) *Regression analysis*

This explores the mathematical relation of other variables with the one under study. It relates the data into a joint equation for all variables having causal relationships with each other. Unrelated data, though interesting and capable of a statistical fit into the formula, usually adds nothing to the results.

(d) Technological forecasting

This is too extensive a subject to be covered fully in this book. Many large books have been published on it. Readers wishing to delve further into this subject should turn to one of these works. It is sufficient to note here that in any high technology economy, technological forecasting, indicating likely future situations in technology, cannot be avoided. While emphasis has been given to trying to predict what will happen, this forecasting is better used to indicate what is possible and therefore what can be made to happen. The main methods are summarised below.

First, there is the *Delphi technique*, in which a group of experts meet to forecast possible future developments through the provision of answers to a series of questionnaires. Successive questionnaires show each expert how his or her opinions differ from the others and offers opportunities for modifications and additions to be made to their original statements. This method stimulates creative thinking and corrects the bias of individual views without leading to the domination of majority opinion.

Next is the formulation of *scenarios*, which attempt to describe a sequence of events and how a particular goal may be reached. They should postulate the various alternative states possible and identify the courses of action needed to achieve the preferred one. It is a creative exercise to forecast what is possible.

Morphological analysis consists of an exhaustive analysis of all the technical requirements of a product and their relationships. These are plotted on a matrix so that possible alternatives can be explored. It is useful in the study of a multiplicity of technical or environmental options but is very difficult to apply in practice.

Impact analysis is a version of scenario writing. It concentrates on the impact various forecasted technological developments might have on particular industries. For example, what would be the impact on the steel-making industry if a new plastic was developed that could safely replace all uses of steel? This method allows companies to spot future opportunities and threats, permitting them to plan to exploit the former or avoid the latter.

Extrapolative techniques are based on study of technological trends and their extrapolation into the future. There are various methods which have obvious links with economic forecasting. The techniques have many faults but have improved validity when applied to genuine problems. For example, what effect will the development of alternative energy sources (e.g. wind power) have on user industries (e.g. electricity generation, ship propulsion and hence design). It becomes a more effective method when linked to studies of the life-cycle curves of each technology and these curves are extrapolated to see when one technology is reaching a turning point or is being overtaken by another.

4.10 MARKETING INFORMATION SYSTEMS

Marketing information or intelligence systems (MIS) have four interrelated functions to perform, as described in Section 4.1. In conjunction with the control systems in operation, executives should also be able to monitor results being obtained, check them against plans and targets and so gain further insight into programme modifications that are necessary. In practical terms the MIS has the prime task of informing executives of what is happening in markets (current and future) of interest to them, what influences are at work and therefore what is likely to happen in the future. Further, it should indicate what the rewards are likely to be for specific inputs of effort and other resources. MIS and control systems jointly have two aims: first, to assist executives to control the present and forecast short-term events and, second, to forecast and plan for the long term.

Therefore, before a MIS can be constructed, the basic questions shown in Table 4.12 should be considered. These in fact require a full-scale review and appraisal of the entire marketing operation, its organisation, strategies and policies. The responsibilities of the executives must be defined to establish how the information should be circulated and when this should be done. The ability of executives to use a MIS and the degree of their sophistication in this respect should be gauged. Further, there must be

Table 4.12 **key questions that determine the nature of the marketing information system required**

1 What types of decision are involved?
2 When and how frequently will they arise?
3 What types of information are required?
4 How much of it is there?
5 How frequently will the need for this information arise?
6 How quickly will the different pieces of information be required?
7 What degree of sophistication is possible?
8 Or should the system be kept as simple as possible?
9 What special studies or requirements are likely to arise?
10 When and how frequently are these likely?
11 What special information needs would arise?
12 What forms of research programmes are likely?
13 What types of data analyses are needed or possible?
14 How flexible should the MIS be?
15 What or when will modifications be needed to the system?
16 What market factors are most relevant and how will they affect the need for, and speed of, change in the MIS?
17 What are the permitted costs for the MIS?
18 What published information will be used and how suitable is it in its raw state for the information, planning and decision needs of the firm?

explicit statements on the planning, decision-making and control processes and procedures that will be used. Finally, the support of management at all levels must be obtained. They should not only be enthusiastic about the system and its potential but be prepared also to assist in, and oversee, its development and evolution.

As firms grow in size and the complexity of their activities, executives become further removed from immediate contact with the scenes of the marketing action. They have to rely increasingly on second-hand information and an increasing amount of it. It is necessary therefore that once a MIS has been developed *rigor mortis* should not be allowed to develop. There must be flexibility of thought and approach that permits the modification of the MIS as the firm's business environment and executives' needs change. Happily the availability of computers, especially minicomputers, makes the processing of data easier and more rapid. The availability of alternative programmes, or the ability to write new ones quickly, also ensures that flexibility can be sustained.

4.11 A CAUTIONARY TALE OR TWO

When marketing and marketing research are first introduced some executives of the firm will accept them, in rational manner, as necessary tools for modern business conditions. Others will resist them and a few may go overboard about them. The last mentioned, and resisters who eventually become converted, sometimes take the bit between their teeth and rush headlong into impossible adventures. The following are some cautionary tales.

There was the chief executive of a firm making kitchen furniture, the built-in variety, who a few years ago, when this equipment was all the rage and there was extensive house building, decided he needed marketing research to help him estimate future demand for his products. He called for an extensive market research, involving over 50 questions, on the annual output of bricks in Britain! His theory was that knowing this and by 'estimating' the number of bricks needed for an average house, he could estimate the number of new homes that would be built and thus the demand for his products. The study would have been costly and difficult to do, as then the production of bricks was not shown as a separate figure in any official statistics.

He had to be convinced of a number of problems. First, it was not known what an 'average' house was nor how many bricks would be needed. This depends on size, design and so on. Then the amount used for non-house building (commercial and industrial) would have to be deducted, as with the amount used for repairs and extensions that would not influence demand for new kitchen equipment. There was also the complication of apartments and bungalows, which presumably used fewer bricks than houses. Nor could it be known by this method that every new house would have built-in kitchen equipment. Council-built houses, for example, in that period, did not.

Most of the new housing where built-in kitchen equipment was installed was being built by major construction firms. It would have been easier, cheaper and more accurate to have mounted a small research study based primarily on discussing plans and intentions of these firms and the few local authorities using such equipment. The chief executive would not be convinced, however, and did not agree that the data required, as mentioned above, could not be obtained. The work went ahead, proved very costly and was utterly useless. It had to be abandoned, but only after much time and money had been spent. The smaller study, then launched, produced sufficient usable data for his purposes.

Then there was the marketing director (newly promoted from sales director) of a company making, amongst other things, teats for babies' feeding bottles. He wanted a consumer profile study of the different customer groups (by income, status, educational background no less) who bought teats, how frequently they bought this product and so on. He felt this would allow him to devise a more effective pricing policy. Since this product sold for 5p each and was about 1p cheaper than the nearest competitor's, the research was pointless, especially as it would be extensive and expensive.

Next there were executives who, new to marketing and forecasting methods, always insisted on the most complex and sophisticated research and forecasting methods being used. They ignored the fact that simpler methods were more appropriate to their needs and that their organisation was not yet sufficiently trained and experienced in handling sophisticated information and MIS. Also, their existing control systems were very slow acting. It took three months for reports to come through in usable form. Having complicated, difficult to interpret (for them) information flows from the market, arriving well in advance of performance reports, was again wasteful. Some were persuaded to think more simply and practically. Others could not be and for years wasted their firms' resources unnecessarily. Finally, there are all those who always want the information tomorrow where three months hence would be soon enough!

4.12 MICRO-ELECTRONICS AND MARKETING INTELLIGENCE

The availability of micro-computers and word-processors offers possibilities of great improvement in marketing intelligence systems. However, certain aspects need careful consideration. First, marketing intelligence needs must be clearly defined so that creativity and intuition are not stifled by complicated, over-sophisticated systems. Producing information more quickly is of no value if the management team is not sophisticated enough to handle this effectively. Second, developing new intelligence systems often means having to replan the organisation. Third, whenever reorganisation is involved, resistance to change will be encountered from some staff.

To avoid these problems it is essential for top management to be seen to be involved in supporting the new system as necessary for improved management efficiency. Decisions must be taken promptly. Next, user participation is needed in the planning and introduction of the new system. To avoid conflict it is necessary to educate executives in the management of (necessary) change. Finally, progress in instituting the change and judging the efficiency of the new system must be clearly evaluated.

ASSIGNMENTS

1 Your company has decided to conduct a comprehensive review of its marketing research needs and methods. Submit your proposals of the various factors that should be considered including the types of data and information required, its relevance to the marketing and other operational activities and the key questions that should be answered by the research.

2 The continuous data collection system will also be revised or modified. How would this affect decisions on the field and desk studies that would then be needed on an *ad hoc* basis?

3 You are retained as a consultant by a large manufacturing company making (a) mass market consumer goods; (b) batch produced industrial products; and (c) capital equipment. You find that various forms of marketing research are necessary. What recommendations would you make (and what justification would you give for your choices) regarding the form and nature of the work; whether questionnaires or personal interviews are used; the sampling frames and samples to be used; the types of questions that would form the basis of the studies; and the degree of accuracy you would expect within any given cost constraints?

4 Prepare a research brief for any two of the studies in Assignment 3 above.

5 You are asked also to submit a paper on the form and nature of the MIS that now seems most appropriate for this group.

MANAGING PRODUCTS AND PRICING

A perennial argument amongst marketing academics is: 'Which comes first, the product or the market?' Acceptance of the product-market concept discussed in Section 1.7(b) should terminate the argument, since it acknowledges the joint and equal importance of both subjects. Provided the concept is followed it does not matter if marketing teams study markets or products first. However, since most firms these days are working with restricted resources, because of their cost, it may be safer to start with the product.

This is not reverting to the old idea 'first find your product and then go and look for a market'. Nor is it tacit agreement with those who should know better but maintain that 'a good product sells itself'. It is just that with limited resources priorities have to be set and it makes sense to study the most difficult area first.

Consider, for example, a firm making high pressure, high head pumps for non-corrosive fluids. If it is tuned in to its markets in its normal activities, it will realise that these products are too expensive for applications where high pressures are not involved. It has some idea of what market opportunities exist, but it should first find out what low pressure, high head pumps it could make. It would then study its markets to see which of the new pumps would sell in sufficient quantity at a profit and revenue which would be acceptable. It can also study which markets of its total market mix would be interested. The ultimate choice would depend on the firm's capacity and other resources.

5.1 PRODUCT-MARKET STRATEGIES

Four basic product-market strategies are available.

(i) *Market penetration*: the firm tries to increase sales of its current products in its present markets by using more aggressive selling, promotions and distribution;

(ii) *Market development*: the firm increases its sales by opening up new markets for its current products;

(iii) *Product development*: the company tries to increase its sales by developing new or improved products;

(iv) *Diversification*: the firm seeks to increase sales by developing new products for new markets.

It is assumed that these increased sales will result in increased profit. Most major corporations and smaller ones needing substantial growth could be active in all four areas at the same time. They would, however, be implementing an agreed product-market policy and not following the above strategies haphazardly. The degree of difficulty and risk involved is least for (i) and gets progressively greater as a firm progresses through (ii) and (iii). Item (iv) carries the greatest risks and uncertainties. This is because the development of a new product is more costly, difficult and uncertain than opening up a new market. If a firm jumps around in random order in this work, it suggests it is not following any carefully thought out long-term plan. Rather it is responding to the urgent needs of each problem or product need that arises.

5.2 WHAT IS A PRODUCT?

This may seem a superfluous question but successful marketing executives know that a product is not just the physical thing that is seen, touched, smelt, tasted, used or consumed. Every product possesses symbolic and psychological attributes to the consumer. All have to be catered for, as far as is possible, if a high degree of customer satisfaction is to be maintained. (With industrial products and equipment, technological and economic attributes must also be satisfied, more so than with the average consumer good.)

For example, consider the case of a camera. To persons not interested in photography it is just a lens, with various moving parts encased in metal and plastic. It may be to them an expensive, unnecessary luxury. To the child in its early teens it may be a more grown-up substitute for toys. It is 'fun' snapping this and that and the main attribute in this case is pleasure. To the serious amateur photographer it is a precision instrument. With it they make time stand still (capture photos of the baby at various ages, holiday capers etc.) and record moments for posterity (at weddings and silver or golden anniversaries or other events). For the professional it is a vital tool of the trade whereby records are taken to satisfy their customers' needs and all their psychological and status pretensions. So products also seem different things to different people.

Take the car for a further example. To the manufacturer it is a collection of parts to be correctly assembled and sold to earn their profit. To the distributor it is an inanimate object that must be sold if he is to earn his living. To the 'young blood' it may be a means to woo (or seduce!) the heart's desire of the moment. To a family it is a means of transport for them and often also the means whereby the wage earner travels to and from work. Which attributes predominate at any time will determine how buyers make their buying decisions and thus the marketing mix that should be used.

(a) Basic terms and meanings

There are various standard terms used in product planning and management work. These are summarised in Table 5.1.

Table 5.1 **product management: some terms and meanings**

Product item	a single product (e.g. a Jaguar XJ6, 3.4 car).
Product line	A number of related products (items) that satisfy a specific need, or are used together, or are within a price range, or are sold to the same customer groups being marketed through similar types of outlets (e.g. all the Jaguar XJ6 cars in that marque).
Product group	All the product lines forming a related group of products (e.g. all Jaguar cars – XJ6, XJ12, etc. – produced by British Leyland (BL)).
Product mix	All the products offered for sale by a firm (e.g. all the cars produced by BL), and the quantities of each to be sold (see also Glossary).
Product management	All the management activities involved in looking after a firm's products; includes *Product planning*; planning items, lines and ranges, prices, etc.
Width	of the product mix, i.e. how many different product lines are produced by a company.
Depth	of the product mix, i.e. the average number of items offered in each product line.
Consistency	of the product mix refers to how closely related the product lines are in end-use, production requirements, distribution methods, etc.

(b) Services

As economies develop and income levels rise, there is increasing demand for services of all kinds. This ranges from banking and insurance to transportation (national, international) for people and goods to leisure (holidays, excursions), recreation, education, medical care and so on. The basic techniques and principles of marketing apply here also, except that their special characteristics have to be taken into account. These are summarised in Table 5.2. Most services basically follow the approach needed for consumer goods but some (e.g. transportation of goods and some aspects of banking and insurance) may be more effectively sold if methods used for industrial products are followed. For service industries the services they provide are their 'products'.

Services can have psychological as well as functional attributes. For example the ladies' hairdresser, besides providing facilities to keep a lady's hair neat and trim will also offer styling which enhances the appearance of the customers. This makes the ladies feel that their natural attributes have been enhanced and so gives them greater confidence and so on. Life insurance gives the insured the happy feeling that provision has been made for dependants should the former die prematurely and so contributes to this psychological need. Holidays meet the similar needs associated with the desire for a good rest or change from the year's toil, the interest in doing something different or gaining a new experience or, when an exotic or expensive holiday is taken, in raising the holiday-maker's status (he hopes!) in his social or work community.

Other special characteristics of services include the 'in-service' nature of the business. For example an insurance company must have all the specialists *in situ* before they can offer the cover they intend to market. In some countries they must also offer some financial guarantees and satisfy the authorities on this. Tour operators have to do the same and in addition must make advance bookings of transportation and accommodation. This, linked with the intangibility and perishability of services, have the following implications for marketing.

First, the forecasting, marketing planning and operations must be done more carefully, with greater precision than say for goods and products. Overestimate demand and therefore have in service more facilities than are really needed means that 'capacity' will exceed sales. Underestimate demand and thus 'capacity' and business will be lost.

Next, the facilities are relatively inflexible. Insurance, experts in life insurance, for example, are not usually able to handle with the same efficiency matters to do with fire insurance. So if demand for the former is not as great as expected, 'spare capacity' will exist and will erode the firm's profitability. An hotel once built is not easy or cheap to convert to other uses. A holiday firm, overestimating demand for holidays in Spain, cannot switch quickly to Italy, Greece or the Far East. Couriers fluent in Spanish and knowing Spain may not have any abilities suited to these other countries. Also, since forward bookings have to be made, it may be eighteen to twenty-four months before the holiday firm can switch its main operations.

Service companies must therefore have more accurate and detailed

Table 5.2 **special characteristics of services** .

Intangibility	Services cannot be touched, tasted, seen or heard, i.e. they do not exist in normal physical form. Cannot be sampled. Potential buyers cannot judge quality before use. Thus reputation of seller plays key role in the buying decision.
Perishability	Their utility is short-lived. They cannot usually be made ahead of time of demand nor stored for peak demand periods. Hotels, transport seats, tourism services, utilities are typical examples affected by these two characteristics.
Standardisation	Difficult if not impossible, for offerings of the same service by different suppliers. Nor can any one seller guarantee consistency in the services offered. Potential customers have difficulty in making definitive evaluations, hence have trouble with making a choice and buying decisions. Creative marketing needed to show how any service meets the unique needs of individual buyers.
Buyer involvement	Sellers must ensure that buyers clearly specify what they want and that these statements are correctly interpreted. For example, what do different people mean when they specify a 'quiet' holiday? Some mean exactly that with lazing on sunny beaches; others may want a few or several trouble-free excursions etc.
Value	Because of the above, it is difficult for customer to judge 'value' before purchase decision and consumption.
Heterogeneity	Services are usually designed around the specialised needs of individuals or firms (e.g. insurance policies; business travel for each executive; etc.) hence heterogeneity of most services. However some services are capable of standardisation (tour operators sell a standard set of holidays to all; public transport services operated on set schedules, available to all) but customers' individualised needs still result in heterogeneity.
Inseparability	For many services, production and consumption occur at the same time (e.g. bank executives 'sell' credit, loans, advice etc. to their customers and the items sold are utilised (consumed) by the latter at the same time). Travel agents, insurance brokers, franchisees have in some cases been able to inject standardisation into the services they sell by offering a limited number of (sometimes specialised) travel facilities, insurance policies and so on.

| Ownership (Lack of) | With services, use of a facility does not mean that ownership of it passes to the user. The aircraft seat, hotel room, computer or photocopying service are in fact only hired for a specific time, or specific use (e.g. to photocopy papers). They remain the property of the proprietors. |

Source: (Adapted or summarised from: L. E. Boon and D. L. Kurtz, *Contemporary Marketing*, 3rd edn (Dryden Press, 1980); D. W. Foster, *Planning for Products and Markets* (Longman, 1972); P. Kotler, *Marketing Management*, 4th edn (Prentice-Hall, 1980).)

knowledge of their markets, customers and demand. Since buying decisions are normally subjective and greatly influenced by personal views and traits, knowledge of human behaviour and motivation and how they affect their business is necessary. Sales staff must be thoroughly knowledgeable about the services they have to sell. Finally, greater care is needed in the selection of marketing techniques used and in their adaptation to the needs of their services. In other words, greater innovation is essential (see Section 9.4).

5.3 PRODUCT MANAGEMENT

Product management is involved in the adjustment of manufacturing capacity and technology and the efficient use of these resources and skills to match customer wants as efficiently and profitably as possible. What the work involves is sketched out in Figure 5.1. Note that the work evolves from agreed marketing objectives and strategies. These in turn are a result of agreed corporate objectives and strategy. Also the co-operation needed with the management of the market side of the firm is indicated, as in the important contribution made by costing and pricing decisions. Note also that double-headed arrows are used to illustrate that co-operation and communications must flow in both directions in every link associated with the work.

(a) Product strategy and policy
Events of the late 1970s and early 1980s have shown that the factors affecting the business environment are subject to change, often sudden, sometimes unpredictable. Executives realised that their firms' strategies and policies, including those concerned with the product-market situation, must be modified and changed from time to time. Static, unchanging ones usually spell trouble if not outright disaster. Examples are all the cases of business failures, small and large. Dynamic strategies and policies are essential if profit, growth and survival are to be assured.

Product strategy is concerned with decisions on the range of products a

124

Fig 5.1 *the product management process*

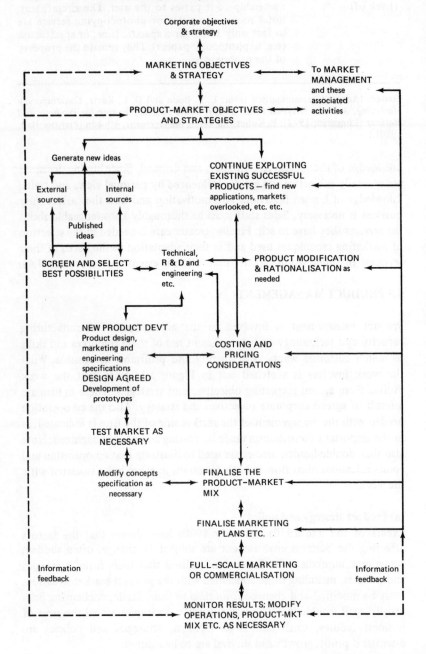

firm must offer to achieve target profit, growth and market shares consistent with total demand and business conditions. This involves studying present and future prospects and the allocation of scarce resources between conflicting and competing objectives. The associated policies will specify the action plans or programmes that would be implemented to achieve the strategy. Policies can be permissive or restrictive. They can be good or bad. A firm that neither defines nor understands its business properly can end up with very ineffective policies. Those that do know their business may adopt similar policies but as they would have been more correctly chosen in relation to the firm's skills and capabilities, they will turn out to be good policies for the company. Also changing circumstances can make what are good and sound policies now into bad policies at some future time. Thus watchfulness and flexibility are required also in product management.

The objectives of dynamic strategies and policies are listed in Table 5.3, with a few summarised notes. What this means in terms of practical work is stated in Table 5.4 in the sub-section that follows.

Table 5.3 **product strategies: objectives**

Growth
To improve total performance, counter competition more effectively and market saturation with current products. Exploit or create attractive opportunities. Stimulate sales of basic products. Attack competition before the company is itself attacked.

Survival
Vital for all firms, especially in difficult times. Need to offset obsolescence of current products, declining demand and profitability due to increasing competition and changes in other market factors.

Resource utilisation
Need for better utilisation of all resources: better use of raw materials, plant, labour and of by-products or waste and use of spare capacity. Firm should make full use of management resources also. Greater use of all special skills, assets. Improve innovative ability and competitive capabilities. Exploit prestige, product quality, reputation, market position and standing.

Stability
Firm must attain some stability for its business: profit, sales, return, earnings per share. Must avoid excessive fluctuations or recession.

Flexibility
So that customers' changing needs can be met. Must also adapt to changes in government regulations, laws.

Profit
Firm must strive to improve profit through improving performance of all products in all markets.

Table 5.4 product planning: points to consider

Profit, growth, stability
How may these strategy objectives be achieved? Usually involves detailed analyses of all aspects of product operations; aims to improve performance of laggard products.

Scope of product range
Requires regular review of product range and product mix to ensure they are meeting customer needs properly, in all respects. All items should also support and enhances sales of each other. Should ensure that all items in a product line help to optimise sales and profit of the whole line.

Marketing and manufacturing efficiency
If the utilisation objective of strategy is to be met, product planning must aim to optimise the efficiency of all marketing and manufacturing activities. Standards for unit costs, quality, output, reliability etc. must be practicable and achieved consistently.

Price and value
These must be in accord with customers' expectations. Should also be considered in relation to what competitors are offering. *Quality* should also be what customers expect, no more and no less. Excessive quality is costly and many not reap any additional benefits to the firm.

Competition
Competitive activity must not only be met but also anticipated, including reaction by them to any actions initiated by the company. Changes in competition (firms leaving a market, new competitors entering and hitherto insignificant ones developing into major threats) must be considered.

Service
Nature and standards required by customers (after-sales, maintenance and technical advice) should also be taken into account.

(b) Product planning
Through product planning executives shape the entire range of products for their selected markets. Their decisions should be based on consideration of the points in Table 5.4. It is a team operation that involves all departments of a firm at certain periods of the work. It is not confined only to the marketing specialists charged with responsibility for this activity. The basic steps are shown in Figure 5.2.

There are several factors which tend to broaden a company's product range. First, a growing number of firms may require products specially designed for their needs. They will not accept 'standard' items. Then

STUDENT RECORD CARD

DEPARTMENT OF BUSINESS & SECRETARIAL STUDIES

SURNAME .... Course ....

Christian Name(s)................................ Tutor ....

Date of Birth .... Admitted ....

Address .... Left ....

....

.... Next
of Kin ....

.... 'Phone No. ....

Tel No. .... Other Info. ....

Last School ....

....

Fig 5.2 *activities of product planning and relationship with other planning*

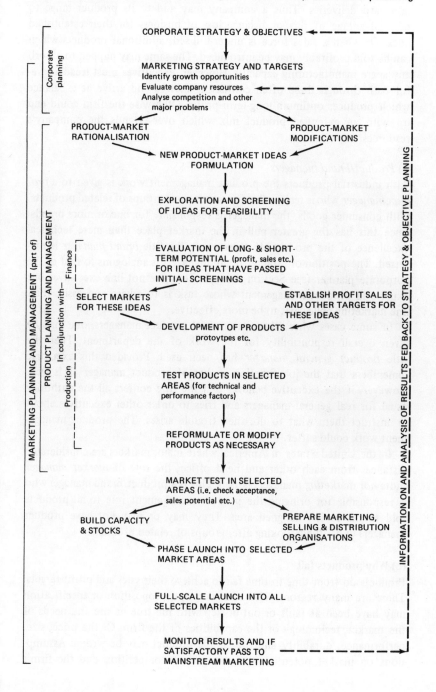

most firms now split their purchases between more than one supplier to safeguard deliveries. Thus a company may add to its product range to take advantage of this or balance loss of business for their established lines. Or when a sales force is under-utilised, additional products which can be sold profitably may be introduced. The same may happen to absorb any spare manufacturing capacity. However, executives must tread a careful path through these often conflicting factors and arrive at a balance which produces optimum long-term profit. Otherwise the firm could end up with an extended product mix which over-extends the company's resources.

(i) *Product/brand managers*

With industrial products the product management work is given to a *product manager* who is responsible for one or more groups of related products. With consumer goods, the manager is responsible for one or more brands, since this has the greater pull in the market place than mere technical excellence of the product. In these cases, the title *brand manager* is preferred. The position of product/brand managers is analogous to that of the corporate planner (see Section 3.1(a)). They are not line executives but experts in product management whose task is to advise and assist their line marketing colleagues to be more effective.

In some cases where there are several product managers, one may be given overall responsibility for the work of the department. Then the title *product general manager* has been used. Provided this executive remembers that the job function is that of product manager all is well. However, if the executive believes that the title confers all the authority usual for real general managers and tries to order other executives about or instruct them what to do, then trouble arises. The product management work could suffer.

In the United States of America, where major markets are considerable distances from each other and head office, the role of *market manager* (note *not* market*ing* manager) is used. This is a product/brand manager who is responsible for bringing the product management role to all products sold to his or her assigned area. They may or may not have product managers under them looking after groups of related products.

(c) Why products fail

Products do from time to time fail to achieve their sales and profit targets. There are many reasons. The basic concept, proposition or specification may have been at fault or out-of-step with the true nature and needs of the market, technology or the capabilities of the firm. Or the price, size, performance, durability and life of the product may be wrong. Assumptions on market potential, the strength of competition and the firm's ability to counter this may have been wrong. The whole product planning operation may have been badly staffed, organised or rushed. There was no systematic programming or control of the work. Technical and production aspects may have been rushed, problems may have been missed or underestimated. All other research activities might have been skimped or rushed. Too much time was taken and competitors were able to leapfrog the new idea into the market with their own ones. The products were 'ivory tower' ones, i.e. satisfied the firm's ideas on technical excellence but were too good or expensive for potential customers. Finally, the international implications could have been overlooked.

(d) The product life cycle

All products have a finite life. Some may be extended over many years, others over a much shorter period. Product managers should have an idea of where on the life cycle curve their products are at any given time. Figure 5.3(a) shows the ideal profile or that for a product with established demand. Figure 5.3(b) shows the profile for a fad or fashion product with a short life. It is because all products have a finite life that new product development (Section 5.4(d)) is so important to a company's long-term survival.

It will be noted that in the first case the product passes through five stages. In the second there are only four, the market saturation one does not really exist. Product managers should realise when their products have reached point A. Then decisions have to be taken whether the product should be modified to take account of changes in customer wants, technology and other market factors so that the life of the product could be extended. Doing this when a product has reached B is too late. There is insufficient time for the work and the product is probably losing credibility in the market. If modifications are made, the ideal profile becomes as in Figure 5.4. Note that the increases in sales and profit and the extended life for each modification diminishes with each successive modification. Thus there is a limit to the number of times this can be done. The cost of the work may also increase as each successive modification becomes more difficult to do.

5.4 SUMMARY OF WORK INVOLVED

The work involved in product management can be divided into four stages: looking after existing products, modifying them, rationalising them when necessary and new product development. These are summarised below. Readers wishing to go further into these areas should read one of the many specialist books on the subject. Some titles are given in the Bibliography (Appendix A.5).

Fig 5.3 *life cycle of a product*

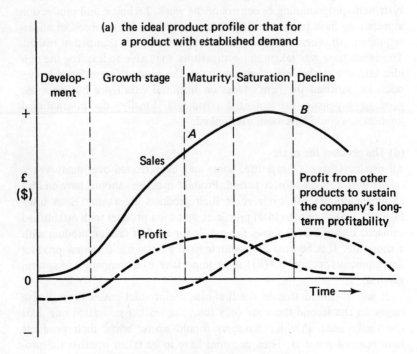

(a) the ideal product profile or that for a product with established demand

| Development | Growth stage | Maturity | Saturation | Decline |

(b) profile for a fad or fashion product

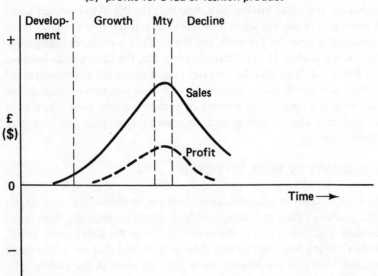

| Development | Growth | Mty | Decline |

Fig 5.4 *extended life cycle of a product*

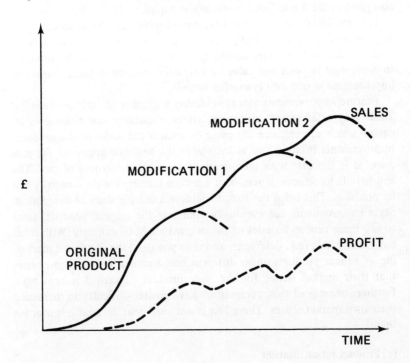

(a) Existing products

Successful though they may be, in the press of their daily round, marketing executives could miss some applications or markets that could use these products. An ongoing part of their work is therefore to seek out these missed opportunities as well as ensure that the market shares, profit and sales of present products are on target. However, they should not push products beyond their 'point of diminishing return'. This is when each incremental increase in sales is producing a decreasing incremental addition to profit. Also the incremental costs involved may be rising. Eventually, overall profit can be reduced. The effort could be more profitably put into other activities. Further, if too large a market share is obtained the products become increasingly vulnerable to competition.

(b) Product modification

Because customer needs, competition and other market factors change, or because the original specification was inaccurate, even successful products need modification at times. (Note the comments in Section 5.3(d).) The work is best assigned to a group of executives drawn from all departments who study the possibilities. A detailed account of the work involved is also given in the books listed in the Bibliography.

It is sufficient here to note that modifications can be of three types: improvement in quality, feature and style. Quality modifications seek to improve the performance, durability, reliability or life of the product. Improvement in perceived value by customers because of these changes or improvement in unit cost is another benefit.

Feature improvements aim at achieving a number of real user benefits. These may offer greater efficiency, safety, versatility, convenience or re-design which can enhance the usage customers can make of the product. Improvements in style aim at increasing the aesthetic appeal of the product, as is the case with modifications to existing marques of cars. The aim here is to achieve or reinforce a unique identity for the company and its products. This helps the firm to achieve a durable share of the market. Style improvements can eventually eliminate the original product, since to sell these new styles sales of the original might be damaged. With some consumer goods (e.g. detergents and soap powders) the continued market-ing of similar products under different brand names by one firm ensures that their market shares for the basic product concerned is kept high. Further, because of this, competitors have greater difficulty in increasing their own market shares. There just is not sufficient demand left over for them!

(c) Product rationalisation

All goods and products have a finite life. Fashion products tend to measure their 'lives' in months. At the other end of the scale, houses, capital equip-ment, hotels, major industrial products have useful lives measured in (many) years. Yet some old and ailing products, beloved by the executives of their firms, or representing some major point of development of the company, like old soldiers, never die. Sometimes they are very slow in fading away even when they are no longer making profits. During this process of reluctant withdrawal, such products can consume a dispropor-tionate amount of managerial time and other resources. They do in fact drain away profits earned by other activities. They add to costs, especially in accumulating inventories and all the price cuts that are needed to move these stocks. The continuance of products passed their prime (obsolete really) can damage the company's image and inhibit the sales of other items. Recent examples include car manufacturers who, for various reasons, continued to make and market obsolete designs and marques.

There really is no room for sentimentality in modern business conditions. When a product fails to earn sufficient profit and it is impossible or too costly to carry out any further modifications to it, or customer demand has declined or switched to other (often new) products, or when it is not still helping to sell other profitable products whose profits far exceed the cost of continuing with the obsolete item, or economic and technical changes have outdated the ailing product, there is only one real answer, rationalisation. That is, it should be phased out of the firm's product mix. However, rationalisation has to be carefully planned and phased-in also with the new product development programme.

Considerable thought has to be given to how and when a product should be rationalised. If too many are deleted quickly or at once, without new items taking their places in the product mix, the total cash-flow position can be seriously affected. While these products may not be earning profits they will still be making some contribution to overhead costs. If other items are not available to take over this load, the overhead costs will fall more heavily on the products remaining in the mix. The profitability of the surviving products will be reduced as will the overall profitability of the firm. While it is not possible to plan product rationalisation and new product development exactly (some new items will be delayed in their launch because of difficulties encountered in their development) it is essential to keep these two programmes in step with each other as much as is practicable.

Again, the detailed work involved is fully discussed in some of the books in the Bibliography. It is only necessary here to summarise the basic approach in Table 5.5 and to make a few further comments. A team of executives, drawn from the major departments, is charged with the task of doing the planning. In most cases it may be the same team that is involved with product modification. They will be the first to identify possible 'candidates' and should possess the basic information needed to arrive at correct decisions. Finally, not all the 'candidates' will be rationalised immediately or even for some time. Decisions will depend upon the overall product-market situation and the full implications of the proposals. Some of the latter have been mentioned at the beginning of this section. Obviously if a 'candidate' is still helping to sell other profitable items and the total gain is advantageous, or if it is keeping out competition in an area sensitive to the firm's future development, its rationalisation will be delayed. However, if it is making no useful contribution, whatever this may be, to the company's business then rationalisation is the only decision.

(d) New product development

The detailed work involved under this heading is also discussed fully in the books in the Bibliography. It should be noted here though that new product development is essential to the survival, growth and profitability of a firm. It counters the effects of the inevitable obsolescence of existing products that arises from natural processes or development or through competition. It helps to improve the overall profitability of the firm and to ensure full utilisation of resources and, as stated, it allows sustained growth and expansion that would not be possible with static or ageing product mixes.

The work involves the entire resources of a firm at different times but some (e.g. product managers or their assigns) are involved throughout the process. A high degree of co-operation and co-ordination is necessary between the team members and all the operating divisions of the company. The team itself is drawn from these departments as necessary and must obviously include marketing and product management executives with representatives from manufacturing and financial departments. It should have a dynamic chairman who is interested in the group achieving its agreed objectives and who will drive them on at a good pace. He or she should be senior enough to be able to persuade the directors of other departments to give the work their wholehearted support and assistance. There should also be a secretary who will be responsible for all the paper-work, making sure it is produced and circulated in time and so on. The new product development team should not be the same as that for product modification, though some executives will be members of both. The nature, scope and content of the work is quite different as are the time-scales involved.

The basic steps have been listed in Table 5.5. Table 5.6 sets out the different stages that have to be followed in practice. Figure 5.5 classifies new product-market activities by product and market objectives.

(i) *Venture management teams*

These teams are sometimes used instead of the new product-development group or committee discussed above. They are comprised of executives drawn from the main operating departments and have the same general responsibilities. However, they are usually assigned to one task and when the new product or venture has been approved or agreed, they remain together to manage and plan the launch and initial marketing of it. Usually they only hand over to the departments when the product has been successfully established and can be moved into the main marketing and manufacturing operations. They are in effect an autonomous section responsible for achieving target profits, sales, market shares and so on for the activity in their charge.

It is an attempt to make innovation more predictable and to minimise the risk involved. It is a corporate effort to manage new developments (products or business) as a perennial activity rather than an *ad hoc*, sporadic or crash operation at times of urgent need. It is also designed to achieve significant developments into new activities.

Table 5.5 **product rationalisation**

Basic steps

1 The team of executives responsible meet to determine the objectives and procedures for the work.
2 They review, study and analyse the position for all products seen as possible candidates for rationalisation.
3 Their initial findings are compared with the firm's immediate and long-term objectives and strategies, especially plans for the future development of the company into new technologies and markets.
4 They consider also the effects that rationalisation of the 'candidates' would have on surviving products' sales and profitability, the resources that would be released for other activities and so on.
5 The team will then make recommendations on which obsolescent products should be rationalised and when and how this will be done.
6 The priorities will be established and a plan of action will then be prepared.

Questions considered

The key questions considered will include the following.

1 How have the products' sales changed in relation to total demand for them?
2 What new or substitute products have eroded the 'candidates'' positions? How has this affected the expectations (life, sales, profit) for them?
3 How has the competitive position changed and how will it change further in the future?
4 How have the demand patterns in the affected markets changed? What will be the future patterns?
5 What gross profit margins and overhead contributions are achieved by these products? How will this slack be taken up if the products are rationalised?
6 What will be the total cost of the proposed rationalisation?

(ii) *Sources for ideas*

Given the need for new products and the fact that many new ideas, for many reasons, may not achieve profitable commercialisation, a firm needs a substantial steady stream of ideas if its new product development programme is to be successful. Thus it must tap all possible sources for new ideas. These range from customers, distributors, research and trade associations to competitors, published information on new technological advances and product ideas.

Every department can make a worthwhile contribution. Obviously marketing and distribution executives will be the main source but manufacturing colleagues can come up with ideas based on thoughts on cost reduction, improved quality or performance, use of better alternative

Table 5.6 practical stages in new product development

1 Prepare long-range forecasts for profit and sales revenue of existing product-market activities based on user requirements, competition and other external factors.
2 Prepare long-range profit plan from the corporate objectives that have been set.
3 Establish profit gap by comparing 2 with 1.
4 From this target (3), which has to be met by new and modified products, select products which can be modified and estimate the profit to be earned by new products if the profit gap is to be filled.
5 Prepare objectives for the new products and make an audit of the company's total resources.
6 From 5, select the new products that seem to be good possibilities from the list of prospects and determine the product-market strategy that would be needed and the markets that would be involved.
7 If necessary, prepare a statement of revised corporate objectives necessitated by the new products.
8 While the above is being done, the work of identifying, assessing and evaluating new product ideas will have progressed, leading to the preparation of a short list of new products that will be developed and the timing for this (i.e. products for immediate, intermediate and long-term development).
9 With these, prepare a long-range profit plan.
10 Assign responsibility for the design, development, manufacturing, launch and marketing of the new products approved in 8. (Adjustments will be needed in 8, 9 and 10, if unforseen difficulties, new market and competitive developments prevent the original ideas from being developed or delay them.)
11 When launched, evaluate the performance of the new products so that any necessary modifications can be made.
12 If the launch of them is successful, incorporate the new products into the main marketing plans/operations.

materials and so on. Financial colleagues can contribute ideas developed from thoughts on how costs could be reduced, prices increased, cash flow and liquidity improvements and better utilisation of funds. Indeed everyone can contribute, even the office boy or girl. Secretaries could suggest ways in which products could be improved, especially if they use them at home. They will have firsthand knowledge of the advantages and disadvantages of present design and the practical needs that current products do not satisfy. The net has to be cast very widely.

(iii) Screening
With a large number of ideas to select from, the development team must have some method for assessing the feasibility and prospects of the ideas. This can be done by screening the ideas graphically or statistically. The

Fig 5.5 *new product-market activities classified by product and market objectives*

OBJECTIVES — PRODUCT MARKET OBJECTIVNESS	NO TECHNOLOGICAL CHANGE	IMPROVED TECHNOLOGY Better use of firm's skills, know-how etc.	NEW TECHNOLOGY Acquire new tech., production & other skills
NO MARKET CHANGE	(Current business)	REFORMULATION To optimise balance of cost, quality, performance of current range of products	REPLACEMENT Seek new & better materials etc. for present products in new technology
STRENGTHENED MARKET Exploit present markets for current products more fully	REMERCHANDISING Increase sales to customers of types now being served by the firm	IMPROVED PRODUCT For greater utility and acceptance by customers	PRODUCT LINE EXTENSION Broaden line on offer to customers thro' use of new technology
NEW MARKET To increase no. of types or classes of customer served	NEW USE To find new classes of customer who can use current products of the firm	MARKET EXTENSION To reach new classes of customer by modifying current products	DIVERSIFI-CATION To add to the classes of customer served by developing new techn. knowledge & new products

TECHNICAL NEWNESS ⟶

MARKET NEWNESS

Source: Adapted from S.C. Johnson and C. Jones, 'How to organize for new products', *Harvard Business Review* (May–June 1957).

latter seems easier to assess objectively (see Appendix A.2). Figure 5.6(a) illustrates the high mortality rate for new product ideas and stresses the need for a continuous supply of ideas if a successful new product development programme is to be sustained. Figure 5.6(b) shows the time/cost relationship. This indicates why it is vital to screen out all the unlikely or doubtful product ideas before the serious design and development stage

138

Fig 5.6 *new product development*

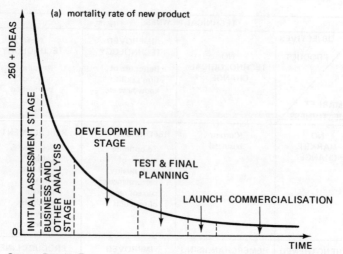

(a) mortality rate of new product

Source: Douglas Foster, 'Most new products die young', *Financial Times* (London) 29 July 1969.

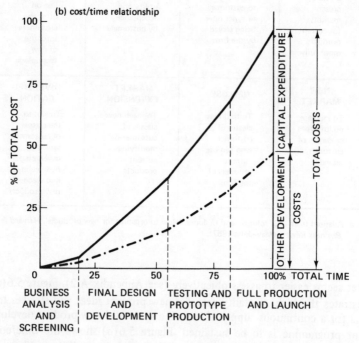

(b) cost/time relationship

Source: Douglas Foster, *Planning for Products and Markets* (Longman, 1972) fig. 5.10.

is reached. It is at this time that total development costs increase very substantially.

Development of the ideas that have passed the second screening can begin. Those set aside can be reconsidered at a later date. Figure 5.7 indicates the process in practice. As the flow chart indicates, if the idea, concept, proposed specification or performance does not accord with the agreed standards, the new product proposal can be referred back to an appropriate stage in the process for further study. Or it can be set aside for future reconsideration.

(iv) *Product tests*

It is often useful to subject new products, usually at the prototype stage, to various product tests. With consumer goods the aim is to check formulation or taste, touch, smell, consistency and so on against anticipated consumer demands. With industrial products, specification, performance, durability, output, life and other factors could be checked against customer needs. The cost of developing and launching new products is high and these tests help to reduce the risks involved.

They are basically of two types, *consumer acceptance* tests and *technical performance* tests. The first try to measure consumer reactions usually by using random samples of potential buyers. In the second, the firm is comparing the intrinsic qualities of the product with those of its major potential competitors. The work covers tests for hardness and durability, abrasion tests for strength and so on.

5.5 PROFIT PLANNING

Profit is not just the balancing item in a firm's profit and loss account or operating statement. No one will deny that capital is an essential requirement for every enterprise. Profit represents an important measure of how successfully this capital is employed. It is the yardstick which financiers, the shareholding public and commentators on business activity use to measure the success of a firm and its management. Besides demonstrating to the world how successful a company is, profit should also be a spur to executives to achieve improved results.

It is only in fairly recent times that most firms have realised it is possible to lay profit plans and carry them through successfully. Many have been relieved to discover that by so doing many of their apparently 'chronic' ills disappear. However if the ills are due to other fundamental problems (in marketing, production or financing) then just making a profit plan may not help. None the less most firms now have set themselves profit and return on investment objectives, with marketing interested in profit/ sales ratio and other financial percentages, and make positive efforts to achieve them.

140

Fig 5.7 *new product development-process and screening flow chart*

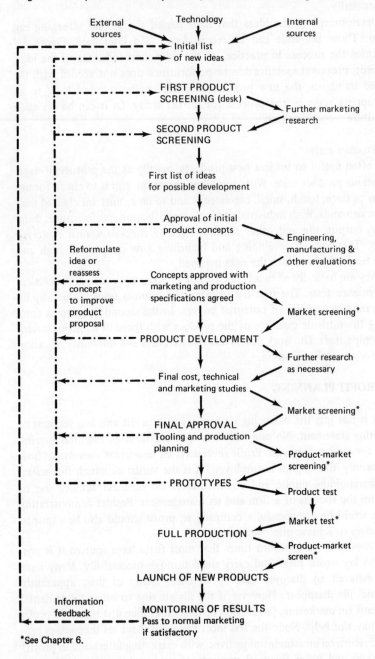

Again, certain important factors have to be considered. First, there is the period of the profit plan. Ideally it should span the same period covered by the corporate plan and the operational ones of the major departments. Stating profit targets for just one year is not really planning for long-term effectiveness. Next, competition, its strengths and estimated plans, reactions to the firm's activities and the market factors affecting the business generally should be studied. Then the profit plan for the firm and even markets and product groups can be established. These will concentrate the minds on the main things they must keep in view, the continued profitability, growth and survival of the firm.

5.6 PRICING

The importance of sound pricing strategies and policies must be stressed. The price of a firm's products is the means whereby it obtains a fair return for its labours, replenishes and increases its wealth and purchasing power for supplying products or services. The profit that can be earned will depend upon the unit selling price, unit product cost and the volume sold.

The first principle to be observed is that pricing strategy, objectives and plans must be consistent with and related to corporate and marketing objectives.

(a) Pricing strategy

Sound strategies and their associated policies must be planned to achieve specific objectives. However, it is not just a question of: 'How much does it cost to make, what profit do we want and thus at what price should we try to sell the product?' Executives in charge of pricing work must consider not only the profit, volume and other social aspects. They have to keep in mind also the type of product and its utility for customers, the stage it has reached in its life cycle (e.g. is it obsolescent? or does it have a long life expectancy?), what market coverage and market shares it is obtaining and can sustain in some specified future period and its versatility.

Then there are the questions associated with its manufacture (how is it made? what resources does it need, and how is it affected by technological changes? etc.) and distribution. Other points include the stage its markets have reached in their life cycles, the turnover (and of course, profit) it must achieve and any ancillary services on which it may depend.

Pricing work is undoubtedly one of the more difficult tasks that marketing executives have to undertake and it is the harder if relevant pricing objectives have not been set. There are several problems to be faced. First, markets are hardly ever in a 'normal' state these days. Changes are almost always occurring so it is difficult to find a 'normal' period to use for control or comparison purposes. There can be sudden fluctuations in demand for 'natural' reasons, some of which can be explained or forecast, but many of which cannot be. Then there are 'unnatural' reasons due to government intervention in business activity. Further, there are dramatic increases in costs, as has been experienced in the late 1970s. These may be due to escalation of raw materials prices, shortage of essential materials, large wage increases, or political developments abroad affecting the free flow of trade. Other factors are the emergence of a powerful new competitor, price wars and market changes due to various predictable and unpredictable pressures.

Then if corporate strategies and objectives call for maximisation of short-term profit, for valid reasons, the resultant pricing should aim for the maximisation of total cash flow (with minimum costs) over the specified planning period. If optimisation of long-term profit is needed, pricing decisions will be aimed at earning the highest total profit for as long as possible (see Section 5.6(c) also). Competitive activity and ruling market prices, market demand, costs and the 'value' customers assign to the firm's products all help to determine what strategy could be followed. Time is also an important criterion. If a firm is early into the market with a new product it should normally be able to command a higher price than at a later period, when substantial competition would probably exist. Figure 5.8 indicates the complicated relationships which exist between different managerial activities and pricing and profit planning. It is obvious that flexibility is needed and strategies, objectives and polices have to be changed when major alterations occur in critical factors.

(b) Pricing objectives
These objectives can be divided into two groups, *general objectives* and *marketing objectives* for pricing. Both cover the profitability, volume and social or ethical aims of marketing. Table 5.7 lists these objectives and the basic information required for price planning. Obviously objectives vary from company to company and will have to be reviewed regularly. Then adjustments can be made to take account of changes in the market-place, as described in the preceding sections.

(c) Pricing policies
The range of policies that are available are shown in Table 5.8 and Figure 5.9. Decisions on which should be followed will be taken by a number of senior executives drawn from the main operating divisions of the firm. It should not be left to a solitary individual, as it still is in some cases.

(d) Pricing process and decisions
Prices represent an important part of the image a firm presents to its markets and cannot be left to the whims and prejudices of one person. However, even with a carefully selected team, setting the 'right price'

Fig 5.8 *planning pricing and profit-associated activities*

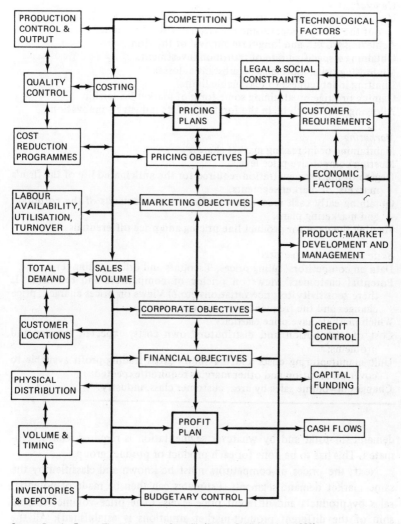

Source: Douglas Foster, *The Management Quadrille* (Pitman Publishing Ltd, 1980).

is not easy. A good team, drawing on their experience and sound judgement, would usually follow the process summarised below.

First, customer demand is analysed and allowance is made for known or forecasted changes occurring. This should be done for different customer groups, classified according to the markets they are in, their size and location and the uses to which they put the products. Likely future

144

Table 5.7 **pricing objectives and information**

General

Maximisation or optimisation of profitability (short- and long-term, without the former jeopardising the latter). Also of revenue.

Achieving growth and long-term survival of the firm.

Obtaining a specified rate of return on investment.

Minimising risks, especially of substantial losses.

Limiting indebtedness to reasonable limits.

Gaining prestige by attaining some form of market leadership.

Allowing the firm to be in the forefront of its industry's innovation.

Marketing

Maintaining or increasing market shares.

Meeting competitive price levels.

Degree of market penetration required for the anticipated life of the firm's markets, or market segments.

Obtaining early cash recovery according to the demands of the corporate and marketing plans.

Meeting the need for product line pricing and price differentials.

Basic information required

Data on competitors' ruling prices, discounts and other trading terms.

Potential customers' views on pricing of competitors and the firm. (Is there sensitivity to price variations etc.?) Views on prices charged, price changes and the frequency of price alterations.

Which markets have price elasticity?

Cost of distribution and distributors' own costs, expected margins and problems.

Unit manufacturing costs and maximum gross trading profit available to cover distribution and other margins required/expected.

Changes in volume sales by area, customer class, industry.

demand, in total and by whatever segmentation is required, can be estimated. This has to be done for each product or product group.

Next, the prices of competitors must be known and classified by the same market demand segments. Estimates can then be made of potential sales by products and different price levels. (The price–volume relationship of the different product-market situations is established). All the other factors mentioned earlier must then be considered and their impact on potential sales estimated. Estimates can also be made on the effectiveness of various price levels in driving out competition. The impact of promotional activities will also be gauged. The existence of substitute products, especially new ones, should not be ignored. Their impact on the demand–price relationship should be estimated.

At the same time manufacturing and financial colleagues will be

(continued on page 146)

Table 5.8 **some basic pricing policies**

Marketing executives can decide which of the following policies they should follow.

Skim pricing: allows early recovery of all costs and total profit required, in early period before competition intensifies; useful for products with a short life (e.g. fashion) or when no patent or other protection exists to shield product from all forms of competition.

Penetration pricing: lower profit margins; used when market expected to have long life and product must build up a reasonable volume of sales, sustained, with reasonable growth, for as long as possible.

Mixed: that is, begin with skim pricing and as competition builds up drop price, sometimes even below cost to eliminate competitors, then go to penetration pricing. (Fig 5.9, p. 146 illustrates.)

Differential pricing: charge different prices for the same product sold to different locations of buyers, different types of customer and large purchases. First takes account of any increased distribution costs to, for example, remote or sparsely populated regions. Second is based on the 'value' of the product to the buyer. Third reflects the cost savings with large orders. Usually worked the other way round; special charge made for small orders. Special discounts for large orders is the alternative approach.

Cost-plus pricing: all costs of a product are calculated, a margin is added to give a profit and the resultant is the price. Where all costs not known, the margin or 'contribution' added is calculated (or guessed!) to cover these unallocated costs and still leave a profit. Takes no account of current and future demand; does not take full advantage of market potential/opportunities.

Single price for all: one price charged to everyone (e.g. in retailing, units of electricity and other utilities, standard fares on transport etc.).

Variable prices: used in industrial markets; similar to differential pricing but bargaining power, potential demand of a customer and their knowledge of market and cost factors taken into account; permits price flexibility.

Variable prices for all: prices altered according to time of use, distances involved etc. but otherwise applicable to all customers. Examples: telephone charges for different distances involved and time of call; season ticket rates for transport fares; etc.

Price lining: takes into account relationships among firm's products rather than viewing each in isolation. For example a clothing firm will have suits, skirts, shirts etc. at different prices reflecting their different quality, use etc. Once made, price lining is not always easy to adjust. If costs rise, the price lining might be changed, often confusing the customer, or production costs of some items will have to be altered (lowered).

Promotional price: a price lower than would normally be if the sales of a product has to be promoted. Used when new products are launched, or to boost sales of ailing or obsolescent items. *Loss leaders* are retail goods priced at less than cost to attract customers who will then, hopefully, buy other regularly priced and profitable items.

Table 5.8 (*contd*)

Market pricing: here the seller has no control over the price. It can fluctuate daily, or during the course of a trading day, according to the demand for the product and the supplies released at the time. This policy is followed in commodities trading (e.g. gold, tin, copper, silver, wheat and other grains etc.).

Fig 5.9 *skim, penetration and mixed pricing*

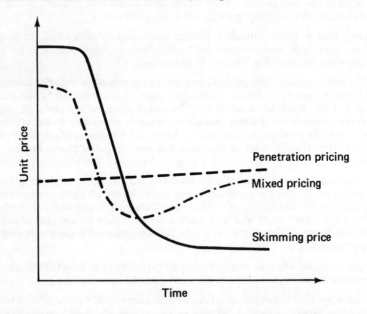

studying the cost, capacity, quality, resource, cash flow, profitability and return implications of Marketing's studies. One aspect forgotten by everyone too frequently concerns the competitive situation and how this is changing. What existing competitors are withdrawing, what new ones are coming in and so on, cannot be overlooked without inviting problems later. When all this work has been done (and there must be constant communication and co-operation between all parties) the pricing team should be ready to recommend the pricing policies and prices that should be applied.

(i) *Pricing new products*
In the case of new products, pricing analysis should begin as early as possible in the product development work. Waiting until the product specification has been agreed is often too late. The application of the new pro-

duct must be known and so must be the advantages it offers over existing, competitive items. The alternatives or substitutes for it should be defined while estimates of possible competition should be estimated. The performance of the new idea should be checked against possible alternatives and against the requirements of potential customers. With knowledge of the potential demand and life for the new idea, decisions can then be taken on the pricing policy to be adopted for it.

(ii) *Initiating a price change*

Executives should start from knowledge of why the change is necessary and the objectives it must meet. One could be to increase market share and volume so that overall profit is increased. However, if the product or firm enjoys a reputation for quality and customers see any price reduction as being impossible without a lowering of quality, then lower prices to achieve these objectives may lead only to loss of volume and market share. If increased profits are pursued by increasing prices, if the quality view holds and customers think there will be a reasonable improvement in quality, sales may increase. However, in hard times, most price increases are viewed with displeasure and many customers may switch to competitors' or substitute products.

The effect of changes in prices on goodwill and competitor reactions must therefore be considered. If a price reduction would take competitors below their unit costs they may not follow, especially if they are already working to optimum output. Any increase in demand for their products may be worthless for them if they cannot supply it. If they see their position in one of their major markets threatened they may make bigger price reductions and could start a price war. If they are not working to full capacity, competitors will almost certainly match any price reductions and often will better them. The initiating firm must also estimate what increase in volume is needed to give a net increase in total profit. Also, if they do not have the spare capacity, price reductions will provide no benefit.

The firm may also raise prices if their capacity is less than demand on them. A reasonable loss of orders may ease the pressures on their order book. Here again estimates should be made on what loss of business would result and whether the higher prices would give a similar, or greater profit than before. A small loss in profit may be acceptable to ease strains or release resources for more profitable activities with a longer future. The view and therefore reactions competitors may take must also be studied. If they match the price increase there may be no loss of business, just an increase in profit for everyone. With all decisions, their effect on profit potential must always be carefully considered.

(iii) *Matching competitors' price changes*

Again the reasons for this should be estimated. If competitors are reducing prices to eliminate accumulating stock it may be best to let them get on with it. Clearance of old stock will only help to upgrade the marketing operations of everyone in the end. However, if the reduction is for other purposes, the firm must consider what might happen if they do or do not follow. If they follow will it mean additional demand which they cannot meet or will they lose business for the quality reason discussed above? If they remain as they were, what business will be lost and what effects will this have on all product-market situations and future prospects?

If competitors raise their prices and the firm does not follow, will it lose or gain business? If the latter, will it have the capacity to cope with the increased demand? If the former, what will be the effect on the firm's business and profitability?

The comments in the preceding three sub-sections suffice to illustrate the delicate and complicated nature of pricing. Readers wishing to study the matter in greater depth should of course read some of the many specialist books on the subject.

5.7 MARKET PRICE REGULATION

There are three basic methods of price regulation in markets. The first is *public regulation*. The second is *self-regulation* and the third *market regulation* of prices.

With *public regulation* of prices the final decision or approval of the prices to be charged is taken by a government department or ministry, or some related quasi-governmental organisation. For example in Britain the prices for utilities such as electricity, gas and water are in reality dictated by the appropriate government department or minister. Other services such as transport also encounter such intervention. With air transport, international agreement has to be achieved involving several governments.

The problem is that political and social considerations will predominate over the realities of the economic situations. Politicians, motivated by the desire to do the right thing for their voters (and perhaps afraid of losing too many supporters and votes at the next election?) are very sensitive to public opinion and attitudes about price levels. The tendency is that any price increases will be less than those dictated by economic considerations. However, they will eventually have to face reality and in a few years swinging price increases just cannot be avoided. The resultant social upheavals are much worse than would have been the case if the right prices had been set in the first place. Thus trying to maintain the *status quo* and social considerations are over-emphasised when public regulation of prices is the **determinant**.

With *self-regulation* of prices, an appropriate professional body or association dictates what prices should be charged for different services. In Britain, solicitors, accountants, management consultants and estate agents are so regulated. Here the prices are often based on the least efficient members of the profession and it could be argued that the public has to pay more than is necessary. The professional bodies counter this by arguing that their aim is to ensure acceptable high standards of operation and so are looking after the interests of their clients.

None the less, there is an underlying dislike of competition, something that would lower the prestige and proficiency of the profession. In most cases, however, self-regulation prevents the worst excesses of any over-charging that might otherwise result. It can be argued that in this form of price regulation prestige goals and social considerations predominate. In Britain some of the professions lay down precise scales of charges while others (e.g. management consultants) may just have guidelines on what represent reasonable fees.

The third method, *market regulation*, is the one that applies to most consumer goods and industrial products marketing. It is also usual for most other services. Here the economic and other conditions (e.g. price sensitivity, customer attitudes to prices, the essentiality of need for an item, competition, total demand and so on) determine what prices can be charged. The concept is expressed briefly in the expression 'what price the market will bear'. Ideally this gives the customer the best prices and customer reactions dictate what the ruling market prices will be. However, when a product has a unique property, higher prices can often be charged than for run-of-the-mill items. This aspect of pricing has been discussed earlier.

5.8 MORE CAUTIONARY TALES

The chief executive of a leading manufacturer of kitchen utensils (pots and pans) with several leading brand names found himself sitting next to the editor of a major woman's journal at a business lunch. Talk came round to the ideas the editor had for promoting her magazine. These included special offers of pots and pans, perhaps especially non-stick frying pans which were then all the rage. At subsequent discussions the chief executive was asked to quote for a supply of 100,000 frying pans.

This was lucrative business. The production run was a long one, so really low prices could be quoted while still leaving the manufacturer with a very big profit. The order was placed and some repeat orders followed. However, even when these ceased the chief executive insisted that production at high volume should continue. The goods were not sold, even at give-away prices and inventories rose alarmingly. Eventually a large quantity

150

of the product had to be scrapped at considerable loss.

Another firm, in a different business, took great care in costing new products. However, when any cost increases came along, these were estimated as percentages of total cost and this percentage increase was added to the unit cost and prices adjusted accordingly. Unfortunately the percentages were rounded off to the nearest half per cent, usually downwards. Several cost increases were experienced in two years. Thus the unit costs used were eventually much less than the actual costs being encountered. Prices were inadequate and profit margins were eroded. It was not surprising that at the end of a trading year the actual total profit earned was less than 'estimated'. Executives panicked and spent a lot of time trying to find out what was wrong!

A third firm only responded to cost decreases if these were substantial. Eventually its prices were much greater than competitors' and considerable loss of business resulted. A fourth firm did not have any real pricing policy as it did not bother to establish pricing objectives for its products. It responded to every action and reaction by competitors. It took little note also of market demand and only scant notice of customer requirements. This was a sad tale. Eventually it was forced into liquidation!

ASSIGNMENTS

1 The group you work for manufactures consumer goods, general purpose industrial products and is also involved in tourism and insurance. The business environments of all four sectors of the group's business are experiencing considerable change. Competition is increasing in consumer goods while demand in the other three areas is declining. You are instructed to consider all the product-market situations and submit proposals for new or modified strategies and policies for the group to follow in the next ten years. What would be your recommendations?

2 How would your decisions above affect product planning activities and thus other planning work throughout the group? How would the use of 'product life cycles' help you to reach sound conclusions?

3 If you were in charge of a non-profit-making organisation (say a charity, mutual building society or a section of a - national - health service) how would your approach to this work vary from that used for the manufacturing case in Assignment 1?

4 A manufacturing company (choose any product group you like) is faced with the need to alter its prices, meet competitive price changes (up and down) and price some new products. What points should be considered and what recommendations would you make on all this to the marketing director?

MARKET MANAGEMENT AND PLANNING

'Market' can be described simply as a group of people able and willing to buy a particular product or service. While with consumer goods and durables 'people' means the consumers, with industrial products and capital equipment the 'people' are in fact commercial firms and business enterprises. Modern usage has given several meanings to the word 'market'. There are definitions based on the type of person buying the product or service (e.g. above, the 'consumer market' and the 'industrial market'). Markets may also be defined by the type of service used (e.g. the 'electrical contracting market') and the product in the selling–buying exchange process (e.g. the 'refrigerator market' or the 'car market'). It can also be designated in money terms (e.g. the market for Product X is £Y million).

To the stockbroker, his or her market is all the customers who deal through him or her but *the* Market in this case is the Stock Exchange, where the transactions are made. To the sales manager the word means the areas and regions of his sales territory, the different types of customers to be served, the different technologies involved and the use to which the products are put. For the accountant the market is all individuals and organisations using or needing these services. To the economist a 'market' is the total universe comprising it. However, for marketing executives the market is not only present customers but *all those persons and organisations who may be persuaded to buy the products or services they offer.* Table 6.1 lists the various classifications of markets used today and gives examples of the products involved. It will be noted that some items can feature in more than one definition, the deciding factor being the use and the properties of the goods in question. The marketing mix used will differ according to the target market.

Table 6.1 **present-day classification of markets**

Consumer goods: goods and services destined for use by the consumer (individuals) or households which do not require further commercial processing.

Mass market: the above that are purchased in some quantity and could be purchased by everyone. Usually these are purchased frequently or on more than one occasion in a trading year, i.e. there is substantial repeat buying.

Convenience goods: Consumer goods purchased frequently, immediately and with the minimum of effort in comparison and buying, i.e. a sub-classification of mass markets (e.g. many food products, soaps and detergents, newspapers, magazines, tobacco products etc.).

Speciality goods: Consumer goods with unique features or characteristics and/or brand identification for which a significant group of buyers will make a special purchasing effort (e.g. specific types and brands of fancy goods, photographic and sporting equipment, hi-fi products and special clothing).

Shopping goods: Consumer goods where in the process of selection and purchase consumers make comparisons based on quality, price, style and suitability (e.g. shoes, women's dress goods, millinery, major appliances, cars, furniture).

Durable goods: tangible goods which survive many uses and have a relatively long life (e.g. refrigerators, washing machines, radio, TV etc.).

Non-durable goods: tangible goods which are normally consumed or used in one or a few uses.

Industrial markets: products, raw materials and consumable items (e.g. cleaning fluids, fuel) primarily for producing other goods or rendering some service or other. Include equipment, components, raw materials, and for maintenance or repair purposes.

Services market: benefits, activities and satisfactions not involving the exchange of tangible products, which are offered for sale (e.g. laundry, transport, travel and tourism services, banking, insurance, hotel and catering facilities).

Government markets: all products and services bought by government departments and agencies for their own use.

Defence markets: all items bought by defence organisations (government departments, army, navy, air force etc.) for use in defence of their countries.

6.1 EMERGENCE OF MASS MARKETS

The history of marketing and the development of markets as we know them today follow closely the history of civilisation and has been discussed in Section 1.7(c). In modern times social changes led to the development of potential mass markets. However, mass markets do not usually occur spontaneously. They have to be stimulated into reality and can sometimes be created by positive marketing effort. As competition increased economies moved from being essentially that of 'sellers' markets' to that of 'buyers' markets'. This required greater sophistication of marketing operations. Studies were needed of such things as the output aspects of the economy, buying power of markets and how this was distributed between customer classes, the expenditure patterns for goods and services and the stability of business activity.

(a) Effects of technological developments

The Industrial Revolution has never ended though at times economic recessions have slowed it down. The present day is sometimes referred to as the 'Age of Automation' and it has had two major effects on economies of relevance to marketing management as explained in Section 1.7(c). The present age is one of surplus and as this increases so does the need for marketing.

Technological developments also have wide reaching effects on economic and marketing activities. Consider, for example, the development of computers for commercial purposes in 1951 and their present-day widespread use. New factories, equipment and engineering were needed. New and better-paying jobs resulted and additional marketing facilities and concepts were required to sell, lease and distribute the machines and their associated software. New markets were created for magnetic tape, paper and other supplies. New facilities were needed for the training of technicians and there was increased interest in knowledge and applications of sophisticated statistical methods to business and marketing. Inventory control was simplified and made more effective, while general record keeping was made more efficient, faster and could be more detailed in the facts recorded. Simulations of various marketing conditions gave very fast indications of possible outcomes and could be repeated very quickly for different values of critical variables. Marketing forecasting and planning became more exact sciences, leading to greater accuracy in forecasts and plans. (However if the computer was used wastefully, this greater accuracy did not always result in improved profitability!)

Companies providing credit services were able to expand and speed up their operations. Design engineering of all kinds (cars, planes, capital equipment and major industrial products, durables etc.) could be done more quickly. Production methods could be simulated and the most appropriate selected, thus improving manufacturing efficiency. Enquiries, reservations and confirmations for travel and hotel facilities could be provided very quickly and (if the computer operators did not make mistakes) more efficiently.

The modern car and public conveyances improved the transport infrastructures and helped to create major cities and increase leisure and business travel. Trucks expedited the delivery of goods. The modern aircraft speeded up internal and international travel, bringing the latter, and associated tourism, to millions who otherwise did not have the time or money for the more traditional and slower methods of transportation. Planes also improved the transportation of goods internationally, necessitated new material handling methods and, because of the latter, reduced the damage and pollution of goods in transit and losses due to pilfering and other reasons. Satellite communications revolutionised international communication links. The availability of instant colour TV transmissions from remote parts of the world extended consumer interests into learning more about these world areas and stimulated interest in long-distance travel and holidays. Xerography also revolutionised office procedures and met reprographic needs that businesses and colleges may not even have realised existed.

All of these and many others contributed greatly to the growth of economies and in marketing opportunities for business. Despite the recession of the late 1970s and early 1980s, technological advances will continue, if more slowly and carefully. More new opportunities for marketing should flow and in their wake, further development of the economies of most countries. The effect of technological changes cannot be ignored by marketing executives. Some may bring indirect benefits (e.g. the computer and its effect on travel and tourism through improved information handling). Remember that improved technology has brought benefits over a wide range of products. These include plastics, transistors, microprocessors, frozen foods, packaging materials, power brakes and steering with automatic transmission for vehicles, air conditioners, tape recorders and antibiotics, to mention just a few at random. In the 1980s microchips may lead to further technological developments.

(b) Stability of markets

The stability of the output aspects of an economic environment has an effect on marketing opportunities and activities. Fluctuations can be recurring or non-recurring. The former are the seasonal and cyclical characteristics of markets and their demand. For example demand for holidays normally peaks during the Summer, Christmas, Easter, other religious and holiday periods. Demand for banking services alter with the fluctuation and incidence of interest and dividend payments. Demand for ice-cream tends to peak in the summer though the promotion of it as a special dinner party treat has tended to smooth out the winter trough. Requirements for hot-water bottles should rise in the autumn (Fall) and winter while demand for air-conditioners should peak in the late spring and early summer.

Non-recurring fluctuations arise because of a major once-for-all change in the business cycle or economic and employment factors. Others arise because of legal, legislative and social changes. Strikes, elections, riots and wars are also other causes. Generally, non-recurring fluctuations are more difficult to forecast or anticipate than recurring ones, especially recurring ones that are based on set patterns. However, these 'set patterns' can be suddenly overturned if a major economic or other development or disaster occurs.

Marketing executives should therefore be interested in this point also. Understanding the stability of markets, especially mass markets, will lead to better, more accurate and profitable results. Thus market management is as critical and complex as product management.

6.2 MARKET DEMAND

Attention is drawn to the comments in Section 4.4(b) (Demand studies). A few more comments are required here. First, the law of demand can be simply stated as 'more goods will be sold at a lower than a higher price', though note the comments in Section 5.6(d). So market demand for a product can be illustrated simply as in Figure 6.1. The slope and shape of the curve will vary from product to product to a certain degree depending on other market characteristics.

First is the principle of diminishing utility. Generally, this means the more a consumer or customer has of a product or service, the less does each additional unit mean to them. Ultimately when they have all they

Fig 6.1 *demand curves*

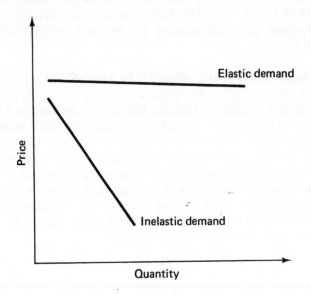

could need they will stop buying until their stock is nearly eliminated, other economic considerations permitting. Second is the customer's ability to buy, that is their income or the amount of money budgeted by a firm for such purchase. The lower the price or the greater their income/budget the more likely customers are to make a purchase. In a recession, when incomes decline, purchases may be delayed or put off permanently. Finally, there is the question of desire. If consumers desire some product strongly (e.g. an exotic, long-distance holiday; a new expensive car) or industrial users have an essential need for a piece of capital equipment, they will usually find the money for the purchase. Usually goods highly desired will have greater market demand than items considered unnecessary luxuries. However, as people's standard of living and associated 'desires' change, so their interest in different goods and hence the demand for them will change. Eternal watchfulness is vital!

In markets having demand elasticity, potential demand will vary with price levels. Changes in the geographical location of populations will also affect demand. Areas major buyers move from will see demand decline; the areas they move to should see an increase in demand. Changes in life-styles will also alter demand.

Forecasting market demand

The attention of readers is drawn to the commnets in Section 4.4(b) (Demand studies) and Section 4.9 (Forecasting). It is only necessary to note here that forecasting market demand is not easy, depending on how easy it is to forecast the demand for associated products. It is easy when the total level or trend is reasonably constant or where competition is non-existent or fairly stable. For most markets, market demand is not stable from one year to the next. The more unstable the demand, the greater is the importance of forecast accuracy and the more elaborate will be the methods used.

6.3 MARKET STRATEGIES, OBJECTIVES AND MIX

Executives have a number of strategies they can choose. The first is *market retention*, which involves maintaining and extending their activities in established markets. Well-established firms with successful products favour this and emphasis is placed on product modification or adaptation to retain their hold on these markets. Then there is *balancing strategy* when the firm attempts to balance costs and revenue. Emphasis is on control of the marketing operation rather than planning major changes. This strategy is preferred for mature products in markets in which the company is well-established and competition is well-known and understood.

The third is *market development strategy*. This is when firms concentrate on market development by producing new products tailored to the needs of new markets. As can be gauged from Chapter 5, this requires considerable time and effort from all the major departments and involves the greatest risk. In product management terms this is diversification. It may employ venture management when it involves efforts to break into an entirely new field or technology.

Finally there is *market growth strategy*. In this the firm is launching a new product or entering a new market while at the same time attempting to expand business in existing markets and carry through product modifications and improvements. Because of the immense amount of work being done simultaneously and the total resources committed, the consequences of failure are more serious. The risks involved are greater than for the first three strategies described above. However, well-managed companies with a good track record will usually be adopting this strategy in the fulfillment of corporate objectives for growth and improved profitability. Figure 6.2 illustrates the relationship between strategies, market opportunities and competition.

(a) Market mix and screening

If used, the phrase 'market mix' (not to be confused with 'market*ing* mix') refers to the planned mixture of markets and market segments to which the firm's products or services are to be sold. For most companies there will be quite a wide choice of potential markets or segments they could serve. Deciding the market mix will need careful consideration.

Usually the possibilities will be listed in some order of priority based on market size, growth prospects, competition likely, ease of access (e.g. nearness to the firm's manufacturing units), ease of market penetration, and so on. It helps if the more likely opportunities are screened just as product ideas are. It is also preferable for a final product-market screening to be made. The purpose of the product-market screen is to make a final check of the points critical to the success of the product in its selected markets, so the important aspects of the latter are also checked in this composite approach. It is then a matter of picking the appropriate one in each group, carrying out the necessary mathematics and comparing results with a predetermined priority scale. The forecasts used are usually those for the 'most likely' outcomes, based on prior marketing research and studies.

(b) Identifying market opportunities

Before the market and product-market screening take place market opportunities and characteristics must be identified. The work needed here is summarised in Table 6.2.

Fig 6.2 *market strategies, opportunities, competition*

MARKET			
STRATEGY/PLAN	OPPORTUNITY	COMPETITION	TASKS
Solidify & extend market share or foothold. Differential advantage. Market segmentation.	ESTABLISHING MARKET SHARE etc.	Limited competition Potential competitors known	Establish favourable product/brand image /preference. Customer loyalty. Good marketing intelligence. Increase mkt share.
Maintain moderate growth. Use new products. Keep relative position.	MARKET MATURITY	Keen competition Pressures on prices Profits squeezed More competitors in market	Stress price, product and package variations. Find new use. Increase promotions. Segment markets further.
Increase use & volume. Redefine segments & extend mkts. Use position to the full. Prepare for new products.	MARKET EXPANSION	Increasing direct & indirect competition in mass markets	Modify prods. Launch new brands. Cut prices. Use mass marketing methods. Sales increase, new product, expand use. Maximise profit.
Keep whatever markets possible. Pull out of the others. Develop new products.	MARKET DECLINE	Strong price competition New product competition Limited profits	Cut prices. Modify the products. Increase promotional activities. Plan for new opportunities.
Gain initial market acceptance. Change method etc. used for achievement of this goal.	MARKET ENTRY	No immediate or forseeable competition for a while	Create primary demand. Gain knowledge. Identify segments. Intelligence on customers. Gain channel support.

Table 6.2 **identifying market opportunities and characteristics with marketing research**

Identifying markets and market segments		1 *Identifying markets and discrete market segments* estimating total demand or market size; identifying significant segments of total market; measuring the coverage of the market by existing products or services (to deduce the new or revised/modified activities the company could consider).
		2 *Market projections* projections into the future (for 5, 10 or more years) to evaluate growth or decline of existing markets; or changes in customer requirements, preferences, etc; or changes in economic, social, political, technological, ethical and other environmental factors which affect market conditions or the services being offered.
	Determining characteristics	3 *Characteristics of market* services required by customers; function or usage of service or products; essential features which the service or product must have; methods used by customers in searching for services/products; competitive position, including share of markets, costs/prices, etc. (should include projections as (2) above); range of services to be offered; functions critical to the success of operations offering services to selected markets; commercial conditions and terms expected by customers; cost/price relationship; price sensitivity; possible pricing policy.
Selecting marketing strategy. Markets and marketing operations + control information feedback		4 *Available market share* estimate of market shares available; projections of market shares as per (2) above; company and competitors' strengths and weaknesses and how these may affect market shares; how to modify marketing operations to improve profitability and gain increased market shares.
		5 *Marketing strategy and market selection* selection of strategy and operations (tactics) to be followed; selection of markets and market segments to be attacked; possible mix to be offered; deciding the resultant marketing plans to be implemented; implementation and control of marketing operations, including analysis of results being obtained, feeding new information and data into marketing planning activities and assessments.

6.4 MARKET SEGMENTATION

Except in special circumstances (e.g. a small, very specialised market, or where the firm has a monopoly through a unique product) it is no longer economically possible to serve total markets. So the need to segment markets has become a reality for executives. Apart from preventing a firm from attempting the impossible and spreading limited resources on too wide a front, market segmentation tries to determine the differences among potential buyers (e.g. buying habits and patterns, preferences etc.) that are consequential to their buying decisions. The rationale is that a total market is not homogeneous (i.e. is not similar) with respect to customer response and preferences for products, price, promotional strategies or the channels of distribution used.

Ideally, total markets should be divided so as to give maximum hetero-geneity (dissimilarity) between segments and complete homogeneity (similarity) within each segment. Thus responses to marketing variables will vary more between segments than within them. If this is to be done well, executives must have clear and detailed definition of the market in terms of consumer needs, wants and problems they are trying to resolve by their purchases. Executives must also understand other problems, however irrelevant they may seem, if these are deemed to influence consumers' buying decisions. (For example South African pineapples are amongst the best in the world but people who have strong political feelings may opt instead to buy fruit of another country even though they do not represent such good value for money. Firms marketing imported fresh and canned fruit would take note of this if they felt they could not market to the whole of Britain and would have to select only parts of it).

The demand characteristics of each segment have to be identified and this requires study of the way different consumer groups perceive the basic need to be satisfied or the problem that has to be overcome. For example, the purchase of expensive capital equipment would be viewed differently by the large firm and a small one. In the consumer market, the need to shave is viewed differently by old and young men. To the former it is a necessity of civilised living. To the latter it may just be a chore to be avoided as much as possible. If they do they could be relatively insig-nificant buyers of shaving requisites.

Then, how a product's attributes relate to customer preferences and how concern or interest in various aspects of the product lead to a buying decision must be known. Next, what trends the different demand character-istics of each target segment are taking should be known and accurate fore-casts made of where these would take demand (i.e. nature, size etc. of demand) into some specified future period. Finally, the worth or size of each segment has to be estimated.

Table 6.3 shows the different variables that can be used to segment consumer goods and industrial products markets. For the latter the items marked with an asterisk are most applicable. Tables 6.4 and 6.5 indicate how two service industries (travel/tourism and investment services) may be segmented, using their special characteristics to arrive at the final groupings. These special features influence potential customers' buying decisions. Figure 6.3 illustrates the use of the family life-cycle concept mentioned in Table 6.3. Finally, Figure 6.4 gives brief descriptions of the different classifications used in the case of the individual consumer and the sort of products and services that would normally appeal to them.

(a) Segmentation resulting from marketing strategy

How a market is segmented is also determined by the type of marketing strategy followed. There are three basic strategies that could be followed.

The first is *undifferentiated marketing*, involving the marketing of one product to all markets using the same marketing mix. The second is *differentiated marketing*, in which many products are marketed with different marketing mixes designed to satisfy smaller market segments. Third is *concentrated marketing*, where the firm is concentrating all marketing resources on a small segment of the total market.

The first strategy is not widely practised now and the inherent danger of it lies in the effort to satisfy everyone. The firm is open to intensive competition from companies offering specialised products to smaller market segments. When competitors hold substantial market shares this strategy becomes unworkable. Where marketing to foreign countries is concerned, there is the added hazards that tastes, preferences and needs will vary. So one product formulation would not be acceptable.

With differentiated marketing greater satisfaction in numerous market segments may be achieved but the costs are greater. With shorter production runs and increased inventories, manufacturing costs are increased. The use of different marketing mixes for each product-market situation increases the time and effort needed from executives and usually requires a larger marketing department with attendant higher costs and greater promotional costs. While concentrating on a single market segment often gives a profitable operation, should total demand in that segment decline, the supplier can experience a critical drop in business volume with subsequent financial trouble.

An example of the latter was a manufacturer of raincoats, the heavyish, traditional, rubberised items. This firm sold all its production, of various styles, to one of Britain's leading chain stores, famous for its name for quality and reliability and having national distribution. The value of this business in raincoats in the 1950s was about £1 million per year. All was beautiful and profitable! Then came the new plastic materials and their

(continued on page 166)

Table 6.3 **market segmentation variables**

Variables	Possible breakdown
Socio-economic group	
Age	1-4; 5-10; 11-18; 19-34; 35-49; 50-64; 65+
Sex	Male; female
Family size	1; 2; 3; 4-5; 6 and over
Income	Either by official groups (e.g. in UK, groups 1, 2, 3, 4) or by actual gross incomes.
Occupation	By official groups (1, 2, 3 etc.) or e.g. executives, professionals, clerical, sales, crafts, etc.
Education	Primary, secondary, higher; public school, university etc.; or no. of years of formal schooling, e.g. under 7, 8, 9-11 yrs etc.
Family life cycle	According to the age and marital status of the family (see Figure 6.3).
Religion*	Protestant, Catholic, Methodist etc.
Nationality*	British, American, German, Japanese etc.
Social class	A, B, C1, C2, D, E, (see Figure 6.4).
*Geographic**	
Region (UK)	Southeast, East Midlands, North etc.
Area (World)	Europe, N. America, Scandinavia etc.
Size of city	Under 5000, 5-20,000, 20-50,000 etc.
Density	Urban, suburban, rural, etc.
Climate	Northern, temperature, tropical etc.
Personality	
Compulsiveness	Compulsive, non-compulsive
Gregariousness	Extrovert, introvert
Autonomy	Independent, dependent
Attitude	Conservative, liberal, radical
Authority style	Democratic, authoritarian
Leadership style	Driver, leader, permissive leadership, follower
*Buyer behaviour**	
Usage rate	Non-user, light user, heavy user etc.
Buyer class	Unaware, aware, interested, intends to try, trier, regular user
Buyer motives	Economy, status, dependability etc.
End use	(Varies with product and service)
Brand and channel loyalty	(Classified by brands and channels used)
Price sensitivity	Indifferent, low, high etc.
Service† sensitivity	Indifferent, low, high etc.
Advertising sensitivity	Indifferent, low, high etc.

*Variables most applicable in industrial products markets.
†Service here = after-sales services or the way a product or service is presented, promoted or sold to customers.

Source: D. W. Foster, *Planning for Products and Markets* (Longman, 1972).

Table 6.4 **segmenting the travel and tourist market**

Segment	Sub-segment
Holiday tourist	fully inclusive package partly inclusive package independent traveller booked via travel agent independent traveller booked privately
Business traveller	booked via travel agent booked by employer's travel dept. or individually (the above could also be divided to show those who go solely for business purposes and those who tag on a short holiday at one end of such trips)
Special or common interest traveller	hobby cultural (art, music etc.). religious archaeological and ancient history ethnic and anthropological flora and fauna

Table 6.5 **market segmentation variables modified for the marketing of investment services**

Standard variable	Special sub-classification
1 *Income groups*	(a) Expected return required (b) Degree of risk acceptable (c) Current investment and amounts and incidence of new funds for investment
2 *Social groups* (*A, B, C1, C2, D, E*)	(a) (b) } As above. (See Figure 6.4 also) (c) (d) Personal characteristics and attitudes to investment and portfolios (e) Possible response patterns to offerings, or marketing and promotional activities
3 *Geographical*	(a) The home locations: region size of community type of community
4 *Personality*	(As standard variables in as far as they condition response)
5 *Buyer behaviour*	(As standard if not taken into full account by 2(e) above)

Fig 6.3 *life cycle of a family*

Bachelor stage: young single people not living at home	Newly married couples: young, no children	Full nest I: youngest child under six	Full nest II: youngest child six or over six	Full nest III: older married couples with dependent children	Empty nest I: older married couples, no children living with them, head in labor force	Empty nest II: older married couples, no children living at home, head retired	Solitary survivor in labor force	Solitary survivor retired
Few financial burdens. Fashion opinion leaders. Recreation oriented. Buy: Basic kitchen equipment, basic furniture, cars, equipment for the mating game, vacations.	Better off financially than they will be in the near future. Highest purchase rate and highest average purchase of durables. Buy: Cars, refrigerators, stoves, sensible and durable furniture, vacations.	Home purchasing at peak. Liquid assets low. Dissatisfied with financial position and amount of money saved. Interested in new products. Like advertised products. Buy: Washers, dryers, TV, baby food, chest rubs and cough medicine, vitamins, dolls, wagons, sleds, skates.	Financial position better. Some wives work. Less influenced by advertising. Buy larger sized packages, multiple-unit deals. Buy: Many foods, cleaning materials, bicycles, music lessons, pianos.	Financial position still better. More wives work. Some children get jobs. Hard to influence with advertising. High average purchase of durables. Buy: New more tasteful furniture, auto travel, non-necessary appliances, boats, dental services, magazines.	Home ownership at peak. Most satisfied with financial position and money saved. Interested in travel, recreation, self-education. Make gifts and contributions. Not interested in new products. Buy: Vacations, luxuries, home improvements.	Drastic cut in income. Keep home. Buy: Medical appliances, medical care, products which aid health, sleep, and digestion.	Income still good but likely to sell home.	Same medical and product needs as the other retired groups, drastic cut in income. Special need for attention, affection, and security.

Fig 6.4 *classifying the consumer*

GRADE		DESCRIPTION	
		General	Services
A		'Upper-middle class' Higher managerial, administrative or professional – has demand for 'quality' and luxury products as well as 'normal' requirements – may be trend-setter too.	Good demand for banking, investment; better grade hotel and restaurant; more expensive tours and independent travel probably with 'special' interests (e.g. music, art, archaeology etc.)
B		'Middle class' Middle to senior management and administration; up and coming professional – often likes to be trend-setter. Requires most products.	Usually has need for investment & banking; probably strong interest in insurance as means of saving as well as protection; good middle grade hotels etc.; more adventurous tours & group travel.
C1		'Lower-middle class' Junior management, supervisory and clerical grades. Tends to ape the trend-setters even if finances overstretched.	Minimal use of banking & investment services; insurance for protection & some 'compulsory' saving; Probably 3-star hotel & restaurants; packaged tours but could also have special interests (music, art etc.).
C2		'Skilled working class' Usually a manual trade. Requires the less costly products usually.	Limited banking (current account); some protective insurance; 2- and if possible 3-star hotels etc.; packaged tours (could also have special hobbies – interests).
D		'Working class' Semi- and un-skilled worker. Mainly interested in the least expensive products.	Very limited use of banking & insurance; probably 2-and 1-star hotels etc.; one holiday a year, if abroad the cheaper package & probably Spain. Could still have special interests.
E		Pensioners & widows	Minimal demand, if any, for all services.

development for use in clothing. New lightweight, inexpensive plastic rain-coats were developed. The public went for them in a big way not only because of their price but also for convenience. They could be folded into a tiny parcel which was light and easy to carry. The demand for the old-style raincoats as a general utility protection against rain vanished in a short time. The chain store naturally terminated its contract with the manufac-turer mentioned and the latter was forced into liquidation. Had the firm developed other market segments (e.g. the military, which still need them in some form or other) and other products, things might have been different. This is a cautionary tale also of the dangers of being a one-product company. When compounded with being a single market segment one the risks are very high and the future very uncertain.

(b) Segmentation strategies

Again there are two basic approaches or strategies. The first is the *consumer segmentation* method where potential customers are grouped according to personal characteristics and product attributes or properties are compared with the former. The second strategy is *product segmentation*, a term open to misunderstanding by newcomers to marketing. In this, product benefits and attributes are first defined and then consumers' personal characteristics are compared against them. The two approaches are not competitive but complementary. The first helps to answer which consumer groups should form the target markets. The second is useful in market definition. It is of particular value to consumer goods as it illustrates what the *brand structure* of a market is and how the different brands are perceived by potential consumers.

(c) Advantages and disadvantages

The purposes of market segmentation are to improve the competitive position of brands and products, attain a more effective position for them in limited markets, identify gaps in the market (unsatisfied needs etc.) which represent new product opportunities and find new customers for existing products. Despite the basic logic of the approach, doubts have been raised as to the viability of the concept. Some markets do not have sufficient heterogeneity of needs. They may have only a need for product variety. Markets can also be too small for efficient segmentation. Further, since three rules have to be satisfied to ensure sound segmentation and these cannot always be met, segmentation can be difficult. The three concern the different consumer groups that could form the basis of segmentation. The groups must be clearly identified (physically and in terms of their needs), they must be easily located and it must be possible to mount specifically designed marketing mixes to appeal to their wants, preferences and so on.

In practice this means that segments must be accessible. It must be possible to focus marketing activities on the segments chosen though this is not possible in every case. For example it would be useful if marketing persuasions could be concentrated on opinion leaders in each segment. Unfortunately their media habits (reading etc.) are usually not distinct from those of opinion followers in their groups.

Then the segment must be substantial, that is, it is large enough to warrant the design and launch of separate and distinctive marketing activities for them. Segmental marketing is an expensive operation. So it probably would not pay for a shirt manufacturer, say, to make and market products specially intended for hunchbacks (with due apologies to those so afflicted!). It is however worthwhile and a great social contribution to design and market special products for the blind (e.g. braille books, 'talking books' and so on).

Finally, the segment should be capable of relevant measurement. Unfortunately many of the characteristics of people, or the variables by which they can be placed in customer groups, do not lend themselves to easy or accurate quantification and assessment. For example, how should a firm measure in a sound way the values different people place on a product? How do consumers measure the true value of a holiday? Sometimes the basic statistics and information needed do not exist or cannot be obtained. Once it was difficult to measure those who were motivated by economy aspects when deciding on the car they should purchase. However, with the startling increases in oil and petrol prices in the late 1970s, many have become economy conscious though estimating their accessibility and measurability is still difficult. Perhaps all that can be done is to isolate those who have company cars and their firms pay for all the petrol used, and the very rich (in the 'A' group) whom, it may be assumed, are not worried by high petrol prices. (They might become so if the companies took effective steps to control the business and private use of their cars or reduced the number provided.)

To cite another example, a manufacturer of desk-top calculators may conceive that it would help left-handed accountants if the control levers and knobs were on the left-hand side of the products. They are normally on the right and are fine for right-handed people. Unfortunately, while left-handed persons are easily identified by observation, as they work in all areas side by side with right-handed colleagues their location cannot be clearly defined. Further, if promotional costs are not to be wasted by the 'scatter effect' (i.e. they are seen by those not interested in or affected by the unique aspects of the market or product offering), promotional activities have to be placed in correct media (ones seen, read or used only by the target customer group). There are no media aimed specifically at left-handed accountants.

Another example is the self-employed artisan. They have the means and interests to go on exotic or expensive holidays. However, their specific needs vary from those in say, the A and B groups (see Figure 6.4). They may read different magazines and papers and watch different TV channels. Ideally the holiday product for them should contain attractions that are of special interest to them. Further, they do not now live in specific areas. According to their financial means they do live in regions once thought the preserve of the B and even A groups. Thus in practice trying to segment the total holiday market by extracting the artisan group from it is impracticable and does not usually provide any benefits to the firm. Blanket marketing of holidays results and the firms just hope that most interested people will be contacted and sold.

The main disadvantages arise out of these difficulties. It is easy to end up with false or incorrect segmentation. For example, the market for housing may be thought to segment into demand for houses, flats (apartments) and bungalows but no specific customer group is interested in only one of these. There are no significant differences in their consumer characteristics expect for the disabled, who will prefer apartments and bungalows designed specially for them. Prices and locations are usually the critical factors so segmenting the housing market by price and region would be more correct and practical.

Next, it is possible to overlook or forget a segment or two, in the rush to carry out segmentation. In almost every marketing situation there is always a customer group or two that could use the product in question but who do not know of its existence. For example there was the firm that developed special gas-tight ceramics for the envelopes of large valves, klystrons and so on used in TV and long-distance communications. Every effort was put into this. It was not until enquiries were received from other manufacturers in the electronics industry for the new ceramic for their own special uses (e.g. for transistors and as bases for micro-miniature circuitry) that the executives realised a much wider market, consisting of many segments, was available for the new product.

Finally, there is the aspect of product variety. Some consumer goods firms believe they have achieved market segmentation through offering a variety of brands. If a brand offers some unique benefit or point of interest to one or two customer groups but not all, then true segmentation may result. However, where there is no real difference in the benefits offered, then consumer preference may just be influenced by the fact that one brand may be 'new' and therefore worth a try. (Some recently introduced detergent powders for home laundry use fell into this category.) Brand switching and lack of brand loyalty may be the only results.

The advantages from true segmentation range from a firm's ability to spot opportunities more quickly and accurately and so compare more precisely the marketing possibilities that exist. Then, marketing effort and expenditure can be more profitably deployed on a selective, narrower front. Fine adjustments to products and marketing appeals can be made. The total effect is the improvement of the firm's competitive stance and more effective market positioning of products and brands. Gaps in the market, or consumer satisfaction should be more easily and accurately identified. (See also Section 6.9.)

(d) Evaluating market segments

If market segmentation, the identification of gaps in consumer satisfaction and the selection of appropriate segments is to be well done, careful evaluation of the turnover, profit (if possible) and future trends in demand are necessary. Assuming the necessary data is available, simple grids can be used for this purpose. Figure 6.5 illustrates one approach.

In Figure 6.5(a) a general grid shows what the total purchases of different groups of customers are for specified product groups. Figure 6.5(b) is a more detailed grid showing how different products in a product group are selling currently to one of the customer groups. A further column shows the estimates of future sales for some specified period and the last one indicates the trend. If possible, and it is not always so, profit figures can be shown. Then subject to the marketing targets for sales, profit, future growth and development, the appropriate product-market segment mix can be selected to fit with the cost constraints applying for the period being planned. A further grid, showing the channels of distribution to be used and the promotional activities needed, with estimated costs, can also be used to help with the planning of the marketing mix for the selected product-market segments.

The benefits of this approach include forcing executives to think systematically about market selection and segmentation and to treat each segment as a distinct entity. They can also make sound decisions on the marketing mix to be used and whether the expected return from a segment justifies the costs. The selection of the correct marketing strategy is more clearly defined and targets and expenditure budgets are in fact built from the bottom up. Strategies and targets are not first imposed and then marketing executives have to struggle to make them fit into the programmes for what is practical.

6.5 MARKET PLANNING

Market planning has to define the markets to be served, the declining markets to be dropped, what new markets should be introduced and the various programmes that would be needed to achieve agreed objectives. There are three stages. First, the market strategies relevant to objectives

Fig 6.5 *evaluating market segments*

(a) *the product-customer group grid for the total market*

Mix	CUSTOMERS	CUSTOMER GROUPS			
PRODUCT GROUPS	Customers / Product	Group 'A'	Group 'B'	Group 'C'	Total
	Product 'X'				
	Product 'Y'				
	Product 'Z'				

(b) *grid for a product-customer group*

		CUSTOMER GROUP 'A'		
PRODUCT GROUP 'X'	Estimates of Product	Current sales & profit (if poss.)	Future sales & profit	Trends (%)
	X1	£	£	
	X2			
	X3			
	X4			
	X5			

Source: Douglas Foster, *Planning for Products and Markets* (Longman, 1972).

must be decided. Second, from all the alternatives available, the most suitable markets must be selected, taking into account the profit, growth, cash-flows and return required and the risks involved. Third, there is planning of the long- and short-term actions required. The critical questions that have to be answered in this work are listed in Table 6.6.

Table 6.6 **market planning: key questions**

Marketing
Which markets/market segments are available and which selected? What products to be sold?
What sales methods and channels will be used, including sales aids, brochures, point-of-sale materials, exhibitions etc.?
What advertising required (kind, media, quantity and quality)?
What kind of sales force is required? What market shares required?

Pricing
What pricing policies are available and which will be used?
What trade terms and discount policies will be used?
What pricing structure will be followed for products, spare parts and servicing?
What ratios of turnover and costs are required?

Physical distribution
What channels and method of distribution will be used?
What standards will be set for delivery times etc.?
What forms of transportation will be used?
Where will depots be located and what size is in mind for the inventory levels for the different products?
Where and what products can be stored? Should inventories be held at own depots and/or with distributors and sales outlets?
How will the dispatch be organised?

Other
What support services are needed?
Will these be provided by the firm or the trade?
What personnel are needed?
What will be the cost of all the above?

It is not usual for there to be separate market managers (or departments) in the sense that there are for product management. In most cases the detailed work will be done by product managers in the normal course of their product studies, since they are the ones most likely to obtain and be able to analyse correctly the intelligence available on this subject. When specialist aspects, such as pricing, physical distribution, costs and so on are involved, other colleagues will assist them. For critical or important matters the marketing manager, marketing and other directors will be involved in the decision-making area if not the detailed work.

When planning for *consumer markets*, executives have to identify the individual consumer or household buyer and the wholesalers, retailers and other middlemen in the distribution channel. With *industrial products markets* the ultimate user, often sub-classified by end-use, technology, size of company or potential demand, has to be identified together with the middlemen who will be used. The latter are specialists too and deal with specific industries for which they have the contracts and technical knowledge. Usually they can also provide limited back-up services such as repair and maintenance.

In the case of *'government markets'*, market planning should differentiate between central government, local or state government and quasi-offical markets. The last include the 'defence market'. In every case the product offerings have to be matched against needs. These offerings cover the good or product itself, back-up services, brand and packaging (for consumer goods), price aspects including credit terms, all distribution methods to be used and the promotional and personal selling activities in mind.

For *service industries* the customers are either consumers or business enterprises. Often both are potential buyers as in the case of transport services. The planning approach will follow either that for consumer or industrial markets, whichever is appropriate. (The marketing activities will do likewise.) However, the special characteristics of services (see Sections 5.2 and 9.4) have to be taken into account. It must also be remembered that industrial buyers keep in mind the profit requirements of their own firms when they make their buying decisions.

(a) Market share

All marketing operations rightly aim to achieve specified market shares. It permits comparison of the firm's performance against that of competitors. It is in fact a comparison *with the average* of all other companies in the industry or market and avoids comparison with just one enterprise. If the latter is the very best firm, direct comparison would underrate the company's performance; if it is the worst, the company would be led to believe it was doing better than it really was.

Market share comparisons also help to indicate whether changes in sales were due to uncontrollable external forces or some weakness in the marketing operations. If market shares are dropping and there are no external reasons for this, then the firm's marketing mix, or its execution, can be judged to be at fault somewhere.

A company that is able to build up its market share is more likely to be able to match, or turn away, the effects of competition. Or conversely, if a firm has a reasonable market share it can safeguard its position. However if it becomes greedy and goes for too large a slice of the total potential available, as mentioned before, it can become vulnerable to competition from smaller companies.

For every operation there is a minimum share that must be held if the operation is to remain viable over a reasonable period of time. What that level is will depend on the industry, products or services, markets, total demand, prices, profit margins and competition at any time. It is not a question of maximising market shares but of optimising them. Executives have to get the right balance for all the company's activities, taking into account the conflicting needs of long- and short-term requirements. At the same time they must obtain sufficient immediate profit without jeopardising long-term survival and growth.

(b) Market leadership

Market planning must also take into account the market leadership a company wishes to achieve. It can be measured in quality of the products or services offered, the 'value for money' aspect, technological innovation, reliability and performance. It can also be measured by the views customers hold of the fact that the firm is playing fair by them. That is, its prices are more than reasonable for the dependability provided and that unjust demands are not being made. That is, when costs increase, the resultant price is not raised by more than is necessary, nor before existing stocks at old costs have been sold. For firms operating overseas, especially in developing countries, strict adherence to the letter *and the spirit* of the law, no matter how inconvenient, is something else that is appreciated by the general public and can lead to the reinforcing of the firm's market leadership or standing.

Market leadership can be lost when marketing plans and actions are not kept up-to-date and when firms are run on outmoded ideas and methods stemming from obsolete experience and maintained prejudices. It can also be lost when the wrong type of executive is allowed to gain control of any of the firm's operations and gain dominance for his or her ideas regardless of their relevance to the conditions and requirements of the market-place. Failure to design and produce products or services in accordance with market needs will also erode the market leadership being enjoyed by a firm. Ignoring any of the points mentioned earlier will also prove disastrous here.

6.6 MANAGING MARKETS

The work of managing markets parallels, or mirrors, that of managing products. First, existing profitable markets must be looked after so that they continue to be so for a reasonable length of time. Next, when performance is dropping off because of some change in market factors – especially consumer preference or customer needs – market modification is required. If it is not possible to do anything on modification, or it would prove too costly, or provide insufficient increased profitability, then market rationalisation may be needed. Finally, if growth is to be achieved and the losses resulting from rationalisation are to be balanced, then a continuous development of new markets is required. Again, as with products, sources for ideas on possible new markets are many, but in this case Marketing and Distribution departments, with middlemen in the distribution network, will usually be the main sources.

(a) Existing markets

Part of the 'looking after' process is making sure that all customers who should be offered the products are being well covered by the marketing activities and that no little, forgotten pockets of potential users exist. Another is to make sure that market share, growth of sales and profit targets are also being met. Then there is the question of improving the profitability of these markets or market segments.

The work could start by taking the total statistics for the market or segment and splitting them down stage after stage, to the smallest denominator if possible to see where performance is falling below target. It is possible for a market segment to be producing the required results in total but some parts of it are not, while others are exceeding expectations. The procedure is similar to that for evaluating new market segments (Figure 6.5). Executives can then investigate the poor performing areas to see what could be done to improve matters.

Perhaps too much marketing effort is being used for the potential demand or market share available, in which case marketing costs would be too high? Or perhaps insufficient effort is being made, or competition is more severe than estimated? Or distribution may be too elaborate and costly, or too slow and losing the firm business and goodwill? Or prices may be too high so that cost reductions may have to be achieved? There are many others but identifying which one is the culprit will indicate steps that can be taken to improve the profitability of a market.

(b) Market modification and rationalisation

There will be occasions when market performance cannot be improved in the ways mentioned above. Perhaps some groups of customers in a market or segment have changed needs or preferences, or are not buying in the quantities anticipated? Then it may be necessary to make modifications to the market by finding other or extra groups of customers in the segment who could be persuaded to buy the products. Perhaps the promotional campaigns may also have to be changed or modified?

However, all markets have finite lives like products though the timescale is often much longer. So eventually a firm would have to withdraw from a market when demand has fallen too low or competition has intensified too much. Again, as with products, withdrawal has to be carefully planned so that the abandonment of a segment does not jeopardise the total potential of important products. The resources saved can be put to the development of new markets or segments offering better long-term potential.

(c) New market development
New markets have to be found, assessed and exploited if the company's long-term objectives for growth are to be realised. All ideas have to be studied and their potential, probable competition, estimated profitability, ease of access and ease of penetration have to be gauged. With these priorities in mind, a list of prospects can be prepared and these follow similar assessment and screening processes as is used for products (see Appendix A.3). Of course during the work executives bear in mind the market objectives and mix that should be achieved. Sometimes new markets that are not immediately profitable or capable of achieving profit targets will have to be developed if they represent areas in which the company believes its future prosperity and survival will be. Or some scarcely profitable markets may be developed if by so doing, the firm prevents, hinders or frustrates the growth intentions of major competitors, or ones who might become so in the future.

6.7 MARKET COSTS

The bulk of the costs that could be ascribed to market management are in fact incurred by selling, promotional, market research and physical distribution activities. Most of these will be discussed in their appropriate chapters but one or two points should be noted here.

First, by operating in a market a firm incurs various costs, the sum total of which can be equal to or greater than manufacturing costs. Therefore there is need for effective cost control and realistic assessments of the benefits that any expenditure would bring to the company's business. Second, it is always possible for some executive to get carried away by the concepts of promotional activities, market research or physical distribution. Then the executive could indulge the company in unnecessarily extensive and costly promotions or research. Or a distribution system could be constructed that was far too elaborate for the firm's needs and thus results in unnecessary expenditures.

Marketing executives responsible for market management work of any sort must remain aware of the cost generation of being in a market. Although the various cost items are the direct responsibility of other line departments, it is beneficial if whoever does the market management work adopts an overseeing role for them. If this person is the product/brand manager or executive, this role would be a natural one since this staff member fulfils a similar one in product management.

Finally, it is in the area of market research costs that good control is vital. It is very easy to embark on an unnecessary piece of research for it may not seem so at its conception. Or in the planning of it and the preparation of the brief, over-elaborations may be allowed to enter into the scheme. Then it must be remembered that even relevant information can become obsolescent in a short time, so how much data is collected for storage and future use must be carefully considered. For critical information it might be better to do the research when the intelligence is needed, assuming time and cost permit, as the facts uncovered will be as up-to-date as is possible.

As shown, management of the firm's markets does not escape the vital need for sound cost control. This includes control of any associated overhead or administrative costs. The number of staff employed in this work can grow alarmingly. Indeed as Professor Parkinson propounded, the amount of work generated will be in proportion to the number of people hired to do it. That is, staff tend to generate work to justify their jobs. It is important that this should not occur.

6.8 COMPETITION

This subject has been discussed in other chapters where relevant and appropriate. A few general comments here are advisable.

Competition is desirable because it tends to improve marketing efficiency. It requires firms to follow dynamic policies and strategies specially evolved for specific conditions. Thus competition promotes greater innovation and the introduction of new products (though all the latter of recent decades have not been seen by everyone as being beneficial to society). It should result (but does not always) in better service to customers. Unregulated monopolies, in comparison, tend to encourage higher prices, discourage innovation, tolerate lower quality of service and product and permits slothful management.

Competition occurs at all levels of business and in all functional areas. Price is not the sole criterion. Non-price competition in product quality and design, promotions, merchandising, delivery and so on is also important. How successful the firm is in these areas will none the less influence the price levels possible. Thus competition can be classified into two types. The first has been called *commodity competition*, where the supply–demand forces of markets establish the nature and extent of competition and hence the prices to apply. The other has been called *enterprise competition*, where the price and non-price factors mentioned above are in play. The latter is normally what is implied when the word 'competition' is used.

The *principle of competitive differential advantage* interprets competition as complex interactions in which a firm's operations are affected not only by its own actions but by the strategies and actions of competitive firms. It is a sequence of initiatory moves by a firm and counteracting responses by competitors and others with which it deals, including customers, its work-force, suppliers and distributors. Thus when a firm offers its customers better prices or quality, or anything else, in order to improve sales volume at the expense of competitors, the latter will retaliate. They do this to redress the balance of sales or to minimise their losses. Competitors try to neutralise or counteract the initiating firm's advantages by offering customers inducements that are as good as, or better than, the initiator's and hopefully increase or improve their own marketing advantages. The time-lag between action and reaction can be a matter of days or years. It depends on the industry and technology, the nature of the markets and the resources of the firms concerned. Instantaneous reactions are more usual in fast-moving, mass market consumer goods. Slowness is unavoidable in high technology products or capital equipment because of the time needed to work out and test product responses. Some new design or concept may be involved and this must be subject to tests prior to offering it to customers. For companies with limited resources, it will take longer for even simple changes to be planned, checked and executed.

6.9 FURTHER THOUGHTS ON MARKET SEGMENTATION

In recent years doubts have arisen about the effectiveness and validity of segmenting markets by socio-economic groups (see Table 6.3 and Figure 6.4).

Social class is defined as the relatively permanent and homogenous division of society into families and individuals sharing similar lifestyles, interests, values and buyer behaviour. The variables involved are power, privilege, influence and prestige. However it has been usual to use occupation only as the basis for much market segmentation. Thus the variables mentioned are not satisfactorily categorised. Now it is appreciated that lifestyles, interests, values, prestige and power can vary considerably within any group. Thus buyer behaviour and propensity to buy any product or service can vary considerably within such a group.

In the last decade or two, major changes have occurred in the economic and social structures of societies in developed countries. Values, lifestyles, quality of life and expectations have changed. They are viewed differently than during the 1970s. It is no longer sufficient to use social class or job status as the sole criterion. (For example, witness the changed lifestyle of self-employed artisans.) It is insufficient to stick to original stereotypes, *namely* that the ABs wish to own their own homes while the DEs are content to rent council houses, nor to consider the C1s and C2s are necessarily of lesser importance than the ABs where 'upmarket' products and services are concerned.

Where demographic discriminators with economic bias are needed, income, age, marital status, size of the household, lifecycle of the family, number of earners in the family, working wives and residential areas are more appropriate. Where the behaviour pattern is culturally related, residential district, standard of education and media usage may be more appropriate. Identifying neighbourhoods sharing socio-economic, housing and demographic characteristics shows greater discrimination than just simple occupational-based segmentation. In other words, use should be made of behaviour-related criteria that are relevant to the marketing task in hand.

6.10 CASE ILLUSTRATIONS

The Eastman Kodak case (Section 1.10(a)) is a good illustration of what sound market and product management can achieve. In the eggcup cases, one firm showed what dangers were inherent in sticking to traditional, outmoded markets unable to provide a sufficient volume of profitable business. The other company showed how sensible thoughts on markets (and products) can rectify even a difficult position.

Then there was the case of a major engineering group that numbered among its products a handmade, expensive sportscar of unique design. It was their prestige product and it sold to wealthy businessmen and others and so served what the group considered were prestige markets. Unfortunately it was not an easy car to make, and being built one at a time, without mass production methods being possible, could not be produced in sufficient quantity. Even with a limited market, there was a waiting list of three years. The result too, in view also of stiff opposition from better-known Continental large sports cars, was that the car had to be sold at a price some £1000 less than the actual cost of production. The group was paying a hefty price for 'prestige'. Yet it took a while to convince senior executives that they should withdraw from those markets and sell the car facility to others more capable of overcoming all the problems.

Finally, there was the case of the manufacturer of construction equipment. The equipment had been designed for the more sophisticated conditions of Europe (e.g. well-trained operators, good maintenance and repair facilities, proximity to manufacturing units so that spares were easy to obtain quickly, ease of access to sites and between sites, etc.) and for working clay, sandy and gravelly soils, relatively non-abrasive substances. With major developments taking place in South-east Asia, they attempted to develop these difficult markets without modifications to the products.

The problems associated with these new markets included the fact that work would be on laterite, a very abrasive substance. Further, most operators were unskilled and, being small, literally had to stamp on the control pedals with some force. Breakdowns were frequent and protracted. The machines had to operate in rough terrain and could not avoid being 'thrown around' severely. Repair and maintenance facilities were few and far between. Sites were less accessible (roads were then limited) and most of the companies using this equipment were, at that time, not very knowledgeable of the technical aspects. Many breakdowns and other troubles arose, aggravated by the fact that the main source of spares was with the manufacturer's plant, some 8000 miles overseas. Marketing results were disappointing to say the least until the machines were modified to fit the market conditions of the new areas the firm wished to develop.

ASSIGNMENTS

1 Your company, hitherto manufacturing industrial products, is contemplating diversification into consumer goods and hence markets. You are asked to review the situation, indicating the change in attitudes and methods required if consumer markets are to be developed. You decide that it would be better to start by outlining how mass markets developed and then go on to discuss the factors affecting market demand, stability and the key role of market segmentation in this new field. You plan to conclude by recommending the various market and marketing strategies and policies that would be required and how decisions here will affect other decisions and the methods of entry and development that would be possible. Prepare an appropriate paper on this.

2 As a result of the work above you are asked to submit a further memorandum showing how consumers may be classified if diversification should be into canned and frozen foods and men's and women's toiletries. You are asked to give particular attention to the advantages and disadvantages that could arise as a result of such classification.

3 You are appointed to the post of assistant marketing manager with specific responsibility for the management of the company's markets. You are asked to prepare a job description for yourself showing what work is involved and how you would decide if 'market leadership' and 'market standing' are desirable for any or all of the company's markets. How will this decision affect the market shares your company should aim to achieve?

THE COMMUNICATIONS MIX

The 'communications mix' in marketing is comprised of advertising, sales promotion, PR (public and press relations) and personal selling. This also embraces merchandising and packaging, which are judged to be sales promotions activities. (The first three of the four mentioned above are sometimes still referred to as 'promotional activities.')

This combination is called the communications mix because in their various specialist ways they are involved in communicating information to customers and potential users about the products or services on offer. Their basic aim is to prompt people to take positive action by placing orders, making enquiries and purchases. The purchaser is supposed to move from awareness of the product or service to product knowledge, liking, preference and conviction with eventual purchase of the item. At each step, it is said, the probability that a purchase will result is increased. The communications mix is intended to prompt the right moves from stage to stage, ending in the purchase of the product being promoted. This concept shows that 'needs' incubate for a time before crystallising into 'wants' and purchasing action. Communications try to limit the incubation time and to prevent a 'stillbirth', i.e. no purchase of the item! However, not all 'needs' develop into 'wants'.

The components of the communications mix are defined briefly as follows. *Advertising* is any paid form of non-personal presentation of products, services or ideas by an identified sponsor. The sponsor may be the firm manufacturing the item (or product group), the distributor handling it, the retail outlet selling it to the ultimate customer, or any combination of the three. Where the cost of the advertisement is shared between manufacturer and retailer (or wholesaler) it is often referred to as *co-operative advertising.* Where two manufacturers of related products agree to a joint advertisement where the costs are shared proportionately, this used to be called *limpet advertising.*

Sales promotions are those activities other than advertising, PR and personal selling that stimulate dealer interest and stocking and customer purchase. They include many of the items in Table 7.1 and exhibitions, demonstrations or seminars to promote some aspects of a product or service and other non-recurring efforts not in the ordinary routine. PR (sometimes referred to simply as 'publicity') includes keeping the public correctly informed about the product and the firm offering it. In the case of 'press relations' PR aims to keep the press fully informed and provide commercially significant news which hopefully will result in free editorial matter appearing. That is, the firm does not have to pay for it; it just appears as editorial matter or news in the appropriate publication, or on radio or TV. (If the sponsoring firm has to pay for it, it is considered as part of advertising.)

Personal selling is (usually) the oral presentation of the product/service offering by one or more representative of the vendor in conversations with one or more executives (or individual consumers) from the prospective buyer. With technical products and capital equipment, several executives from the potential purchaser are usually involved in these conversations.

Table 7.1 **some popular promotional activities**

Advertising
Audio-visual sales aids
Brochures
Catalogues
Company visits
Competitions (for customers and the trade)
Design (product and packaging)
Direct mail
Directories
Financial incentives
Free gifts
Guarantees
Incentive schemes (trade and own salespersons)
Leaflets (technical and other)
Merchandising
Off-premises displays
Packaging
Point-of-sale displays
Premiums
PR (public and press relations)
Price reductions (and pricing strategy)
Special offers (price etc.)
Telephone selling
Tent cards (hotels, restaurants, departmental stores)
Vehicle livery
Year books

Those shown in italics have been the most used.

This activity is what most people mean when they refer to 'sales' or 'selling'.

The items forming this mix are not mutually exclusive. In all cases the vending firm will require some mixture of two or more of them. This will depend on the type of product being sold, the market conditions applying, especially competition and the type of potential customer forming the target market. The amount of money (budget) available and the other resources of the vendor will also affect the decision. How much total expenditure should be put behind the total effort and what relative usage should be made of the various activities form the substance of this chapter.

In meeting its basic aim, the communications mix has to respond to increasing competition in domestic markets. With the increasing internationalisation of business, this domestic competition may come from home-based enterprises, which may be national or foreign in ownership, and direct imports from overseas. Usually it is now a combination of both types. Then if the firm is active itself in overseas markets, foreign competition has also to be met, in those counties. The communications mix used must be modified to counter all forms of competition. Having got the mix 'right' at any point in time for the home market does not mean that marketing executives can sit back and have an easy life. Competition now is volatile and with sudden economic changes can change quickly, often unpredictably. Thus the effectiveness of the entire mix and its components must be reviewed regularly so that modifications to it all can be made as seems necessary. When entering a foreign market for the first time, a mix different from that being used in the home market may be necessary (see Section 9.5). Also, for similar reasons, the effectiveness has to be monitored and the necessary changes made to the mix. It is a very challenging but interesting task.

7.1 MASS PRODUCTION, MASS MARKETS AND MASS MEDIA

Large batch and eventually mass production evolved as market demand, for an ever-increasing number of products and services, increased. Competition intensified on an international basis. 'Selling' was not enough, the whole panoply of 'marketing' had to be used, especially in mass markets. The continued existence and growth of mass markets sustained mass production and led to further technological developments such as automation and now micro-miniaturisation of all kinds of equipment involved in the business cycle. The mass media evolved to facilitate more effective communications between vendors and buyers. This mass media included the development of TV, commercial radio and the press (national or large regional newspapers, both daily and Sunday editions; magazines; trade and specialist publications).

This development and associated technical advances (colour photography and printing, the computer for commercial uses of all kinds, electronic news gathering and transmission equipment, and so on) allowed new methods of communications to be evolved, especially in new concepts of advertising and sales promotion, until we have today mass communications methods. Mass production predicated mass consumption which in turn predicated mass communications. Any one is not possible without the other two and in a highly competitive economy mass communications, efficiently and effectively used, are vital for business survival. Even with industrial products and capital equipment, the extent and nature of the communications mix used today is more extensive than half a century ago. It is not only the consumer goods market that has been affected by this chain-reaction development. This is why students of marketing have now to understand what is a relatively complex communications situation today.

7.2 ADVERTISING

Modern commercial advertising is the persuasive force that aims at changing customers' attitudes and patterns of behaviour to a product or service (by use of the mass communications media) in ways which would be favourable to the vendor. This is necessary since consumers' needs and wants change as their economic position improves and as they pass through the different stages of the family life cycle (see Figure 6.3). In persuading them that certain products satisfy these changing needs better than others, advertising and the other components of the communications mix provide an effective way of reducing marketing risks by giving greater control over changes in demand. They seek to cushion the disruptive effects of economic and other changes beyond the direct control of the vendor firm and also to initiate or facilitate the process of change as in product-market development.

Advertising, with help from the other components of the mix, also has to develop and establish distinctive or unique product or brand identities which will prove attractive to potential customers. The ideal situation is when these identities are seen by customers as synonymous with quality, dependability and the performance of a particular function. For example Hoover became synonymous with vacuum cleaning using a reliable appliance, so that many housewives still refer to 'hoovering' their homes even when they were using a different make of appliance. Xerox became synonymous with fast, efficient reprographic services.

The three basic aims of advertising are (1) to inform potential customers and users of the existence of the product or service and the benefits they can bestow on the purchaser; (2) to remind established users of the continued existence and/or improvement of the products and services; and (3) to regain lost customers and accounts. The first aim is concerned with winning new customers or accounts while the second is seeking repeat orders and trying to establish product or brand loyalty. With mass-market consumer goods customers sometimes switch from one brand to another for valid reasons and often for no rational reason at all. Advertising must then seek to limit this brand switching if viable business is to be assured.

By communicating sales-motivating information to selected customers, advertising can accelerate the demand process by creating customers for a product or service more quickly than would be possible without advertising. This is vital when it is necessary to gain an early foothold in competitive markets, especially when technological, economic and other changes are occurring at a fast pace. Unless reasonable demand can be created relatively quickly so that profitable levels of business activity result, fewer new or improved products and services could be offered. Thus these promotional activities help a firm to look well beyond the next immediate sale.

The effects of advertising are not necessarily limited to the time when it appears. Indeed good advertising has a long-term, durable effect in that it builds goodwill between the firm, distributors and customers. How well this is done depends also on the product not being competitively inferior or failing to match the claims made for it. Bad, misleading or ill-judged advertisements can, however, damage customer goodwill that might have taken years to create and can undermine the entire work of the communications mix (see also Section 7.3).

The second aim of advertising, reminding customers and potential users, is necessary because the total of products and services is changing due to economic and other changes, new incentives to spend money in other ways being devised and the average customer not being able to remember everything or keep abreast of all these developments. Also markets are not static organisms. New potential customers are drawn into them from newly employed, newly married and newly retired persons, from families changing homes and localities or moving into a new stage of the family life cycle (see Figure 6.3). Further, fresh interests and needs are being created. Without advertisements reminding people of the availability of products (especially mass market ones) or services, demand for any one would soon decline.

(a) Objectives

The general goal is to improve the likelihood of customers buying a particular product or service. The specific objectives will depend on the nature of the product, the stage it has reached in its life cycle, competitors' advertising strategy and the purpose of the proposed advertisement. The more usual purposes are listed in Table 7.2. Objectives will also be influenced by content, type of appeal, intended effect, geographical coverage and other factors. A possible classification is given in Table 7.3.

The setting of advertising objectives is fundamental to the formulation of advertising strategy. Unfortunately, firms have trouble in identifying the correct objectives with precision. There may also be arguments about the real purpose of the campaign. The sales manager will see the prime purpose as helping his people to sell. The chief executive may be preoccupied with creating a good corporate image. The technical directors may wish to see the firm's technical abilities properly put across to potential users. And so it can go on. While having a multiplicity of goals is not of itself harmful, the relative importance of each goal or purpose must be known and made clear to those who have to organise the campaign.

(i) *Consumer goods advertising*

Sometimes referred to as commercial advertising, the specific objectives here are (1) increasing sales; (2) introducing new products/services; (3) counteracting competition; (4) increasing usage and applications; (5) increasing off-season sales; (6) maintaining brand loyalty; (7) building a good corporate image; (8) securing leads for the sales force and (9) gaining the support of dealers and distributors. Because the individual consumer lacks detailed knowledge of the products on offer and does not have the time to study in depth the pros and cons of the many competing offers being made, or lacks experience of the type of buying decision to be made, advertisements intended for consumers (individuals) should generally observe the following guidelines. They should:

- be specific in expression (message), clarity of thought and direction; be brief;
- be authoritative and present an argument which can be accepted as factually correct by the consumer: it should not mislead, or be untrue or factually incorrect;
- have impact; be distinctive or individual in approach with a sense of urgency; the message should be relevant to the product, situation and the needs of the consumer;
- be correctly timed for its main purpose.

Table 7.2 **common purposes of advertisement**

Announce

Location of stockists:	to support dealers and encourage selling-out of stock.
New product/service:	announcing new brands, insurance, holidays, unit trusts etc.
New pack:	pack identification at points-of-sale is important.
Modification:	to product or service to revive sales.
Price changes:	to keep customers fully informed.

Assist

The sales force:	by providing back-up support of their effort.
The stockists:	critical when dealing with supermarkets and chain stores to get dealer support; helps stockists to move goods down the line; persuades them to hold stocks.

Attract

Enquiries:	so as not to miss any opportunities.
New business:	to expand markets and increase profit.
Return of lost accounts:	to reverse negative sales trends.

Challenge

Competition:	to hold market shares etc.; to reduce impact of new/substitute products etc.

Educate

Customers and stockists:	to explain anything that needs it.

Expand

Markets to new buyers:	to ensure full exploitation of all opportunities for a product/service.
Stockist network: (or develop)	find new stockists to improve market coverage.
Direct sales:	to reduce distribution costs and increase market shares.

Make

Special offers:	to counter competition, off-peak demand; to increase sales, launch new product.

Maintain

Sales:	to hold market shares etc. (usually by reminding customers about the product).

Test

A market:	checking response before a national launch.
A medium:	for effectiveness, readership etc.

There have of course been celebrated departures from the above (e.g. the famous Rolls-Royce/Bentley advertisement in New York by Ogilvy and Mather in the 1950s) but this needs care, calls for excellent knowledge of the target audience, especially their behavioural traits and requires considerable creativity in designing the campaign.

Table 7.3 **classification of advertisements**

By appeal	Factual
	Emotional
By content	Product advertising
	Institutional advertising
By demand influence	Primary product level
	Selective brand level
By geographical spread	National
	Regional
	Local
By intended effect	Direct action
	Delayed action
By sponsor	Manufacturer
	Distributor
	Manufacturer-distributor, co-operative advt
	Joint by two manufacturers
	Retail outlet
By target market	Consumer
	Industry
	Trade
	Government agencies

There are several obstacles to be overcome. First, there is the indifference, slackness or laziness of the potential customer. There may be market attrition due to the movement of customers by emigration, social changes, death and so on. Third, there may be antipathy because potential consumers have rejected the advertisement, or its predecessor, as being unbelievable, irrelevant or inappropriate. Then there is the problem of lapse of memory or distortion of the image due to competitive advertising and demands made on the consumer from other directions. Or activities by competitors or competing products (not necessarily of the same 'family', e.g. new synthetic materials v. natural ones) may have fuzzed the issues. Finally, there may be incomprehension on the part of consumers as a result of defects in the advertisement due to ambiguity of phrase, lack of precision, vague orientation and so on. Thus considerable thought and care is needed in designing advertisements for consumer goods and services.

(ii) *Business buyers*

Advertising under this heading must take into account the four main groups of business involved: industry, trade, the professions and the agricultural community (mainly farms). They are customers for consumer goods, services, industrial products and some capital equipment. In the case of *industrial buyers,* purchases cover all the items required in the conduct of their businesses. The advertisements should stress such qualities as economy, efficiency, durability, reliability, strength, performance of the bought item and convenience of purchase and use. With *trade advertising*, aimed at wholesalers and retailers of all kinds, the objective is to encourage purchase and assist the trade to move the items through the distribution channel. Profitability and ease of selling the items because of substantial established consumer demand should be the main themes.

In the case of *professional advertisements*, aimed at lawyers, accountants, architects, doctors, dentists and so on, the usage of the bought items and the requirements for quality, dependability and value for money (cost) will indicate what the themes should be. Finally for *agricultural (or farm) advertising,* the users should be judged to be similar to industrial buyers in their purchase of farm machinery, pesticides, fertilisers, other chemicals and agriculture-related products. The advertisements would stress similar points to those shown for industrial buyers.

(iii) *Industrial products*

Further comments about these products and their advertising needs would be helpful to the student. The markets are generally smaller in number of potential customers (but not necessarily value) and are more specialised. Then, in industry, the profit motive rather than personal gratification is the prime buying consideration and rational rather than emotional appeals should be stressed.

The first problem is demonstrating to potential customers that the product or service advertised will decrease costs, increase production, be economical without sacrificing quality below permitted limits, improve the saleability of customers' own products or otherwise increase profits. A product which cannot be demonstrated as helping to improve profitability of the purchaser's operations is a difficult product to advertise and sell.

Another problem arises with a component or raw material which loses its identity in the final end-product. It is then difficult for the supplier of the raw material or component to build a solid 'brand image' with associated 'brand preferences'. Then there is the need to pitch the appeal not only to the primary customer but also to that firm's customers. This is essential for new and improved products where considerable resistance to change may be met, especially if the improved benefits, at first consideration, appear to be marginal. The advertisement should convince the ultimate user of the merits of the product. It should influence that company to specify the new or improved product on new orders for the complete equipment or plant. With expensive products and capital equipment, the importance of them, their high cost, performance, durability, minimal maintenance needs, quality and reliability are all points on which potential buyers have to be convinced.

Thus industrial advertisements should

make clear to the recipient what the sponsor makes or does;

describe the firm's functions and specified product advantages without ambiguity;

stress correctly the competitive advantages of the product; markets seldom know as much about a product as is imagined by the manufacturer; it is not safe to assume that everyone knows and appreciates the attributes of the product or service;

consider long- and short-term objectives for they often clash; quick sales of cheap plant can damage long-term intentions of say establishing the firm's products as leaders in their own field.

These must be taken into account with the other points mentioned earlier about advertisements if effective industrial products advertisements are to result.

(b) Style

The various types and classes of advertisements and their different purposes or goals have been discussed. Consider now the styles that are adopted and the results they are expected to achieve.

(i) *Persuasive advertisements*

These are sometimes referred to as the 'hard sell'. This type forms the greater majority of the advertisements seen daily in non-Communist countries though even the latter use them, if to a lesser degree. (All political advertisements and blandishments on posters and in the press are however, 'persuasive' in nature.) It is the inevitable companion of industrialisation and mass-production societies. There is no point in having production machinery if the output cannot be sold (a reality that quite a few firms do not appear to understand fully). These advertisements' primary aim is to find the markets and, by keeping up demand, help to keep the wheels of industry turning.

These advertisements must perform five functions. The first is attract attention to the product or service advertised. Second, they must command attention and interest. Third, by so doing, create desire in potential users. Fourth, they must inspire conviction and so, fifth, provoke action by users. The creation of these advertisements calls for a considerable range of skills.

(ii) *Informative advertisements*

All products and services are not bought instantaneously, as soon as consumers or firms have seen an advertisement. Some require careful consideration and thought and often detailed analyses of quite a bit of data and information. There may be need for considerable 'shopping around' and budgeting before a buying decision can be made (e.g. important industrial products or equipment; a car; the next holiday; a new suit or dress; a purchase of a product or service not bought before, for instance life, household or fire insurance). In these instances informative advertisements have to be used inviting readers to obtain more information by obtaining a brochure or leaflet, or discussing the important facts that potential users will want before a decision is taken. There may be more copy to read, more pictures to study and they may appear less compelling than persuasive advertisements. None the less they must still be attractive (to catch the attention of readers), interesting (to hold that attention) and convincing (to bring about a purchase). Some consider that this type of advertisement is in fact more difficult to do effectively than persuasive ones.

One form is the advertisement which stimulates the editorial style of the medium carrying it. Such advertisements are very informative but because they can be mistaken for editorial matter the *British Code of Advertising Practice* stipulates that these must have the heading 'Advertiser's Announcement'. All informative advertisements are believed to be the 'soft sell' approach but in reality they can often be nothing more than a cleverly disguised 'hard sell'.

Advertisements frequently combine the persuasive and informative approaches. Also the former tends to be used on TV and commercial radio and in the popular press, while the latter appears in magazines, specialist and trade publications and the Sunday editions of the press. The exceptions are advertisements for those products that are sold on hard facts or where the ethics or self-regulation rules prevent or frown on pure persuasive advertising. Examples include proprietary medicines and treatment where lengthy copy on evidence and testimonials supporting the claims are needed. These then are purely informative advertisements within the definition of them.

(iii) *Institutional advertisements*

These are more usually called *corporate* or *prestige* advertisements. They are used to present and promote a company's image or sometimes the image of its activities and major products. This type is used by oil, chemical and pharmaceutical companies who take space to describe their skills and contribution to society, or their attempts to minimise pollution or support conservation. The aim is to gain increasing support from the public, especially potential users of its products and to tempt young graduates and other skilled workers to join their work-forces.

(c) Designing an advertisement

First of all, the objectives, aims, purpose and style of the advertisement needed, the product or service to be promoted, its special or unique attributes, and the target audience must be known before the design of the advertisement can begin. The impact it is to have, the media to be used (see Section 7.3) and whether the product is subject to brand preference or switching are other basic facts that should be established at the outset. Table 7.4 lists the key questions involved.

Table 7.4 **designing an advertisement: key questions**

---

1 *What product or service is to be advertised?*
  (i) What performance/properties/attributes does it have?
  (ii) What unique selling propositions (USPs) does it possess?
  (iii) How, where and when does it meet competition?
  (iv) What product/service does it replace or act as a substitute?
  (v) Any guarantees etc. involved?

2 *How should/will the product/service be advertised?*
  (i) To what market segments?
  (ii) When and how frequently?
  (iii) Using what media? (National/local press? Trade and technical press? Exhibitions, demonstrations, seminars? Technical leaflets and data sheets? Free editorials in press? Displays at special centres or points-of-sale? Direct mail?)
  (iv) What theme and copy platform should be adopted? Any tie-in with other interested associations (industry, technical or research)?
  (v) What would seem to be the most effective (total) copy? Use of colours and if so how many?
  (vi) Best size for advertisement and frequency of exposure?

3 *What sales promotions and PR activities will be used in support of the advertising campaign?*
  (i) Receptions for press and other interested organisations? (For example travel trade for tourism subjects; supermarkets for new convenience food; major industrial users for new industrial product or equipment?)
  (ii) Demonstrations (and to whom? e.g. (i) above)?
  (iii) New releases, with/without pictures?
  (iv) Visits by distributors, retailers, or key consumer groups to factory etc.? (For tourism, visits to new resort area being developed?)
  (v) Any free samples (or special price offers) to important potential users for practical usage tests?

Note: Most of the items, other than the press, listed in 2(iii) above are sales promotions but are shown here as they have relevance to decisions on the form/nature of the advertisement).

(i) *The creative task*

The creative group (see also Section 7.3(e)) will first establish how aware the target audience is of the product, what knowledge it already has about it (i.e. how well informed it is), the degree of desire enjoyed by the product, the degree of attention that must be created and how original the advertisement should be. The creative group will require unity in the layout and presentation of the advertisement (headlines, text, pictures and so on, must hold together as a visible whole). There should be rhythm and harmony so that the eye of the reader will flow easily along the advertisement, not be jarred by excessive use of jargon or ambiguous statements and the advertisement should be pleasing to the reader. Type sizes and measures should harmonise so that the copy is pleasant (and easy) to read. Then the emphasis which has to be placed on the advertisement or parts of it, the proportions of it (the size and shape) and the scale (or visibility), with the colours and numbers of colours to be used, have to be established.

Then there is the question of the headline to be used. Generally (consumer goods especially) this should be a short, catchy phrase or slogan that will stick in the mind of readers and be easily remembered when they are next called upon to make a buying decision. The text (or copy) of the advertisement and supporting illustrations should be attractive to look at and have a style of writing and presentation that fits the personality of the target audience so that they find it pleasing. Careful consideration is also needed regarding the choice of typography to be used. The need for clarity of print should not be allowed to lead to monotonous use of the same typeface.

(d) Measuring effectiveness

The advertising budget, especially for consumer goods and durables, is one of the larger components in the total marketing budget. It is substantial in the communications mix budget, generally being exceeded only by the personal selling costs. So assessment of the effectiveness of the advertising and control of expenditure on it are vital necessities. However, advertising expenditures are difficult to assess for these purposes. As a rule, advertising is held accountable for achieving certain levels of sales but a strong body of opinion believes that the sole use of this criterion gives an uncertain base of assessment.

The problem is that the casual relationship between advertising and sales is limited and often unmeasurable. How far did sales rise because of the new advertising campaign? What would have happened if there had been no advertising? Was the sales increase due to a rise in total demand? Or how did advertising influence total demand? These are some of the questions that need answers. If any answers are to be validated, there is need for a past 'normal' sales period when market conditions were 'normal' and whose sales statistics can provide the control mechanism. Thus if a new campaign was launched in the present period and sales increased, compared with the 'normal' period selected, there are grounds for believing that the first caused the second to occur.

However, this need not be correct! Other marketing factors affect demand and sales including product or service features, packaging, distribution, personal selling effort, prices, special offers, point-of-sale displays and merchandising. Further, no marketing activity exists in a vacuum. Competition, changes in customer needs, attitudes, preferences, tastes and seasonal factors, changes in conditions affecting an industry and in the economic climate of a market or country all have some effect on demand. These items are themselves usually in some state of flux. So if sales fall after an advertising campaign is this due to the programme being faulty in some way or because, say, the economy has nosedived or a new, more aggressive competitor has entered the market? Would the fall in sales have been greater if the new campaign had not been tried? Perhaps too much marketing effort (and hence total costs) had been used, providing a downward trend in profits, or if the prices were above average this might have caused sales to decline? Or was there insufficient total marketing effort?

Modern attempts to overcome this hurdle are based on two approaches, *pre-testing* and *post-testing* of the advertisement. The first involves testing the advertisement in carefully selected test markets before the campaign is launched nationally. There are several methods. First, there is the 'sales conviction test'. Here interviewers ask heavy users of the product to identify which of two possible advertisements would convince them to buy the product. Sometimes the sample of respondents may be drawn to represent the cross-section of the customer makeup of the whole market or market segment.

Then there is the 'blind product test' where a sample of respondents is asked to select unidentified products on the basis of advertising copy available. Or they can be put in studios where they are asked to press one of two buttons, one representing a positive response and the other a negative one. Or an eye camera can be used to record eye movements and thus how people read the advertisement to determine where headlines and key statements should be placed. Or advertisements can be cut out of advance copies of magazines, the ones to be tested are stripped in to these in no set order and the impact of all these are checked.

Post-testing assesses the impact of advertisements after they have been used. Considered not as helpful as pre-testing (for reasons already stated), this approach helps in planning future campaigns and modifying existing ones. The most popular method is where interviewers ask readers of selected magazines whether they have read certain advertisements. With large advertisements, specific questions on headlines, text, illustrations and so on may be asked. A copy of the magazine is used as an aid in this method, which is often called *readership or recognition tests.*

Unaided recall tests is a variation of the above. With this, respondents are asked to recall the advertisements from memory and may be asked to comment on key aspects of them – e.g. did they notice this or that? The respondents list the ones they remember and also why they remembered them. Then they are asked about their potential purchase of the product.

Further, *enquiry tests* can be tried. Here the advertisement incorporates a free offer and the number of enquiries received is checked against the cost of the advertisement. However, since a large number of readers may not be attracted by the free offer and there is no way of checking what the typical response should be, these tests give only a rough measure of acceptance, especially if consumers can purchase the item without having to return the coupon. Finally, *split runs* have been used. In this the magazine is printed in two runs and a different advertisement is put into each. The response to the two editions is then compared. The limitations are again as suggested above.

(e) Advertisements v. telephone selling v. personal visits.

Especially in the case of industrial products, the perennial question exists as to which form of communication should be used or is most effective. Is there any mileage to be gained from advertisements? Or would results be better if telephone selling was used? Or are personal visits by representatives, especially technical ones (i.e. those trained and experienced in the technologies of the product and its users) best of all?

The advantages and disadvantages of *advertisements* have been discussed earlier. While they are not cheap these days and do not necessarily lead to an instant flow of orders, they do prepare the ground for the sales force. They keep information flowing to key and sometimes difficult-to-contact personnel in the buying firms and so could help to reduce the number of calls or visits made. Sometimes a smaller sales force may be used or can cope with the work (see Section 7.8). Given that a salesman or woman now costs an average of £16,000+ each a year (*Financial Times* London 17 July 1980) any saving here is worthwhile.

With *telephone selling* a suitably trained and experienced member of staff telephones preselected customers on an agreed day and time to solicit orders. The system has to be agreed with customers before hand. Usually customers introduced to this method like it. It saves their buyers having to spend time seeing visitors. The end-result can be better order response including orders for items not hitherto placed with the soliciting firm. Even at today's telephone charges, the return (value of orders received/cost of the telephoned enquiry) is better than for advertisements and even personal selling. However, it cannot replace personal visits; they can just be made at longer time intervals. Of course when an important problem or technical point arises, sales and other technical experts must visit the customer involved as quickly as possible.

Personal visits or selling calls seem to be the best method despite their cost. A face-to-face discussion allows the sales proposition and associated matters to be discussed fully on the spot. The sales response should be good. However, research has shown that as many as 40 per cent of all calls in a year may be non-effective, i.e. they do not produce orders. Where *missionary or pioneering* calls are necessary (e.g. when opening up a new account or market) then the successful order–visit rate will be even lower.

For services, consumer goods (especially mass-market) and durables, a carefully planned mix of all methods is usually necessary. To make the right decisions the executives should conduct cost–benefit studies. What would be the total cost of each method and based on past experience, what value of orders would be received? Again from past experience, the total effect of a mix of these three methods (in various combinations) can be estimated. Whatever the resultant mix chosen, the order value being obtained should be carefully recorded. If results are falling below expectations and there are no external factors (e.g. economic decline) that could account for this, the mix being used could be altered. Experiments in varying the mix, perhaps in test market areas before introducing the changes nationally, can also be helpful.

7.3 COMPONENTS OF AN ADVERTISEMENT

The essential components of any advertisement are discussed below, together with brief descriptions of advertising agencies, and the ethics, laws and regulations controlling advertising activities. The first six items discussed influence the impact advertisements have on their target audiences.

(a) Copy or message
To the advertising industry, 'copy' is the text or wording in the advertisement and 'copy platform' is the basic theme of the campaign. To printers and publishers and marketing executives, 'copy' is the text, pictures or other illustrations and artwork that make up the total content of the advertisement. (To complicate the issue further, in America, what is 'copy' to the advertiser in this country is usually referred to as 'the message'!)

The difference in preparing copy for consumer goods and services and industrial products stems from a fundamental difference in the interests of the respective readers. A consumer reads for pleasure and can be expected to be attracted to read advertisements that catch the attention or create interest. Good artwork and catch-phrases are often needed to attract and hold the attention of the consumer-reader.

With industrial users advertisements are read primarily to keep the readers informed of developments of interest to them in their work or business. They maintain an objective attitude to reading, which is often in company time as part of their work. The resultant purchases can of course be substantial in value. Most industrial readers read advertisements intensively. So, while these advertisements must also create interest for their readers, the interest centres on hard facts and relevant technical or other information.

Most industrial readers are in fact looking for the following in the advertisements they see:

nature and distinctive characteristics or properties of the product/ service;

advantages over competitors' items;

adaptability to the needs of the buyers;

dependability of claims made for the product (delivery promises; maintenance; repair and replacement services; etc.);

experience of other users;

gains or advantages/benefits resulting from purchase.

(b) Media

The various media available in Britain and some other countries are shown in Table 7.5. However, it should be noted that some countries do not as yet have, commercial radio or sometimes even commercial television. Yet others are too large and diverse in demographic and other details (e.g. the United States of America) or have limited distribution and transport facilities, or have too many languages or dialects (e.g. India) to make a national newspaper, in the United Kingdom sense, possible or viable. Of course in America, the major newspapers published in New York, Chicago, Washington DC and some other cities, and *U.S. Today* launched in 1983 from several centres, can be purchased in the major cities and towns. However, they do not give national coverage in the way newspapers in Britain do. Here all the major ones can be obtained, as a matter of course, in every town, hamlet or village.

The lack of a truly national newspaper creates problems for advertisers. More than one paper has to be used and sometimes the content and style of the advertisements may have to be changed to meet the needs or attitudes of the different ethnic groups. Where different dialects or languages are involved, the changes in copy will be substantial. Also some statements in one language may be totally unacceptable in another for religious,

Table 7.5 **media available**

Newspapers
National/regional/local; weekday and Sunday editions.

Technical press
Technical magazines and 'newspapers'.

Magazines
General (of general interest to readers e.g. women's magazines etc.) and special interest (e.g. sport, recreation, house and furnishings, hobbies etc.).

Commercial television

Commercial radio

Poster sites
Outdoors generally, at transport termini etc.

Display cards
On transport* (e.g. in trains, buses); in hotels and restaurants.

Cinema and theatres
In programmes and displays during intervals.

Direct mail

*Sometimes referred to, in America, as 'Transit Advertising'.

Above-the-line advertising. This is where advertisements are placed in media which, having 'recognised' the agency, pay the latter a commission on the purchase of space, sites and air time. These media are the press, commercial TV and radio, transport organisations and (some) cinemas. They provide the bulk of an agency's income.

Below-the-line advertising involves media that do not normally pay a commission or fee to the advertising agency. The latter must add a percentage to cover handling charges, profit etc. The fee can also be based on the time spent on making use of these media. The media here include merchandising, exhibitions, direct mail, printers, package designers, film makers, producers of display material.

---

ethnic or social reasons. For example in the Far East, for a long time, an advertisement showing a man and a woman embracing – however innocently – might be tolerated in an English language paper but was taboo for the local language one. So a different advertisement had to be designed. If the circulation and readership of the local language paper was not too big, the extra cost was a burden on the (probably limited) budget.

(i) *Media selection*
Apart from the basic matter mentioned above, other factors have to be considered. These are summarised in Table 7.6. Of the major media available, TV and radio offer opportunities for national coverage with

Table 7.6 media selection: points to consider

CIRCULATION

Normally means the audited net sale per issue, i.e. the number of copies sold. Advertising rates vary according to audited net sales. Usually the number of free copies distributed has been subtracted from the total copies issued. (For *exhibitions*, certified attendance figures are the equivalent. However, what is more important here is the quality and calibre of the people attending rather than the total attendance figures.)

READERSHIP

The total number of people who see or read the publication which is usually greater than the number of purchases, i.e. the circulation. This is the better figure to work to when considering the media to use and the cost effectiveness of advertisements. *Quality aspect*: refers to the type of people seeing or reading the publication (income, age, sex, social grading etc.). National Readership Surveys usually give these details but have to rely on publishers' statements especially for the lesser publications. *Quantity aspect*: refers to the fact that readership can be from three to fifteen or more times greater than the circulation figure.

PROFILE

This refers to the proportional breakdown of the readership by social or income groups. Useful when matching media selection to market segments.

PRIMARY OR SUPPORT MEDIA

Refers to whether the media gives an initial, powerful impact by reason of its coverage etc. (e.g. *The Economist*, leading women's magazines, *Radio Times*, Sunday papers etc.) or plays a supporting or secondary role (e.g. local press, direct mail, window bills and displays etc.).

PRODUCT LIFE CYCLE

The stage a product has reached in its life cycle can also be a guide to the media that should be used. There are two aspects.
Staircase effect: This refers to established products whose life cycle is extended, or takes off from the maturity stage as new uses, markets or applications are found for it. Various plastic products were examples.
Leapfrog effect: Products with a long life may not suffer any real decline in sales but do encounter periodic market challenges which are often met by product modification, repackaging, restyling and merchandising. In these cases it is necessary to leapfrog the new challenge by such developments. The choice of media will then depend on the nature and scope of the challenge and how best this can be countered or overcome.

PENETRATION

The degree of market penetration achieved will depend on a blend of creativity in the design of the advertisement and the effectiveness of the media used (assuming the product has the right attributes). How well media assist successful penetration of any market is important and must therefore guide executives in their selection of media.

TV capable of regionalisation, according to the company chosen and its regional franchise. For example, in Britain, London Weekend Television and Thames TV cover London and the Southeast at weekends and on weekdays. Obviously there will be some overlap of the areas covered by each company. Advertisements can be tailored to match regional needs more precisely.

The disadvantages include the fact that radio lacks 'visibility' and TV is very expensive and requires the viewers' full attention – they should not be away from the set making some tea or attending to other personal needs. These media are very effective for consumer goods and services, durables and simple industrial products (e.g. electric drills and small motors) which are used by individuals, especially do-it-yourself buffs. They are also said to be good for corporate image advertising, especially where the aim is to attract skilled staff. They have been used also, in some countries, to advertise degrees and other courses offered by tertiary educational establishments (colleges, polytechnics and universities).

Newspapers offer wide coverage, especially where national editions exist. Regional papers allow firms to select regions or market segments of interest to them or of prime importance to the items advertised. However in America there were, at the last count, some 1800 dailies and over 8000 weekly publications, indicating the selection problem faced there. However, with care, properly selected papers can provide precise coverage for a given product-market situation. Relatively inexpensive, this medium is effective for most purposes but the varying standards of printing can detract from the effectiveness of the advertisement. Another is that as newspapers carry a large number of advertisements, more care is needed in the design (layout, print size and size of advertisement used) and the location within the paper, for each advertisement placed.

Magazines are more expensive, especially if colours are used. However, if carefully selected, matching product uses to type of reader, they can be very effective. The trade publications are favoured by industrial enterprises. For example, manufacturers of chemical processing equipment would in Britain use *Chemical Age*, which is read or seen by chemical engineers, especially those involved in buying such equipment. Tourism products could be effectively advertised in travel magazines or the travel page of major newspapers. One disadvantage is again that any advertisement may have to compete against a number of others for similar products or services, so design and location must be carefully planned here also.

Magazines and some newspapers (e.g. the Sunday editions) that lie on tables in appropriate places for some time are particularly attractive to advertisers. For example, in Britain, the *Radio Times* and *TV Times* get into most homes and some offices, and being weeklies, lie there for seven days. Readership possibilities are high, especially for the front and back covers. The competition for space here is intensive.

(ii) *Media planning*

Media planning is based on the advertising objectives agreed for the product or service which are themselves determined by the agreed marketing strategy. Factors influencing media planning include the location and accessibility (in media terms) of prospective customers, the frequency with which the item is bought or used, the seasonality of demand, distribution, strength of competition and economic, social and psychological makeup of the target audience. Thus decisions on media will take the following into consideration:

size of the media budget;
suitability of the medium;
degree of flexibility required;
nature and scale of competitive media activity;
effectiveness of the medium;
the importance of coverage and frequency.

Ideally the size of the budget should be such as is necessary to achieve the advertising objectives most economically and effectively. However, for economic and other reasons, this is not always possible. For example the wider the purchase of an item, the more difficult and expensive it is to reach all potential customers. Where colours are needed (as in advertisements for foods, toiletries, fashion and cosmetics) the costs are increased. If primary and secondary media have to be used this also increases total advertising costs. The budget should also be based on the sales the campaign is to achieve, not the sales of the previous year. The percentage used varies. For consumer goods for example, 5 to 10 per cent is usual with more when a new product is being launched. With industrial products the figure is from 3 to 5 per cent. For expensive capital equipment it is usually 2.5 per cent or less. However, wide variations from these figures are often used, depending on the firm's resources, strength of competition and demand.

Competitive media activity will guide firms on the difficult subject of which media to use. Should the company plan to reach the same audience as competitors by using the same media, or would a different mix of media reach a more appropriate or wider audience? Many advertisers consider achieving identification with and dominance in specific classes of media important. This assumes of course, that the selection of media is correct in the first place.

The degree of flexibility of media planning required is primarily dependent on the nature of the product and its demand. For well-established products having continuous use during any year, the degree of flexibility needed is not great. For products with predictable seasonal peaks (e.g. sun-tan lotion, cold remedies) or when sources of supply are subject to the vagaries of climate (e.g. fresh fruit and vegetables, imported canned foods) there is greater need for flexibility in media planning. In the case of the appropriateness and effectiveness of media, the factors in Table 7.6 have to be considered. The effective cost (per thousand readers/listeners/viewers) of each medium and the effectiveness of the message or copy have also to be taken into account. The *impact* of an advertisement depends also on the following four points.

(c) Coverage and frequency

'Coverage' refers to the number of potential customers reached by the advertisement. 'Frequency' is the number of times the message is exposed to each of these people. Coverage can be increased by adding to the number of media used. Frequency is increased by buying more insertions in the media first selected and/or by increasing the media used while keeping the number of insertions per medium unchanged. Given the fact that most persons have short memories and it is necessary to keep reminding them of the existence of a product or service, a firm should achieve the greatest frequency possible within budget limitations and other marketing considerations. However, continuity of advertising is essential and most firms rely on the experience and knowledge of the media planner in their advertising agency to advise them on these two points.

(d) Colour and size

The use of colour, as mentioned, is necessary for some products but is generally advisable for most, where the extra cost can be met. Coloured advertisements attract more attention than black and white, and certain colours produce particular emotional responses. The latter vary with ethnic groups. For example red to a European usually means danger but to some Eastern races it is a very auspicious colour. Gold (rather than yellow) is favourably aspected with most people. The psychology of colour is one that successful advertising executives have found useful to understand.

The size of an advertisement will first depend on the amount of copy that is required, the size of the budget and thus on the creative ability of the advertising agent or department. Large-sized advertisements certainly attract attention and there is a limit as to how small an insert should be. Too small for its purpose or message and it will be overlooked by readers or swamped by competing advertisements. Also large inserts are very expensive, especially if colours are used. Given that potential users have to be reminded often about the product or service, smaller advertisements placed say weekly or fortnightly into a publication are usually disproportionately more effective than one whole- or half-page insert placed once a month or once every two or three months. Each case requires careful consideration by executives expert on the subjects of media effectiveness and related aspects, as every solution could be different.

It is also believed that when a campaign starts a large advertisement should be used but that smaller ones should be used subsequently. This is based on erroneous thinking, since potential users will not be aware that a specific campaign starts on a given date. It has been found that three insertions of the same size, content and style are needed before potential users begin to notice, the campaign makes an impact on customers and creates sales. Thus the sizes selected will depend on the mix that is believed will build up good coverage and achieve the necessary penetration as the campaign continues. Sales should then also build up and achieve for the product the desired market penetration.

(e) The advertising agency

The specialist staff of an advertising agency are listed in Table 7.7. According to the size of the agency and the 'accounts' they handle, some of these tasks may be done by one person. Two examples are noted in the table. Figure 7.1 shows one way in which a typical agency may be organised. Again, variations of this structure are used by some agencies, according to how they believe they work best and the resources they have available for their activities. The agency is a team of experts appointed by clients to advise on, plan, produce and place agreed advertising campaigns. In fact they act as agents of the media.

Although the advertiser appoints an agency to do its advertising work, the agency is responsible for all the bills incurred in doing it, while the bulk of its income is received from the media organisations. Strange as this system may appear, it works well. While much discussion occurs, most agencies are reluctant to do away with the 'commission system'. However, some do arrange to be charged net for the space bought and then charge a fee to clients. In inflationary times, when a 15 per cent commission may not in fact cover an agency's rising costs, especially overheads, the net charge plus fee approach may be better. The fee can then be adjusted to take account of the 'fruits' of inflation. It is also more practical when a campaign with a small budget has to be handled. The commission from the limited space bought may be insufficient to

Table 7.7 **the advertising agency: staff members**

1 *Plans board*: a committee of departmental heads who meet clients and discuss new assignments; they meet to consider final schemes or as other needs arise; ideal when agency can present schemes to client top management.

2 *Review board*: which may exist instead of, or in addition to, a plans board; group of agency staff who have not been involved in planning or creating a scheme who meet to criticise proposals before they are presented to clients.

3 *Creative group*: favoured by large agencies, consists of appropriate staff responsible for one or more clients.

4 *Account director*: responsible for a group of accounts (i.e. clients); will have a number of *account executives* working under them.

5 *Marketing manager*: recommends to clients the market segments to which campaign is aimed, or new markets that should be developed, or the product presentation, pricing and packaging needed.

6 *Marketing research manager*: advises clients on this and the data or information available; also buys and oversees any research services needed.

7 *Copy writer*: very creative individual responsible for writing the copy; may also think up the theme and presentation required.

8 *Creative director*: combines ability to write and artistic abilities to produce complete advertisements; may direct creative groups or buy outside freelance services.

9 *Visualiser*: produces rough ideas called *visuals, scamps* or *scribbles*; interprets copywriter's ideas and shows ways they could be presented.

10 *Layout artist*: (could be the visualiser) produces designs closely resembling the printed advertisement; 'lays out' text and pictures etc., producing a drawing to the exact measurements of the advertisement which typesetter, engraver, printer, platemaker can follow.

11 *Typographer*: an expert on type faces etc., selects most suitable and instructs printer about spacings etc.; good work here can make an advertisement original and attractive in appearance and a pleasure to read (the layout artist may perform this function).

12 *Finished artist*: draws or paints the finished artwork; much of this work is done by famous names who find the commercial work adds to their income while still being interesting to do.

13 *Production manager* with *production assistants*: responsible for buying original blocks, typesetting etc. for letterpress printed advertisements, and for supplying text and artwork for photogravure and offset-litho printed ones; also organises the flow of work to meet timetable that has been set after clients have approved proposed campaign. larger agencies have *traffic controllers* responsible for directing the work flow.

14 *Accountant* or *finance director*: controls the despatch of bills to clients; these have to be supported by vouchers (copies of publications in which advertisements appear as proof of insertion) which are usually issued by a VOUCHER CLERK. This work is important if the agency's cashflow is not to suffer, especially during credit squeezes when overdrafts are restricted or high rates of interest are charged to borrowers.

Fig 7.1 typical advertising agency organisation

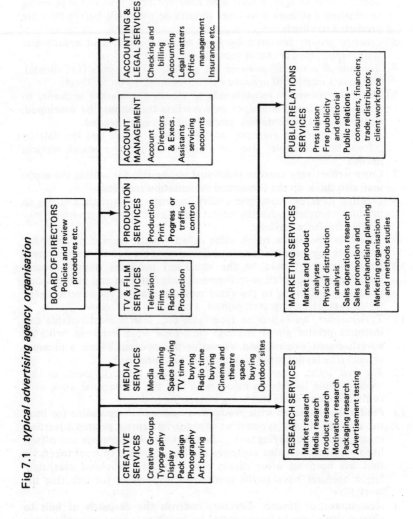

cover the agency's costs and leave them a reasonable profit on the deal. It should be noted also that even with substantial campaigns, while the total billings (costs) may be very large, the net profit margins for the agency can be quite small.

Selecting an agency is an important marketing task. Pick the wrong one and the entire marketing effort can be ineffective, wasting considerable resources of all kinds. Executives must consider the experience and knowledge of the agency in relation to the product or service to be handled and the target customer groups or market segments to be developed. Then the track record or performance of it in these areas must be carefully assessed. Next, the additional backup services that can be provided must be investigated. Help under the headings in Figure 7.1 of 'Media Services', 'Research', 'Marketing' and 'Public Relations Services' may be crucial to the success of any campaign. (The complex positions regarding media and media selection have been noted in preceding sections.)

The acceptance of the 'marketing concept' has made executives realise that they must overcome not only problems associated with the manufacture of their products (or services) but also those of presenting products effectively to potential users. Customers, instead of being on the periphery of management thought and planning, secondary to manufacturing aspects, now occupy the centre of the stage. This requires firms to have greater and more detailed knowledge of customers. As a result agencies, their functions and services, have had to be developed to meet clients' increased needs. Further it was realised that the many skills involved had to be properly integrated into a balanced whole if the advertisement or campaign was itself to give balanced and integrated support to the rest of the marketing effort. The advertising industry has come a long way from the days when agencies were just space-buying and -filling companies.

The agency plays a very important role, through its specialised skills of providing important practical help and advice to clients on a wide range of marketing problems. It brings an independent mind and considerable expertise to bear on such matters as client's marketing strengths and weaknesses; the effectiveness of the firm's current communications mix, especially personal selling; the level and quality of product mix, product distribution and display; the effectiveness of the distribution system generally; and the effects of specific promotional activities at trade and consumer or customer levels. The agency's involvement in clients' marketing planning and thought on a continuing basis increases the chance of more effective advertising being created and used, while giving greater stability and integration to the client-agency relationship.

On the other hand there are agencies which do not offer such comprehensive services. They might just be small operations or ones, usually, specialising in one particular aspect of the work. They make useful contributions to the work and are very useful to firms which may have limited need of advertising or have some special problem which has to be resolved independently of the mainstream campaigns. Also, they provide useful aid to small companies who cannot afford a large budget, but here the agency would have to charge a fee to cover its costs and profits. The space or time commission would not be sufficient for the work that has to be done. However, the main advantage of large agencies over small ones is the former's complete commitment to clients' needs. Further, whatever size the agency may be, clients must remember that there is a very big difference in the return obtained with a good strategy as compared with a bad one. Thus the agency should be given a precise brief, while the client keeps a close eye on progress during the resultant campaign.

Some major organisations have their own advertising departments. Today's costs, however, make it almost certain that in most instances the total cost of what is virtually an in-house advertising agency, cannot be justified. A small department may then be used. The purpose of such departments is to assist marketing colleagues to establish advertising strategy and goals, help to select an appropriate agency, brief it thoroughly on what is required, explain the firm's policies and philosophies to the agency, decide how the total advertising budget should be allocated, monitor operations and make recommendations if results are not as planned. Sometimes one executive, usually called the 'advertising manager' will do all this; at others there may be a few assistants to help with the work.

(f) Types of campaigns

The type of campaign to be used will depend on whether a 'hard-sell' or 'soft-sell' approach is needed, the nature and style of the advertiser, the product or service concerned and the target audiences involved. As mentioned in Section 7.2(b), hard-sell campaigns will usually use persuasive advertisements. The 'harder' the sell, the punchier or more aggressive will be the style and copy of the advertisement. Soft-sell campaigns would use informative advertisements. Between these two extremes there are other possibilities.

A hard-sell campaign, but one not aggressively so, may use a *product differential type* insert. This will try to establish one (or two) key differential of the product which establishes it as superior to competitor products. (For example in the early 1960s, Hotpoint's advertisement for washing machines which began 'Hotpoint washes cleanest because it cannot tangle clothes', established the point that other makes did tangle clothes badly and housewives had great difficulty in unravelling a mess of wet clothes.) These inserts or advertisements can carry much stronger copy if a truly hard-sell is intended.

Then there is the *pioneering approach*, which shows how a task may be done more efficiently with the product advertised. This is usually a soft-sell approach, especially if by using the product customers would save on labour and lay-off or redundancies would result. Campaigns using *testimonial, prestige* and *catalogue page* type advertisements can be soft- or hard-sell in concept. Usually with testimonial inserts (aimed to gain confidence of consumers, as with pharmaceuticals and even toiletries) and catalogue page ones (easy and simple to prepare) a soft-sell campaign is intended. With prestige advertisements, the campaign can be of either type depending on the text and illustrations or artwork used.

(g) Ethics, laws and regulations

With advertising there are ethical aspects to consider concerning the honesty and truthfulness of the satisfactions offered and the information given. Truth in advertising is a controversial and much discussed subject. Whilst in many advertisements promises are made which no rational person would expect them to deliver (i.e. the often hinted promise of joy, happiness and a fuller social life, usually with the opposite sex, if 'Product X' is used), ironically most factual statements made are true. Further, with TV advertising, the fictitious examples given are not to be taken literally but many do, as witnessed by the letters of complaint to the controlling body (in Britain, the Independent Broadcasting Authority – IBA).

In Britain this aspect of 'misleading' or 'untrue' claims is well controlled by law (*Trade Descriptions Act*; various *Broadcasting Acts*) and voluntary controls through the *British Code of Advertising Practice* and the *Advertising Standards Authority* (see also Table 7.9). Other countries of the European Economic Community also have laws controlling advertising.

In 1972, Belgium passed a Law on Commercial Practices which outlawed misleading advertisements, while in 1974 Denmark enacted a similar law with an identical aim. West Germany's law against unfair competition was first passed in 1909. This makes it an offence for any business or trade to indulge in market practices which were contrary to good business ethics. (Companies have been convicted recently under this old law.) In 1973 France enacted the *Loi Royer* which not only imposed severe controls but also empowered courts to compel an offender to use advertising space to admit when some previous claims fell below the required standards. Eire's 1978 Consumer Information Act introduced very specific controls and provided for the appointment of a Director of Consumer Affairs with power to initiate court proceedings.

America has several Federal and State laws which control or affect advertising directly or indirectly (e.g. those on various aspects of pricing and unfair trading practices). False and misleading claims are specifically controlled under the Wheeler–Lea Act. The Federal Trade Commission, set up in 1914, can restrain advertisements which seem to have the ability to deceive. The FTC can also act against *bait advertising*. This is an insert which attracts buyers' interest under false pretences. The popular one is where a particularly good buy is advertised and then the advertiser finds some excuse why it cannot be supplied. A substitute product, more profitable to the advertiser, is then offered.

Another ethical aspect is a more subjective area of advertising: the attempt to be helpful to the consumer when the latter is faced with the need to make a choice. Questions of relevance, good taste and other factors cannot be controlled by any set system but must be left to the honesty, good sense and sensitivity of advertisers and the agencies. None the less these aspects are also subject to the same laws, regulations and ethics as mentioned earlier. One change in British practice is worthy of note. Until fairly recent times it was considered unethical to mention the competitive product which compared unfavourably with the item being advertised. Hence the use of the famous phrase 'Brand X'. Now this is no longer so and it will have been noticed how car manufacturers compare their product quite openly with named competitors. The facts given, however, must still be (reasonably) true and demonstrable as such. Hence the frantic quoting of official and quasi-offical test results.

The advertising of bad products or unnecessary services is bad ethics. However, the urgent search for additional sales may lead an advertiser to promote a product for purposes outside its normal range or for which it was not designed. Then the value of the item to buyers may be dubious. However, good, sound marketing, properly planned and controlled, should have no need for this 'sell at all costs' advertising.

7.4 SALES PROMOTIONS

Sales promotions normally include merchandising and packaging activities, but as the latter is an important subject it is discussed separately in Section 7.5. The more usual sales promotions are listed, with Advertising and Public Relations, in Table 7.1. Not shown there are coupons redeemable by the purchase of the product, free trials and samples, 'budget' packs with extra content or reduced re-sale prices, banded packs of related products giving customers a net bargain and self-liquidating offers.

While the basic purpose of advertising is to build sales over a long period and so establish the product in its markets that the sales gain is held when the campaign ends, the basic aim for sales promotions is much more limited. The effect is short-term in concept and reality. For example they help to launch a new product, revive demand for an ailing one or boost sales during peak sales periods. However, when this campaign ends, sales normally drop, often below previous levels, and may take some time to pick up again. The different effects are shown in simplified form in Figure 7.2. None the less, advertising and sales promotion form integral and important parts of the communications mix and should be planned as related, supporting activities which also jointly support the total marketing effort.

With consumer goods and durables and services used by consumers, the activities fall into three groups:

(i) *trade promotions*: aimed at distributors to persuade them to handle and sell the product; these often take the form of special discounts (especially for quantity sales volume), other cash incentives, one or two free bottles etc. per pack and competitions (e.g. free holidays for the winner and friend);

(ii) *consumer promotions*: used to persuade consumers to buy particular goods at specific times (periods); used extensively for mass-market goods but also for some services (e.g. holidays, travel) and on occasions for other products bought by individual consumers (e.g. for do-it-yourself buffs); include special retail price offers, two-for-the-price-of-one, banded packs, in-pack premiums, send-away coupons, competitions, etc.

(iii) *display*: product display and/or demonstrations with related point-of-sale material (posters, banners, placards, showcards) at the point-of-sale (or point-of purchase in America).

With industrial products, modified versions of consumer goods promotions can be used for items sold to individual users (e.g. screwdrivers, hammers, small drills, screws and other fixing devices etc.). For items sold to business and industry and for capital equipment, other methods are available. More useful for heavier plant (e.g. machine tools, earth-moving and road-building equipment, cranes etc.) are *demonstrations* of the item in use. The aim is to show in a practical and definitive way the claimed advantages offered by the product. Demonstration of the product's prowess and cost-saving potential is more convincing to potential users than any relatively marginal price offers or discounts. With really expensive items, better *hire-purchase terms* can prove the most effective sales promotion. Users would be attracted by lower interest rates and/or longer repayment periods, especially during difficult economic times.

Another possibility is the use of *industrial shows and exhibitions*. Here potential customers are met, discussions in depth can take place,

Fig 7.2 *advertising and sales promotions: effects on sales volume*

(a) advertising

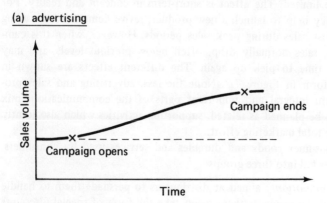

(b) sales promotions

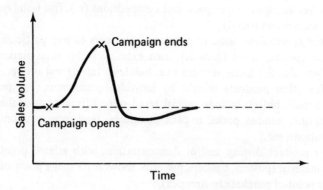

(c) combined effect of integrated programme

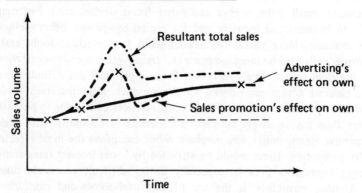

new applications explored and competitive products can be studied more closely. *Direct mail* has also been found useful, perhaps surprisingly, for some industrial products, provided the special correspondence used has been well and appropriately designed for the purpose and the target audience. In America direct mail has been used very effectively to achieve quick, widespread distribution of new products, to pave the way for sales visits and in building institutional prestige for the firm and its products. It has proved helpful too in testing the acceptability of new products, following up sales visits with specific emphasis on key points made in the oral presentation of the product and as an encouragement for distributors to stock and sell the item.

Catalogues, technical and other leaflets and *special seminars* are other sales promotions which are used. If the product is small (e.g. microchip) or not too expensive (e.g. special alumina ceramic slips that form the base for miniature circuits etc.) a limited number of free samples could be distributed. Or to selected potential users, a small supply could be given for them to test the product under operating conditions. This allows users to appreciate fully the product and their reports give the manufacturer a sound insight into customer reactions to the product, problems which may be encountered in its use and any sales resistance that might be met when the marketing operation is launched to all market segments.

Sales promotions are important facets of the communications mix. Besides being useful for the special situations mentioned at the beginning of this section, they make valuable contributions to marketing effectiveness by supporting the advertising and personal selling activities. In most instances this is the role that they perform. When used on its own, the effect of sales promotions on sales volume is as shown in Figure 7.2(b). When it is part of a carefully planned and integrated communications programme which includes a related advertising campaign, the total result can be as shown in Figure 7.2(c). The effects of the advertising should ensure that some of the additional sales gain from sales promotions should be held into the longer term.

(a) Point-of-sale material

This is material displayed at or near places in retail or other outlets (e.g. wholesalers) where customers will make their purchases, that is, where the sale is made. It is most effective when used as a supplement to other promotional activities with which it should be integrated. Its function is to attract the attention of the potential customers as they pass by or through the outlet. This is necessary since today there is such a great variety of products competing for customers' attention. A good example of this problem is found in the tourism and travel business. There are so many countries, regions, resorts, packaged and other holidays, carriers and so on to choose from that a good point-of-sale display could sway purchasing decisions to the item being promoted in this way.

Careful thought must be given to the display. The posters, banners, show-cards and other display material, besides being apppropriate for the subject and within the ethics and laws of the land, should also be attractive and suit the décor of the outlet. They should show off the product effectively, give the vital information that would attract attention and achieve a favourable decision to buy, while making the item look valuable or worth at least the price asked. For example, two escorted tours to the same places might have different prices (and they can be very different these days). What does the more expensive one offer that makes it more expensive than the other? The display should make this clear, whether this is having a very knowledgeable guide (e.g. a professor of archaeology for a visit to Egypt), using better hotels, or more comfortable transport (e.g. only four to a safari minibus) or that some important excursions are included in the price. With mass-market items in a supermarket, the strategic placing of bins, stands, floor and end-of-counter displays, overhead and wall signs must also be carefully planned.

With industrial products careful attention must be given to the presentation and layout of catalogues, leaflets and technical sheets. Apart from the general rule that this should be easy to read and understand, the information imparted should be relevant to potential users' needs and avoid irrelevant material (or 'puff'). In addition the size of paper used needs careful choice. Usually the International 'A' sizes are preferred and as the information has to be stored for future reference there should be uniformity of size and the items should be capable of easy filing. 'Bastard' shapes and sizes must be avoided.

Good print design and selection of print sizes and type are other valuable contributions to the aim of 'intelligence made visible'. The good design of important brochures is therefore necessary. Again, thought has to be given to the purpose of the publication, the target audience for which it is intended, how they read it, what information they would be seeking, how much time they have for studying the information presented and thus the best presentation required. The budget available will influence the final decisions and thus the permitted cost for each publication.

Then there is the arguable point of fashion. Should publications follow the latest fashion in layout, print and so on, when it might be indistinguishable from many others? Or should a firm develop its own style? Generally having its own house style is effective. Also, care must be taken with publications in foreign languages. The points above apply but the exactness of the translations must be checked carefully also.

(b) Merchandising

Until the development of major supermarkets and chain stores, major manufacturers of mass-market goods (e.g. Heinz, especially for baked beans and sauces; Procter & Gamble for soaps and detergents; Unilever for soaps, detergents and other major products) provided a merchandising service for retail outlets. Now, with major supermarket groups and other retail outlets with their massive purchasing power and turnover, there is not such a great demand for manufacturers' merchandising help. The retail outlets prefer to do their own thing and perhaps do not wish to be dictated to by their suppliers. The retailers believe they know their customers well and therefore are in the better position to decide what merchandising activities to use to gain maximum benefit in improved sales.

Merchandising has been defined as the total effort to move goods at the point-of-sale (i.e. make sales) by exploiting the product, its packaging and pricing through the use of planned displays, display material (i.e. point-of-sale and other specially produced material) and any related special consumer buying incentives (e.g. free gifts; increased quantities at reduced prices; offers of specially reduced prices on another product, related or not and so on). It is a *selling out* process and is specific to each retail outlet. It calls for considerable creativity on the part of 'merchandisers' (people who organise, arrange and run such activities), retailers and manufacturers. The last have to give special attention to presentation and packaging design.

For most consumer goods, the consumer buys only what can be seen. They do not always make a straight line to a particular brand or manufacturer's product. With the wide choice available, they tend to take the first item to hand provided the price is acceptable. Merchandising aims to steer their attention to a specific product and so make a sale. Many 'events' can be used as pegs on which to hang merchandising displays. 'National ... Week', 'Book of the Month', 'Record of the Month', 'Summer Cruise Competition' and 'Win a Dream House' are some examples. Another is the use of a loss-leader. For example, sugar may be marked down to below cost and positioned around the item being merchandised to attract attention. Or there could be provision of special credit facilities or dividends on purchase for the item being merchandised.

The modern merchandiser must understand retail shop management and operational problems. Above all, there must be sound understanding of the personality and buyer behaviour of the different classes of customer using the outlet. While merchandising operations appear to be popular and effective, two points must be noted. First, if there are a number of competitive offers being made, then brand loyalty can be destroyed. Consumers may be weaned to accept a competitive brand if the latter's merchandising is more colourful and effective. Second, many consumers are soon annoyed if there is unjustified delay in the dispatch of the free gift, premium offer or in the announcement of the winners in a competition. However, merchandising seems particularly effective with mass market goods that are bought on impulse (i.e. there is no brand or product preference).

7.5 PACKAGING

How well a product sells in its markets, especially consumer goods, will depend on the packaging and brand name used and how these are integrated into the other associated marketing activities. The main functions and goals of packaging are summarised in Table 7.8. The selection, design and use of packaging are highly skilled jobs, especially for mass market

Table 7.8   **packaging functions and goals**

FUNCTIONS

Identification: packaging (and labels) identifies the product and brand and by its distinctive nature attracts the attention of potential buyers; tempts them to look at and handle the item which it is claimed is 'halfway to making a sale'.

Containment: offers customers pre-weighed, pre-measured, pre-assembled or pre-sorted contents at clearly indicated prices.

Protection: in conjunction with the protective wrapping or packing materials (e.g. corrugated paper, waterproof paper or plastic wrapper/bag, wood or plastic box or carton etc.) packaging helps to protect the product in transit, in store or when on display.

GOALS

Attractiveness: to enhance the appearance of the product to catch consumers' attention. Use of colour is important. Some associations are: blue = distinction/coolness; green = quiet/nature; yellow = sunshine/warmth; orange = warmth/movement; red = excitement/heat; purple and gold = royalty and richness; white = purity/cleanliness; brown = utility. Note that different ethnic groups interpret the meaning or significance of colour differently.

Economy: overpackaging is expensive and wasteful. But if the item is expensive or prestigious, more elaborate packaging may be justified. If the economics of packaging are properly assessed, economy in wrapping a product for protection and attractive display can be achieved.

Convenience: Correctly designed, packaging of easily handled quantities provides convenience to customers: also to manufacturers in manufacture and distribution.

LABELS

Important that these are right for the packaging used. Must identify ingredients, who and where made and how it should be used.

goods. Firms are advised to seek expert advice and help, but too often some eager amateur amongst the executives will attempt it all, usually with poor results if not outright disaster.

(a) Branding

The two goals of branding are the achievement of *product identification* and *control* of the marketing operation and pricing. The first is important when there are many competing products with very similar characteristics and prices. A *brand* or *brand name* identifies a firm's product and helps to differentiate it from those of competitors. Brands create confidence in a firm's products and assure consumers that they can rely on the product and thus encourage them to make repeat purchases and eventually develop brand loyalty. Where a firm markets its own branded products it is assured of control of the pricing, advertising, sales promotions and distribution activities. A well-established brand has considerable promotional value.

Choosing a good brand name is not an easy task. Points to note when this has to be done include: the meaning (and spelling) should be closely associated with the product (e.g. 'Brillo' cleaning materials); should be capable of translation into foreign languages important to international marketing operations; and should be appropriate for the product and its target markets. For example, the makers' names for some women's clothing have become associated with certain age groups. 'XL', a very successful allusion to the high quality of the tinned goods, is another successful example. *Trade marks*, which are really brand names given legal protection and granted to one firm for its sole use, can also be used (e.g. Coca-Cola). Establishing a brand name requires adherence to the points made above, good packaging and the use of appropriate promotional message. Obviously, also, the product must live up to the claims made for it and there must be well-planned and effective marketing generally.

7.6 PUBLIC RELATIONS

Public relations is the deliberate, planned and sustained effort to establish and maintain mutual understanding between a firm and its public. This must be founded on correct information and true facts. It is not a casual or *ad hoc* activity and should not be a means of attempting to excuse company failings. The 'public' varies too from consumers and customers to financiers and shareholders, employees and the public at large. Public relations must also inform the company of any changes in public opinion about it or its products. Thus it helps to indicate the implications for company policies and actions.

Public relations influence the opinions of various groups. It can show the firm to be a leader in its industry or as an innovator. Or it can illustrate that the company is public spirited and aware of its social responsibilities or is a vigorous organisation that gets things done (worthwhile ones, that is!). Well thought out public relations activities can enhance employees' sense of pride and so improve their performance, critical in the case of the sales force.

Public relations, although using similar media to advertising, unlike advertising does not normally promote a single theme. It is a highly personalised activity requiring a constant flow of press releases about the company, its operations, products and employees. These releases are adapted to the needs and style of the chosen medium. It is a sophisticated technique of communication to a much wider range of audiences than advertising or sales promotions. Nevertheless it must form an integrated part of the entire communications mix and indirectly support its sister activities in this mix.

In cases when the advertisement of a product may be prohibited (e.g. cigarettes in Britain, Scotch whisky in France), public relations activities can be useful. Here the release would feature the firm or factory where the product is made, related advances in research and development or some human interest story about the employees. This helps to overcome the difficulty in establishing the brand name for products so afflicted.

7.7 THE PROMOTIONAL MIX

A few concluding words on this subject are appropriate here. Selecting the most appropriate mix from the six components of communications calls for careful consideration. The size and nature of the personal selling effort will be dictated by many factors and these are discussed in the following sections. Assuming therefore that the amount of selling effort required is fixed, the remaining question is: How much support does selling require from advertising, sales promotion packaging, merchandising and public relations? The answer will determine the mix, extent and nature of these.

Where the emphasis should be placed (on selling, or advertising and sales promotions) depends on the nature or type of products (consumer goods or industrial), the target markets involved and the value and profit margins of the products. (The same considerations apply to most services.) For example, low value consumer goods sold on a national basis would normally rely heavily on advertising and sales promotion while the personal selling content would be low, probably restricted to distributors and concentrated on retailers including supermarkets and chain or departmental stores. Consumer goods of high price or value sold into a more limited number of markets could use promotional and selling activities, both to a high but not necessarily equal degree.

An example of the first group is inexpensive processed foods of all kinds. The second group includes expensive escorted tours sold to the 'B' and 'C' social groups. In the latter case, the tour company does the advertising and the retailer (travel agent) does the personal selling, as well as some advertising perhaps on the local press. With the former example, the manufacturer advertises the products and sells into the retail outlets and the only selling involved as far as the consumer is concerned is the availability of the products in the shops or supermarkets they use. The expensive end of women's toiletries can use advertising and personal selling equally, though the emphasis is usually on the former through impressive advertisements in the glossy women's magazines. Personal selling would be by canvassers to the homes and by salesgirls in the more expensive departmental stores.

For screwdrivers and hand tools (relatively low value, industrial products needing national coverage) almost all the expenditure would be on advertising (including a few mail shots). Again the only 'selling' might be the availability of the products at the retailers, with suitable displays. For most other industrial products (high value sold on a more selective basis to various customers having different or specialised needs), the emphasis is usually on personal selling with sufficient advertising to make users aware of the existence of the products. Much of the effort would also be on sales promotions (leaflets, catalogues, etc.) especially where considerable technical information is needed by customers. For capital goods or plant and equipment (very expensive items sold almost on a one-off basis and tailored to individual requirements), the communications mix would be comprised of almost all personal selling and negotiations. Advertising would be minimal, again just to keep the firm and its products in the eyes and minds of potential users.

Seldom can there be reliance on one component of the mix. While advertising is probably the most effective for creating awareness, personal selling is more effective in producing conviction in customers' minds that they need the product or it will make a considerable contribution to their business or needs. Advertising, sales promotions and selling are usually equally important in creating customer comprehension of the product or service. Finally, the optimal communications or promotional mix will depend on the stage that a product has reached in its life cycle (the 'older' it is the more selling it may need), the promotional strategy of competitors (if they are advertising heavily it may be advisable to follow suit) and the nature of the buying process (with industrial products of high value, so many persons are involved, personal selling is of greater importance; some vital person may not see, understand or believe an advertisement).

(a) Promotional budget

Because it is difficult to measure and forecast the results produced by promotional activity, promotional budgets tend to be 'calculated' by rule of thumb. Theoretically the total budget should be at a level where the marginal profit obtained from the marginal £ spent on promotions equals, or exceeds, the marginal profit that would be obtained by using the £ in other non-promotional alternatives. In practice this theory is of little value, except perhaps when trying to measure the effectiveness of previous budgets. The ratio of promotional budget to total marketing budget does not, necessarily, provide a useful basis for planning either. A high ratio may just mean the firm is compensating for inadequacies in some aspect of the product or service and its price. A low ratio could mean that promotional expenditure is too low for the job that has to be done or the company is using the product's superior quality as a promotional aid.

In arriving at a budget, consideration must be given to the task to be accomplished, the nature and complexity of the products/services, the size and nature of the markets served, the composition of the customers comprising them and the nature and extent of competition. The composition of the communications mix (how much selling, how much advertising or sales promotion?) must also be taken into account. Now some activities are more expensive than others and, especially with industrial products, there is a tendency to go for the cheaper activities. If the latter are inappropriate for the task or product, then using them would just be a waste of money. On the other hand, using expensive methods because they are fashionable would also be a waste if they were inappropriate.

Having considered these basic points, the methods available are as follows. First, there is the *ratio method*, where the budget is calculated as a percentage of the sales revenue to be earned, based on an analysis of the effectiveness of this approach in previous years. Next is the *competitive comparison method*, based either on what major competitors are spending or on the industry's average rate of expenditure. The disadvantages here include the difficulty of assessing what these comparative budgets or expenditures are and that little consideration is given to the objectives that must be achieved.

Then there is the *unit method*, where a fixed rate per unit of sale (e.g. 20 pence per case or £2 per installation) is used. This means that as sales increase the budget grows and when sales decline the budget is reduced. This is in fact the reverse of what is usually needed. As sales decline, promotional expenditure may need to be increased to counter competition more effectively and ensure that the firm gets a fair slice of a decreasing 'cake' of total demand. Finally, considered by many as the most effective, is the *task or objective method*. This is based on careful evaluations of a firm's promotional and sales objectives.

There are two basic steps. First, the company must define clearly what goals or targets the promotional effort must achieve (e.g. increase profit by x per cent or £x, or market share by y per cent, or gross sales revenue by z per cent or £z, or any combination of these). The company must then determine by experience and past performance the extent, nature and mix of promotional activity needed, their cost and thus the total budget required. In practice there may have to be some compromise with the ideal because the funds available may be limited. However, if the results over the years are carefully monitored and analysed, this is perhaps the most effective method of budgeting in modern circumstances. In the end the firm 'pays its money and must make its choice'!

7.8 PERSONAL SELLING

Selling involves the personal presentation of trangible products or intangible services and ideas of significance to potential customers (consumer, trade and industry). In its work it receives back-up support from advertising, sales promotions and public relations and all four should form an integrated plan and an integral part of the total marketing plan. Personal selling makes a valuable contribution to a nation's economy. Besides providing work for many persons, in and outside the selling function, it is a major creator of demand and thus economic activity. In competitive situations the survival and prosperity of a firm depends on the success of its selling activities.

While selling as part of marketing becomes more effective as a result of the close integration with the other promotional activities, marketing research and product-market planning, it is also enhanced – not belittled – by the adoption of the marketing concept. The aims, objectives and targets for the sales function are more precisely and clearly defined. The sales staff know what has to be done, when, where and by whom. They know what support will be given by promotions, distribution and other integrated, planned marketing activities. Sales prospects are better defined and sales people do not just have to maintain the 'same old slog', knock on doors and request people to buy their products. They know who needs them, what use is made of them, the competitive position and thus who are the better prospects and what sales pitch should be used. In short, they are fully informed on the marketing and sales situations.

Accepting the marketing concept does, however, require some restructuring of the sales task and sales management. Until the sales manager is promoted into general marketing management, this executive may lose some autonomy – the price for being a member of a team and not a lone individual – with less direct control of promotional activities, pricing, distribution, product design and credit control. However the gains in greater effectiveness, greater success, having more – and more purposeful – support, making worthwhile contributions to the overall marketing planning and control activities and so on, should compensate. The sales job becomes more satisfying and rewarding.

Selling and marketing (not just advertising) are subject to voluntary and legal controls. In most countries there are many laws controlling or affecting business activities directly and indirectly and new or amended ones reach the statute books in an almost continuous flow. Some executives believe that all firms now need at least one lawyer full time on their staff just to guide them through the legal mazes that confront business people. A short list of the British laws affecting business activity, with those relevant to marketing, advertising and selling in whatever way shown in *italics,* is given in Table 7.9.

(a) Sales objectives and targets

Personal selling covers a very wide range of activities. The range of possibilities is shown in Table 7.10. During any business day numerous salespersons are explaining the merits of their products or services to executives, consumers (housewives and others), wholesalers, retailers, officials of government and quasi-governmental organisations, doctors, lawyers and 'Indian chiefs' of all kinds. Still more are making various follow-up calls, making deliveries and taking orders for future deliveries, as, for example, confectionery sales staff making routine calls on shops in their territory.

Because of the variety of selling tasks, more than one of which may be needed in any firm, setting sales objectives needs considerable thought. What tasks have to be accomplished and what methods have been found to be the best to use? What will be the cost and return? Can the company afford it? These are just some of the questions to ponder. Remember too that besides the choice implied by Table 7.10, cost, limited resources and other reasons may make it necessary for a firm to work through agents (especially overseas), franchise holders (for remote areas) or on a mail-order basis (though current postal charges in Britain have put up the cost of this operation).

The starting point for this work is the corporate objectives in the corporate plan and from these, the marketing objectives as defined in the marketing plan. The marketing targets which set the parameters for sales objectives include the profit to be earned, the sales revenue to be

Table 7.9   **some laws/regulations controlling business activity in Britain**
(those particularly relevant to marketing are italicised)

Advertisements (Hire Purchase) Act 1967
Banking and Financial Dealings Act 1971
Bills of Sale Acts 1878, 1882, 1893
Carriage by Air Acts 1961, 1962
Carriage by Railway Act 1972
Carriage of Goods by Road Act 1968
Carriage of Goods by Sea Acts 1920, 1971
Carriers Act 1830
Consumer Credit Act 1974
Consumers Protection Act 1961 (amended 1971)
Copyright Act 1958
Exchange Control Acts (various)
Fair Trading Act 1973
Food and Drug Act 1955 (and amendments)
Hire Purchase Act 1973
Insolvency Act 1976
Medicines Acts 1968 (and associated regulations)
Mercantile Law (Amendments) Acts 1856, 1894
Merchant Shipping Acts 1894, 1904, 1967, 1974
Misrepresentations Act 1967
Race Relations Acts 1968, 1976
Resale Prices Acts 1964, 1976
Restrictive Trade Practices Acts 1956, 1968, 1976
Sale of Goods Act 1893 and amendments
Sex Discrimination Act 1975
Statute of Frauds 1677 and Amendment Act 1828
Supply of Goods (Implied Terms) Act 1973
Trade Descriptions Acts 1968, 1972
Transport Acts 1962, 1968
Unfair Contract Terms Act 1977
Unsolicited Goods and Services Act 1971 and Amendment Act 1975

(This is not a complete list! Other countries have equally complex laws controlling business activity.)

obtained, the annual rates of growth and market shares needed and the markets to be served. Thought must also be given to the need to balance long- and short-term requirements, the relative emphasis to be given to market shares and profit and the degree of customer satisfaction required.

In addition, marketing strategy must be taken into account for this indicates the different emphasis that will be placed on promotional activities. The extent, nature and timing of the latter and their ability to open doors or help to make sales will help to define the size and nature of the selling tasks needed. For example, in mass-market foodstuffs, it is usual to place the emphasis on advertising when the selling activity required is that of the in-field order taker. Sales staff then see that retail stocks

Table 7.10 **activities of salespersons**

1 *Delivering basic products*: bread, milk, fuels etc. Actual selling is a secondary role but a pleasant manner and good service enhance customer acceptance and should lead to more sales. Only originate new sales occasionally, as a general rule.

2 *Taking orders*: relative routine business (e.g. soaps, cleaning fluids, tinned goods, nuts, bolts, small industrial products) of established items bought for general use; works in the field and contacts buyers in supermarkets, and retail outlets and in industry for items that need little selling; the 'hard sell' is often discouraged. Pleasant personality and good service enhance sales but little creative selling involved.

3 *Inside order-taker*: counter sales staff at retail outlets, travel agents etc. Customers have usually made up their minds and only suggestive selling (e.g. helping consumers decide which holiday to have) is involved besides just serving the customer. Opportunities to do more than this are few.

4 *Technical selling*: putting across the attributes of technical products providing information or advice; really a 'consultant' to 'client' firms. Involves many contacts and conversations to make sale.

5 *Building goodwill*: educating the actual or potential customer as with 'missionary' selling (opening new accounts); sometimes excluded from taking orders and only opening doors for (4) or (2) above.

6 *Creative selling*: of intangible services (e.g. banking, insurance, investment services, tourism/travel, advertising services etc.); more difficult task since intangibles are difficult to demonstrate and consumers have difficulty in gaining good comprehension of them.

7 *Creative selling*: of tangibles such as household appliances, encyclopedias etc.; first makes prospect dissatisfied with present products then sells his/hers.

are adequate for anticipated demand, the goods have good and effective shelf exposure (or space) and appropriate sales promotions activities are mounted at the right times. The sales strategy then emphasises 'pushing' products into the retail outlets while advertising aims to 'pull' them through to the customer.

With industrial products, personal selling creates interest and seeks orders while advertising paves the way for the sales staff. They do not walk 'cold' into prospective buyers. Advertising here creates awareness while selling creates preference leading to orders. Depending on the services to be sold, the selling–advertising relationship can follow either course. For example with professional services (banking, insurance, etc.) the industrial approach may be best. For travel and holidays, the consumer goods one is usual in that retailers (travel agents) hold stock (an allocation of holidays or facilities) and advertising usually by tour operators generates consumer interest. The marketing and sales strategies will once again be of the 'push-pull' type.

interest. The marketing and sales strategies will once again be of the 'push-pull' type.

The size of the sales force needed will be determined by the volume of sales and market shares to be obtained and the costs that can be afforded. From this will come decisions on quota (per territory and salesperson) for sales volume or revenue needed and, if possible, the profit to be earned. Thus sales objectives will be quantitative in nature (hard figures specifying sales, profit, market shares etc.) and qualitative (specifying coverage, frequency of contact, degree or level of customer service and satisfaction required) and both will be influenced (or restricted) by the pricing strategy and policy that will apply. In the case of industrial products and capital equipment, the degree of essentiality of these for prospective buyers will also influence the sales objectives that could be set. The more vital an item the greater should be demand and emphasis would be placed on the attributes of the product, especially the benefits they would confer on buyers' own business activities.

To summarise, sales targets are usually derived by taking the company's marketing targets and then breaking them down by territory according to their potential, the degree of competition that would be met and the sales coverage that could be provided with the back-up from promotional activities. Thus if London and the Southeast are believed or known to account for 25 per cent of total demand or has traditionally provided that amount of total company business, then this could be useful starting point. However, trends and developments must be considered. If total demand in the area is known to be increasing how should future sales targets be adjusted? Should they maintain the same market share or, if competition is slacking off, should the company strive for a larger market share? If demand is declining, should effort be switched to other areas leading to lower sales targets for London and higher ones elsewhere? When the quota for a territory has been agreed, the individual ones for the salespersons will be similarly deduced. However, if more salespersons are being added to an area, or some are being withdrawn to the more profitable ones, the final quota will need adjustment.

A more sophisticated method which is not always easy to use involves the projection of demand trends for major individual companies, factories, retail groups and so on. Then the total demand for an area can be compiled, market shares agreed and quota set. The difficulty lies in making these projections. The firm and its marketing staff must have extensive knowledge of the individual units on which these calculations are based. How is their business changing? How will this affect demand for established and new products? What new items will they need? What is their opinion of competitors and ourselves? In practice it is not easy to find the answers to such questions.

(b) Roles of the sales staff

The basic roles and duties of field sales people have been discussed above and summarised in Table 7.10. Two more aspects of *retail selling* need to be mentioned. Sales staff here have two possibilities. First, they can use the technique of *selling (or trading) up*, which seeks to convince customers that they should buy a more expensive (better quality?) product than they intended originally. Then there is *suggestion selling*, which seeks to broaden the original purchase with related products (e.g. if buying golf clubs why not buy a new golf bag?). Usually this ploy would be assisted by special promotional campaigns and/or price offers. Now consider the basic roles of some other sales staff.

The *field sales manager* usually controls the operations of a field sales force though sometimes this unfortunate may have to control more than one group of salespeople. This manager must organise the sales force, the disposition of it and the allocation of money assigned to him or her for the sales tasks to be performed. The manager should also motivate the team to achieve, and if possible exceed, agreed targets provided that by exceeding targets problems are not created elsewhere (e.g. depriving another area of stock).

Then there is the construction of clear and concise plans to establish the timing, cost and co-ordination of all the activities of the sales force. This includes the identification and use of precise controls needed, including cost budgeting. Finally, direct responsibility for the appraisal of individual performance and the training and development of salespersons cannot be avoided. In addition the manager makes contributions to the identification of strategies and objectives for the sales force. Other contributors will include the sales force itself and other interested marketing colleagues, including the marketing director or manager.

Where a sales force is widely spread geographically, or the volume of work is heavy or technical and other complexities arise (usually on some regional or industrial basis), field sales managers can be assisted by one or more *sales supervisors*, or *area managers*. They ensure that the points mentioned above are correctly carried out. Because they are in close contact with the salespersons in their area of responsibility, they play a vital role in the motivation of their part of the sales force. They help to overcome the feeling of isolation that field sales staff can feel if they are at a distance from the sales office.

Sales managers are usually responsible to the marketing director (sales director if the selling function is separated from the rest of marketing) for all aspects of the selling task. They also supervise the field sales managers and provide essential back-up when this is necessary. They maintain close liaison with other marketing, manufacturing and financial colleagues in all aspects relevant to the selling role. They also control and manage the sales office and make sure that the procedures (correspondence to customers and field force; invoicing, billing; attention to complaints and enquiries) are followed efficiently. They liaise with colleagues responsible for the distribution side of the business. For those directly responsible to them and for others via field sales managers and supervisors, sales managers are responsible for performance appraisal, training, development, recruitment and remuneration of all the sales staff.

The *sales office* is responsible to the sales manager for keeping all the systems and paperwork operating efficiently and as planned. This is an important role for mistakes in the paperwork (invoicing, billing, stock records etc.) can dislocate, badly, an otherwise good sales operation. Where there is a lot of work involved, a *sales office manager* can be appointed to take direct control of the work. This person is usually responsible to the sales manager but on occasions may report direct to a sales director (if existing) or the marketing manager or marketing director. It depends on the importance of the work but as a rule bypassing the sales manager is not preferred as it can lead to resentment on the part of the latter and subsequent administrative difficulties. There may also be an *export manager*, who is usually responsible for the export sales of finished products but could also control shipments of components to overseas assembly or manufacturing units. If distribution is not under a separate department, a *distribution manager* would control this work including having responsibility for stock or inventory control.

(c) Organisation

The sales work can be organised in various ways, shown in Figure 7.3. There can be one sales force or separate ones reflecting the general organisational structure. If special technologies or market conditions exist it is usually advisable to have separate sales forces for each important one. Decisions on the organisation and sales forces required will depend on the nature, scope and scale of the selling task. Where products are not homogeneous, or involve different technologies, a more complex organisation and sales methods are needed.

For example, the functional type is common among small and medium-sized firms selling a single product, or a limited range of homogeneous products through similar distribution channels or to similar types of customer. The work is then divided into functional groups or departments. In Figure 7.3(i) the sales manager is responsible for home sales, exporting and international business being handled by some other marketing colleague not shown in the chart. This organisation becomes untenable when the range of products, customers and distribution channels are extended. Dissimilar products requiring different selling and distribution

Fig 7.3 *types of sales organisation*

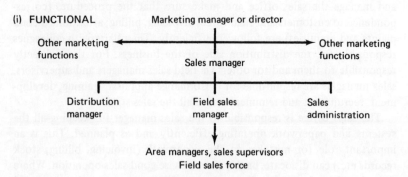

(i) FUNCTIONAL

Marketing manager or director

Other marketing functions ← → Other marketing functions

Sales manager

Distribution manager | Field sales manager | Sales administration

Area managers, sales supervisors
Field sales force

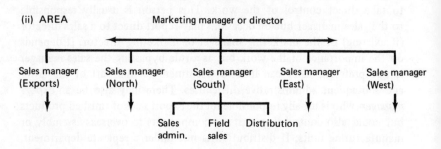

(ii) AREA

Marketing manager or director

Sales manager (Exports) | Sales manager (North) | Sales manager (South) | Sales manager (East) | Sales manager (West)

Sales admin. | Field sales | Distribution

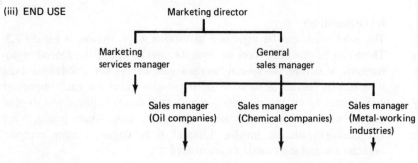

(iii) END USE

Marketing director

Marketing services manager | General sales manager

Sales manager (Oil companies) | Sales manager (Chemical companies) | Sales manager (Metal-working industries)

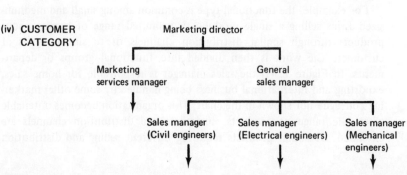

(iv) CUSTOMER CATEGORY

Marketing director

Marketing services manager | General sales manager

Sales manager (Civil engineers) | Sales manager (Electrical engineers) | Sales manager (Mechanical engineers)

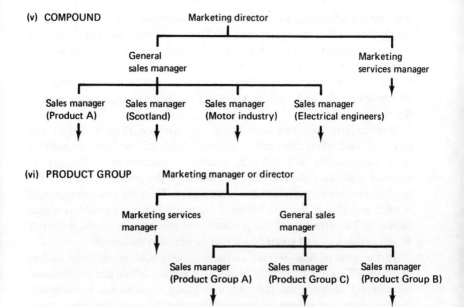

(v) COMPOUND

Marketing director

General sales manager — Marketing services manager

Sales manager (Product A) — Sales manager (Scotland) — Sales manager (Motor industry) — Sales manager (Electrical engineers)

(vi) PRODUCT GROUP

Marketing manager or director

Marketing services manager — General sales manager

Sales manager (Product Group A) — Sales manager (Product Group C) — Sales manager (Product Group B)

methods for disparate groups of customers involves more work and detail that such a simple organisation can handle efficiently.

The area or regional organisation (Figure 7.3(ii)) is one in greatest use by companies with a limited number of relatively homogeneous products in widespread distribution through many outlets. The nature of the product, methods of distribution, the degree of dispersal of the manufacturing units are other factors that must be considered. For example national brewers, bakeries, petrol companies and most major mass-market consumer goods organisations have area-based sales organisations. However, where diversification has tended to make the product range hetero-geneous in parts, at least, evolution to a compound structure (Figure 7.3(v)) would be used.

Industrial goods which can be manufactured in several locations, usually with a good geographical spread of users, are also best handled by an area organisation. Again, if there is some disparity between some products (e.g. involving different technologies, or having different appli-cations requiring specialised knowledge) some form of a compound structure will be used. In Figure 7.3(v), 'Product A' is one of these special items, all the rest being, presumably, in general demand.

Most public utilities (gas, electricity) use the area method as do many services (insurance, investment services, travel and tourism). Area sales organisations are able to exploit local brand loyalties, regional differences in preferences and taste and the strengths of, or relationships with, local distribution channels, as well as make maximum use of localised, or nearby, expensive manufacturing facilities. General functional services (marketing research, product and promotional planning etc.) are usually centralised at head office or the main factory for economy. However, if the regional demands are large enough to justify it, small offshoots of marketing research and promotional departments can be located in the regions.

The end-use and customer group organisations (Figure 7.3(iii) and (iv)) are used when firms sell to different kinds of customers or markets with very specific and differing marketing requirements. The greater or more specialised the technical requirements the greater is the need for specialised sales management and sales forces. Then the end-use approach is used and this is the one favoured by many industrial products manufacturers. The diversity of the products and their service needs are better served in this way and greater customer satisfaction should result.

In the case of mass-market consumer goods sold to different outlets or customer groups there may be need for various selling and promotional techniques. In this case the customer group organisation is preferred. In both cases, the volume of business with the different customer groups or for each product group must be large enough to justify the expense of these methods. Again, the functional services in general use may be located at head office for economy, or in the regions if this is justified and gives more efficient or effective results.

The product group approach (Figure 7.3(vi)) is preferred by many industrial products firms and multi-product consumer goods and durables companies. Here different product groups are sold to different markets or customers through different distribution channels and involve different strategies, pricing and packaging policies, promotional activities, sales forecasting and budgets. With very large firms with considerable turnover in each product group, there may be a separate sales force and manager for each of them. For example a pharmaceutical products firm may split its sales organisation into three, one selling ethical products to doctors, hospitals and dentists, another selling proprietary items to chemists and retail outlets (departmental stores) with chemist counters and a third dealing with sales to veterinary surgeons, animal hospitals and specialist institutions (e.g. RSPCA homes, kennels and catteries). Sometimes, for economy, one sales force may be used for the first two product groups (ethical and proprietary items) but the greater knowledge and expertise required for the first may in fact be wasted on the second.

While increasing competition of all kinds has led to greater diversification of the product range by many firms and thus created the wider use of compound organisations (Figure 7.3(v)), some companies have always needed it. For example a soft drinks firm selling through the usual retail outlets *and* to homes, door-to-door, would have a manager and sales force for direct sales to the home, usually operating out of local depots and vans. Sales to wholesalers and retailers would be handled by another manager and sales force, with deliveries by the firm's vans out of the various regional depots. If the business is large enough, the trade sales might be organised on a geographical or regional basis. There may be more than one sales force covering the trade in different parts of the country, each with its own field sales manager. This gives better coverage and control and again builds rapport between distributors and the firm. It is able to respond more effectively to local requirements also.

It is necessary now to illustrate the basic sales organisations or 'hierarchies' which can be used. These are set out in Figure 7.4 with qualifying notes. Working from left to right of the illustration, the first organisation is used by firms having a single sales force operating in various markets. The implication is that the business allows the company to be organised on a functional basis (see Figure 7.3 and accompanying text). The second is useful where the market coverage is more extensive but one sales force is being used (no technical or other complications) but it is advisable to break down coverage into smaller areas for better control. Where the sales coverage is wide and more than one sales force is being used, the third organisation is preferred to improve the chain of command and control. The fourth method is needed when the technical or other factors of the products or goods vary considerably and require different marketing and promotional approaches and/or support services.

There is no 'one best' organisation. The right one depends on the tasks in hand, the extent, nature or complexity of the selling job and the markets or customers to be served.

(d) The nature of the sales task

The nature or content of the sales task to be performed varies according to the type of points-of-sale used and potential customers' expectations at the different points of the distribution network. First consider the distributors.

When selling to the distributors, the salesperson's task is to persuade the former to hold adequate stocks for the territory and outlets they serve and to mount a continuous sales campaign on retailers and other outlets (supermarkets, departmental stores) to 'push' sales along to the ultimate consumer/customer. Where products are bought by customers direct from wholesalers the firm's sales staff should be prepared to assist wholesalers in this. Associated tasks include helping to deal with complaints of all kinds, servicing the accounts, persuading retailers to take stock from the wholesalers and sometimes working with distributors'

Fig 7.4 *some sales management 'hierarchies'*

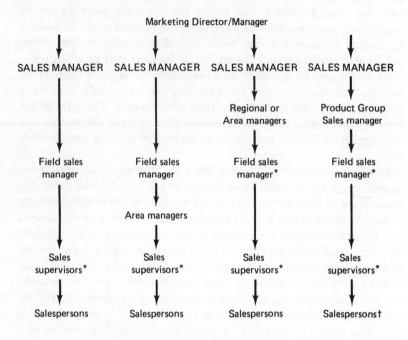

Marketing Director/Manager

SALES MANAGER SALES MANAGER SALES MANAGER SALES MANAGER

Regional or
Area managers

Product Group
Sales manager

Field sales
manager

Field sales
manager

Field sales
manager*

Field sales
manager*

Area managers

Sales
supervisors*

Sales
supervisors*

Sales
supervisors*

Sales
supervisors*

Salespersons

Salespersons

Salespersons

Salespersons†

* Optional appointments depending on the extent,
scale or scope of the work to be done.

† For industrial products and capital equipment
this role may be divided into two: (1) salespersons
doing routine selling job (seeking orders etc.) and
(2) technical sales engineers handling the more
complex technical queries and after-sales needs.
Sometimes the sales supervisors are replaced by
technical sales engineers.

Note: There are many variations on these basic themes.
For example, in end-use or customer category
organisations the product sales manager could be
replaced by either of the 'sales managers' shown
in the lowest level of organisational charts (Figure
7.3 (iii) and (iv). Area managers usually look
after a smaller territory than regional managers and
may report to the latter.

salespeople, even helping to train them. The last is important when technical products, capital equipment and household appliances are the items handled.

Thus selling to wholesalers requires not only good knowledge of the products being offered and their uses but high sales skills and knowledge of the typical organisational structure, methods and aims of operation of wholesale enterprises. Apart from the usual economic and financial aspects, the wholesaler is concerned about the reliability of the supplier in respect of assured quality and above all delivery promises. The salesperson must convince the wholesaler on these points and that demand for the product exists. Some firms use missionary salespersons who obtain orders from retailers for placement with specified, prospective wholesaler buyers.

When the ultimate user or consumer buys anything direct from the manufacturer the implication is that the former have already made up their mind on the make, brand, quality and price of the item they want. Usually they are looking for price savings through cutting out the middleman. However, they may or may not accept the possibility of lower quality of the item (though quality is normally as good as that for the item bought through retailers). Customers will certainly expect the same back-up services as they would obtain from retailers. However, when customers buy direct from wholesalers, it means that while they are expecting some price savings and adequate after-sales services, they have not yet made up their mind about the make or brand to choose. Wholesalers usually carry more than one make or brand. The manufacturer's sales staff in direct selling have to ensure that the contact with customers does end in orders. They are then primarily interested in closing the sale successfully. When customers buy from wholesalers, the manufacturer's people must persuade customers that their products are better than competitors' but must take care not to undermine too forcefully sales of competitive or substitute products. The latter may in fact be of greater importance or profitability to the wholesaler. Company sales staff operating from wholesalers' premises must employ considerable tact. When operating from their own premises (factory, shop etc.) they can employ more 'hard sell' methods and when customers are still doubtful about the item being considered, or are definitely unfavourable to it, then the sales staff must attempt to interest customers in the firm's alternative offerings.

In the case of retailers, most have their own sales force employed in selling their stock. They use various degrees of aggressiveness for this, depending on the importance of the product, the attitudes of potential customers and the competition to be overcome. The firm's staff is then involved in assisting the retail sales force where necessary or requested and in persuading retailers to take and hold sufficient stock from wholesalers or direct from the manufacturer. The latter's people then take their cue from the retailers without sacrificing the objectives and needs of their employers. Where the manufacturer's sales staff are operating from the premises of the retailer (e.g. a 'shop-within-a-shop' in departmental stores), the sales staff will use all the usual ploys to close a successful sale but must not deter potential customers from considering competitive products if they wish.

The most frequent example is with women's clothes. The ladies may start by looking at one brand or make but if the style, colours and price do not suit them they must be free to move on to other makes. In these instances helpful suggestions of other makes to consider often build up the goodwill of customers to the brand of the helpful saleslady. Sometimes the customer, having looked at the alternatives, will return and make a purchase at their first choice. Usually customers have good personal reasons for looking at one make first. They may have been pleased with the quality and style of earlier purchases. Or they may consider the price represents good value after all.

When selling to retailers, salespersons have to stress patronage motives, in particular the support services provided by the seller. Consequently emphasis must be placed on the more competitive credit terms, delivery charges (if any) and assured prompt delivery that may be on offer. Frequently they may have to spend a good deal of time assisting their retailer customers with window and in-store displays and any full-scale merchandising activity that may be considered necessary and suitable for these outlets.

When selling to industry and commerce, the various points discussed in preceding sections apply. With technical products, the sales staff will have to prepare technical presentations to prospective buyers. A separate presentation may be needed for different end-uses or types of customer. The sales decisions are often based on rational considerations. When involved in *executive selling* (i.e. selling a wide range of items to more senior executives) considerable creativity is needed with knowledge of all aspects of the items being offered and the uses and technical aspects of interest to the customer.

At exhibitions, the selling task is more one of providing information on the company and its products. Studies have shown that about 40 per cent of enquiries are from unidentified persons seeking a wide range of information. The remainder are serious enquiries from identified individuals or organisations and the information they need is more detailed and precise than from the former group. Usually they have a problem to solve or a new idea and are looking for the means to overcome or carry them through successfully.

In the first instance, salespersons should provide the information with the firm's name and address clearly displayed. They should try to identify the enquirers or at least urge them to contact the firm more formally at a later date. With the second group, identities are known and follow-up visits arranged. With technical products the necessary back-up should be available though very difficult points are normally referred to an appropriate executive at the firm for later follow-up visits after the matter has been investigated or researched.

In all cases at exhibitions or on personal visits, the salesperson forms an essential communication link between the firm and its customers. Salespersons advise the customers on the products or services available and their attributes. They also keep the firm informed of what is happening at the users' end, changing needs, relevant technical developments, what is happening with competition and so on.

7.9 SALES PLANNING AND CONTROL

In planning the sales operations, executives must be aware that conflict can arise between the firm's objectives, those of customers and the sales staff. Salespersons advise customers on the products available and aim to sell the best product mix to optimise the volume of sales achieved. The company is interested in optimising profit and return as well as long-term growth, not necessarily sales volume. Customers on the other hand are interested in meeting their own needs, satisfying their wants at the highest quality and most economical prices possible. They are interested in prices that signify value for money spent. Generally they are not interested in the implications of these points on company needs and *vice versa*.

Thus in trying to achieve its objectives, the firm may not in fact be making acceptable marketing offerings to customers. The products may be of too high a quality, or be too long lived and thus more expensive than customers require. For example in the late 1950s some shipbuilders were still making ships to old designs, which offered a long life but did not match the changes taking place in longdistance haulage and handling needs (e.g. use of containers requiring new mechanical handling methods at termini; need for faster loading and unloading; and higher speeds to give shorter transit times; etc.). The time taken to build the old-style ships was also too protracted. Customers turned to builders producing vessels of more modern and appropriate design.

On the other hand, firms have to keep a balance between satisfying customers' needs and their own financial requirements consistent with the resources and capabilities of the company. The sales and marketing tasks may be redefined as generating a satisfactory income for a sustained period of time, of 'buying' revenues in the markets at lowest possible cost. Many of customers' wants may not be practical (for technical and other reasons), they may be too costly to produce or they may involve the firm in putting too much of its resources into less profitable items at the expense of more profitable ones. They could lead also to producing large volumes of some items, creating problems of stocking and distribution. Much capital may be tied up unproductively, giving problems of liquidity and cash flows.

Salespersons, however, may be interested in selling items which can be sold easily allowing the easy attainment of sales quota. They will also be interested in pushing products which earn the best bonus or commission for themselves, at the expense of other items of equal or greater importance to the firm's total activity. In so doing they may overload the factory and thus there would be insufficient capacity for other items. They also prefer to avoid competition when perhaps facing up to it may be necessary for the long-term survival and growth of the company. The firm itself has to balance customer needs with their own short- and long-term needs. Obtaining the right balance between the last two items is a common problem facing all companies.

As mentioned elsewhere in a different context, the task of the salesperson is not limited to just 'selling'. Potential customers have to be advised or 'counselled' on many points. The more technical or complex the product or service and the buying procedures, the greater will be this counselling. Then the sales force is the additional eyes and ears of the marketing department. If properly briefed and if necessary trained, salespersons can collect a wide range of useful market information which the company needs in its marketing planning and decision-making processes. They help also in the work of merchandising. Then there are the numerous liaisons which the sales force must create between technical and other specialist colleagues and themselves and potential customers. This is particularly important when users complain about any aspect of the product in use. Finally, there is all the help and assistance they must give to wholesalers and retailers as explained earlier. Thus the sales job today is a much more widespread one than before and provides staff with many interesting and challenging opportunities.

(a) Sales methods
Section 7.2(e) compared the merits and functions of telephone selling and personal selling with advertising. A few more words here are in order.

Personal (face-to-face) selling is the most effective method of obtaining orders but it is also the most expensive. With technical products or where complicated matters are involved, this method cannot be ignored. Indeed with intangible services it is vital that face-to-face selling is used and it cannot be eliminated entirely whatever has to be sold. However, because of the costs, judicious use of *telephone selling* is helpful. The benefits, as explained earlier, are direct and indirect (i.e. can increase sales volume for existing business and tempt customers to put new business the firm's way). There is need for some, more limited, face-to-face selling none the less (used on individuals, telephone selling exerts unacceptable pressure on them.)

Selling by correspondence, whether personalised letters or by *direct mail* shots is cheaper than the other two but the order response may be lower. It depends on the attractiveness of the product and the offer, whether the offer is contrived or too 'gimmicky' and so on. With personalised letters great care is needed to ensure the message is clear and unambiguous and does not offend the recipients' susceptibilities in any way. The paperwork with direct mail shots must also observe these rules. Attempts to personalise what is obviously general promotional material by the insertion of the recipient's name can offend, or put off people from making a favourable response. This method has been used extensively in recent years and there are signs that the public is beginning to resent it.

(b) The sales interview
Most firms now realise the importance of the interview and the need to train salespersons in how to plan and conduct them. Particular attention has been given to how to open and close an interview and meeting objections. Basically, besides knowing all that is relevant about the product, its attributes, the uses customers have for it and the relevant technical and competitive situations the salesperson must consider the following.

The *presentation* or *sales pitch* must be thought out carefully. It describes the product or service's major attributes and relates them to the customer's needs or problems, making clear the benefits or assistance that should accrue as a result of its use. The presentation must be concise, positive and free of ambiguity and waffle. It must instruct, advise or assist potential customers to come to the right decision, not confuse or irritate them. In Britain and other countries it is usually considered 'bad form' to plunge into the presentation on meeting. Some social chit-chat breaks the ice and gets the atmosphere right for the sales discussion. This preliminary should not be too long (though in Japan it can be long and quite formal).

Salespersons have to use their judgement and experience to gauge when the *formal opening* of the presentation should take place. This is easier to do when the salesperson has established personal relationships or rapport with buyers. Some openings can be stronger than others. Whether a soft-sell approach is needed or a more aggressive style is necessary has to be established by careful thought and planning. The salesperson should collect as much information as is relevant to deducing the nature and style of the person to be interviewed and thus the best approach to adopt.

In every presentation there is a chance that the prospect will make excuses for not placing an order or will raise some objections to the proposition. Where the latter may be based on hard technical or economic facts, the salesperson must be fully briefed on the subject to be able to counter the objections effectively. Generally every objection should be used as an opportunity to present more relevant information. Thus it is often advisable not to shoot off all the shots at the initial presentation. Also careful assimilation of the type and nature of the questions put by a prospect will guide the seller on how the rest of the presentation should go and the additional information that should be provided.

Closing the sale, when the prospect is asked to place an order, is the crunch point for salespersons. Many encounter difficulty in asking for an order. The approach should follow naturally from the presentation and discussion and should be positive, delivered unhesitatingly. The basic techniques include telling the client that orders should be placed immediately if the required delivery times are to be met, or that because of demand (if true) the product may not be readily available at a later date. Or an appeal can be made to a relevant emotion (e.g. pleasure and enjoyment when a holiday or car has to be bought; pride in ownership as with a prestige product; essentiality in regard to the customer's business; etc.). Then there is the use of alternative decisions when the customer is asked to choose between several possibilities, or extra inducements (e.g. special cash terms for immediate orders; special servicing support; etc.) can be offered. Finally, use can be made of silence, that is the salesperson stops talking and the client realises a decision has to be made. If the client appears to have formed positive views of the presentation, likes the product and its attributes, this method will work. However, where there are doubts remaining, or economic factors make a decision to buy difficult and so on, silence may just produce a rejection of the offer.

(c) Buying–selling models

Several models have been devised to explain the buying–selling relationship. Some will be described briefly here, but those wishing to study them in detail should refer to specialist books on the subject. The simplest model is the *Buygrid* illustrated in Figure 7.5. It was devised by P. J. Robinson and C. W. Faris and attempts to categorise buyer behaviour to enable significant implications for marketing to be drawn. For example, the most difficult problems arise with a new task and the anticipation of associated problems. The customer needs substantial information to define the problem. Since a new task may involve a number of policy decisions, several feasibility studies may have to be conducted and several senior executives consulted, placing unusual demands on the supplier.

Although a useful approach, it does not describe the behavioural

Fig 7.5 *the Buygrid model*

Buy phases	Buy classes		
	New purchase	Modified rebuy	Straight rebuy
Anticipation or recognition of a problem.	✓	✓	
Determination of characteristics and quantity needed.	✓	✓	✓
Description of characteristics and quantity needed.	✓		
Search for and qualification of potential sources.	✓		
Acquisition and analysis of proposals.	✓	✓	
Evaluation of proposals and selection of supplier.	✓	✓	
Selection of order routine.	✓	✓	✓
Performance feedback and evaluation.	✓	✓	✓

Fisher's model of involvement in purchase decisions

COMMERCIAL UNCERTAINTY	PRODUCT COMPLEXITY	
	High	Low
High	Total involvement	Policy-maker emphasis
Low	Techno-logical emphasis	Buyer emphasis

PRODUCT COMPLEXITY: Standardisation of product; technology; previous purchase history; newness of product; after-sales service; ease of installation and use.
COMMERCIAL UNCERTAINTY: Size of investment; order size; timespan of commitment; potential effect on profit; ease of forecasting effect.

processes involved, or their influences. R. W. Hill in 1972 postulated a simple descriptive model for organisational buying behaviour with three components. These were (1) the sequential buying stages in time; (2) factors likely to affect the behaviour of individuals or groups involved in the purchasing decision; (3) functional areas in the customer firm likely to be involved in the purchasing decision.

Another simple model was devised by L. Fisher in 1969 which integrated the factors influencing buying decisions and the involvement of different functional area of the firm. The two factors were product complexity and commercial uncertainty. This model is also illustrated in Figure 7.5 and the various aspects of the factors normally used are given below it.

Then there are several models of the advertising process based on an understanding of the buying behaviour of consumers and how these may be influenced by advertising. These are listed in Figure 7.6. The first three assume that the consumer moves sequentially along a scale of commitment to the brand or product. The probability of purchase increases as the consumer moves through each stage. Studies done so far have found no empirical evidence to support this theory. The last model shown (ATR) was proposed by A. S. C. Ehrenberg in 1974, based on his extensive studies of consumer brand choice behaviour.

Many other models of buyer behaviour have been devised. These include the Howard–Sheth model based on four considerations. First, there are the internal state variables and processes which characterise the state of the buyer. Second, consideration is given to the inputs of the marketing environment. Third are the inputs from the social environment and fourth the outputs, the dimensions of buyer behaviour.

Fig 7.6 *AIDA, DAGMAR and other models*

AIDA	DAGMAR*	Hierarchy of effects	ATR
Awareness	Awareness	Awareness	Awareness
Interest	Comprehension	Knowledge	Trial
Desire	Conviction	Liking	Repeat
Action	Action	Preference	buying
		Conviction	
		Purchase	

* DAGMAR = Defining advertising goals for measured advertising results.

The Sheth model for industrial buyer behaviour, enunciated in 1973, assumes three distinct aspects of organisational buyer behaviour. These are the psychological aspects or characteristics of the individuals involved; the conditions that precipitate joint decision-making; and the conflict resolution procedures necessary when a joint decision has to be taken. Other models are based on the rating or standing of vendors in the eyes of potential customers, source or brand loyalty and socio-economic and demographic variables as they affect buyer behaviour.

(d) Domestic and international markets

While the basic concepts and techniques of selling apply to any market, note must be taken of the special characteristics of the economic and social environments of foreign or international markets. How much these vary in foreign (*host*) countries from conditions in the domestic (*home*) nation will determine the degree of modification required for the subjects discussed in the preceding sections. Table 7.11 lists the major preliminary questions that must first be answered. Tables 7.12 and 7.13 summarise the economic and social environmental factors that must then be considered.

The level of economic development achieved and thus the wealth of the country and the distribution of that wealth will indicate what pro-

Table 7.11   **selling overseas: points to consider**

1   What overseas markets are available? Where are they located? How accessible are they, geographically and in terms of distribution and selling needs?
2   How large is demand in each market and how is this growing or declining? What factors affect demand?
3   How geographically concentrated is each market?
4   What commercial freedom exists? (Can the firm operate freely against local competition, set its own prices, or will it be subject to government control?)
5   What views exist or what attitudes are apparent towards selling, advertising and sales promotions? Are they accepted as normal commercial necessities or viewed as exploitation of the innocent public (by opinion leaders and government)? What laws etc. exist to control or restrict these activities?
6   Are exports to other countries permitted if local assembly or manufacturing is set up?
7   Will sales have to be done by local nationals or organisations?
8   Must the firm go into partnership and what proportion of any capital must be provided or held by local nationals or organisations? Any special tax laws, rules?
9   What is the possibility of nationalisation or expropriation of the venture at some future date?

Table 7.12   overseas markets: economic factors

1 *Subsistence economy* (sometimes referred to as a primitive self-support-ing economy); majority engaged in simple agriculture; consume most of their own output; barter or sell surplus for other needs; limited monetary system; general standard of living low, concerned mainly with essentials only; limited opportunities for exporters.

2 *Raw material exporting economy*: rich in one or more natural resources, poor in other respects; most of income from exporting these, though in recent decades many insist that some processing takes place in their country (e.g. oil refining, tin smelting etc.). Standard of living and wealth depends on nature and extent of these operations and foreign involvement, investment and number of expatriates working in country. Also depends on number of wealthy landowners, mine owners etc. in country. Export prospects vary accordingly, as do chances of local assembly or manufacture of more sophisticated products. The same thoughts apply to services needed.

3 *Primary manufacturing (or industrialising) economy*: manufacturing beginning to play major role; product and service needs becoming more sophisticated; but not yet at mass manufacturing stage; more wealth, more widely distributed; promotional media available but limited or primitive in parts; new rich class forms but small if growing middle class; total demand limited but growing; emphasis on essential goods and services, especially those assisting industrialisation, with increas-ing demand for some sophisticated items (e.g. cars, radios, furniture, clothing, toiletries).

4 *Industrialised economy*: good industrial base established; may be growing still or limited to certain industries; relatively substantial wealth, reasonably spread; middle class established; demand for wide range of goods and services, subject to social factors (see Table 7.13). Good but selective export/international marketing prospects.

ducts or services could be sold and the degree of technological and other sophistication possible. Provided the factors listed in Figures 7.12 and 7.13 are taken into account, the work and approach of salespersons will be similar to that for the home country.

In host nations a greater degree of educational work (of local nationals, colleagues, distributors, consumers) is usually necessary. Also, because of the size of the countries, or the wide geographical spread of the populations, with many sparsely populated areas, greater use of area or regional sales agents may be unavoidable. Then the missionary and educational work of the sales force will increase. Finally, it is also pre-ferable to have salespersons resident in the country, whether local nationals or expatriates. However, today, most developing nations limit the time expatriates can be used and the firm is expected to train local nationals for this job as soon as possible, subject to educational standards and so on.

The similarities of markets, home or overseas, lie in the general

(*continued on page 242*)

Table 7.13　overseas markets: social and other factors

1 INCOME
   Subsistence economy: usually very low family incomes; little demand
   for sophisticated products and market saturation soon reached.
   Raw materials exporting economy: most families poor but some are
   rich; demand for consumer goods varied; poor supplement own
   production with imported foods and textiles; right live on expensive,
   imported items, cars etc.
   Industrialising economy: mostly low family incomes; government
   forces any surplus from working classes for capital formation; general
   drabness, bureaucrats live austerely usually; most consumer goods
   produced locally; imports depend on government economic and other
   policies.
   Industrialised economy: at first the low–high income spread persists
   but as middle class arise income structure tends to even out; eventually
   institutions develop that tend to even out extremes. Middle class have
   some net discretionary income left over for more sophisticated items
   (cars, consumer durables, expensive furniture etc.). As more skills
   required, low income groups decline and artisan middle class grows.
   Demand for a wide range of products and services grows.

2 FAMILY
   Style: patriarchal, matriarchal, democratic; determine who makes
   buying decisions and life-style (with income).
   Size: average size of family, with income, determines purchasing
   power and thus market demands. As socio-economic developments
   advance, autocratic control of the family declines and purchasing
   possibilities increase.

3 EDUCATION
   Usually the better educated gain skills that permit higher earnings and
   thus wider demand for increasing range of products/services. If education slanted to totalitarian political views this restricts growth of consumer expectations and thus demand.

4 RELIGION
   Has strong impact on what can be marketed and how it may be. For
   example apparent nudity and kissing scenes usually taboo in countries
   where religion is strong; pig products should not be offered to Muslim
   countries; beef should not be offered to Hindu countries; attitudes,
   rules and regulations here must be fully understood.

5 LANGUAGE
   All phrases not capable of exact translation; tragic misunderstandings
   and offence can result. Essential for sales staff to be fluent in host
   country's language; preferably to be truly bi-lingual, i.e. thinks in the
   language, not thinks in English and then translates; in former case all
   the nuances of language, life-style, attitudes etc. are more likely to be
   understood; if just fluent, these nuances may be missed or lost in
   translation. With difficult languages, suitably trained/experienced
   nationals of host country preferred for the selling tasks.

Table 7.13 (*contd*)

6 CULTURAL FACTORS
Must be appreciated; set tone, style or level of life-style. Affects demand for more unusual items.

7 SOCIAL STRATIFICATION AND CLASSES
As in developed countries, this (with income) determines what items are wanted and how, why and where bought, i.e. reveals possible demand structure. Norms of behaviour will again assist in deciding how to market items, what communications and product-market mix needed (incomes indicate possible price levels).

8 POPULATION
As for developed countries, population size, growth and other related demographic details help marketing planning and decision-making. Determines size of demand.

9 TECHNOLOGY
Level of technology and technological trends will also indicate the nature of demand and demand trends. Depending on skills available or that can be trained so will be determined what can be made locally and what must be imported. In poor countries with mainly unskilled labour and high unemployment, sophisticated manufacturing processes not favoured. Old methods using large numbers of unskilled preferred. With limited skilled labour, methods requiring 'intermediate technology' (semi-sophisticated) may be best. Indicates the product mix possible; also the productive capability of host nation.

10 LITERACY
Low literacy with limited media choice restricts marketing and communications possibilities. Simple products/services, sold in an unsophisticated way may be all that is possible. If many languages or dialects, communications problems increased especially with restricted media.

11 TAXATION AND IMPORT CONTROLS
Can enhance or obstruct business opportunities and prospects. May favour some classes of products/services but not others. Some countries offer 'tax holidays' to industries they want but are too capital intensive for them to develop on their own.

approach to them. First, possible markets must be identified. Then, through market research or other detailed assessments, the target markets and customer groups are defined and the possible size of demand, how this is growing or declining and the factors influencing this must be studied. Competition, price, distribution and promotional possibilities are estimated. Also, consumer or buyer behaviour has to be analysed in as much detail as possible (sometimes the basic information is just not obtainable) so that usable consumer profiles can be formulated. Then the marketing and sales planning and decisions that suit local conditions can be taken.

However, buyer behaviour varies from country to country and indeed between ethnic groups. Thus as with countries in East and West Africa, India and some others, where the population is made up of various ethnic groups, special problems are posed. One marketing and sales strategy and policy, especially the one used successfully at home, usually will not suit such markets. New strategies and policies have to be evolved to suit local needs, habits, preferences and taboos. They must also conform with local customs, laws and buying practices. The conduct and activities of salespersons must comply with local ethics, or offence will be given. So when entry into a new overseas market is contemplated, there is need for considerable research and study. Where the necessary intelligence infrastructure does not exist, the final decision may have to be based on 'hunch' and past experience of similar market situations.

International sales management can involve (1) responsibility for sales through agents; (2) managing a team of travelling export salespersons based at the firm's head office; (3) management of salespersons based abroad within their sales areas; they can be either expatriates or nationals of the host countries; (4) ultimate responsibility for the nationally organised and managed sales forces of overseas subsidiaries or branches. While (1) and (2) are usual where *direct exports* (shipment of finished goods overseas, or components for overseas assembly) are concerned, (3) and (4) are more usual with full *international marketing*. (See Sections 9.5 and 9.6.)

Apart from having comprehensive knowledge of the products handled, their technology and the technologies of the users, or the needs of consumers and linguistic ability, salespersons in international markets should possess the following. First, there must be managerial competence, for salespersons overseas will frequently have to make prompt decisions, often with limited information and little consultative support. The operation is inherently more risky than home sales activities. Then the salespersons must be competent in research work. In regions limited in usable information and marketing statistics, they must know how to seek out advice and intelligence and to interpret it correctly. All this calls for dependability, the ability to work well without supervision in frustrating and testing circumstances.

In addition salespersons overseas must be culturally adaptable, able to identify with cultures very different from their own. They must learn to think and act like the local nationals they deal with if they are to get the maximum, in sales terms, out of the exchanges. Finally, they must have good health. Travelling overseas and living abroad in many countries are physically demanding. Many major and minor local epidemics have to be survived. They must know what to eat and drink and what not to and the necessary health precautions that should be observed. (For example, in countries with uncertain water supplies, do not drink unboiled water, or milk, or from rivers or streams.)

(e) Sales control and reports

Like all other managerial activity, if sales activities are to be successful over the long term they must be controlled and monitored so that any necessary alterations to plans can be made. Regular reviews of results are needed (how frequently depends on the business: mass-market goods usually fortnightly, others perhaps monthly) so that in due course modifications can be carried out (usually about every three reporting periods). Only then will effective control be possible. It does not matter how good the planning may have been, if activities are not well controlled the results obtained will not match objectives.

The basic aim of sales control is to ensure that targets (volume, revenue, profit, market shares, salespersons' quota) are being achieved. In addition management wants to know if target markets are being covered and contacted effectively and at the agreed rate. Who is being contacted? How frequently and when? How many are being called upon by each salesperson? What are the call ratios and what revenue is obtained? How effective are the salespersons (their 'cost/benefit' to the company perhaps)? What is achieved when salespersons are face-to-face with customers? And so on.

To be able to judge this, certain basic paperwork is necessary. First there is the *salesperson's report*. This can be done on a daily basis (when the volume of business is substantial as with mass-market goods) or weekly or monthly (as with industrial products). The reports should inform the sales manager of the accounts contacted, when and for what purpose, the success and results of the visit and bring to the firm's attention any deficiencies in its products or marketing services. They should also inform the company of changes in customer needs or expectations, especially any complaints. They should also indicate from time to time the current level of customers' business activities, and new developments in the market or relevant technology that could affect demand and the activities of competitors and customers' general views and reactions to the general state of the market. Reports should be promptly made, be brief and accurate. It is possible to devise forms which record the essential details of a visit. Then any special points, problems or developments could be covered in a supporting memorandum. This saves sales managers from having to wade through a mass of daily or weekly reports.

An equally important document is the *complaints report*. From time to time customers will have occasion to make a complaint on something or other. These must be dealt with speedily. Delays in attending to them irritate customers and can lead to loss of goodwill and orders. Then there is the salesperson's *expense sheet* through which legitimate expenses are claimed. These cover travelling, hotel and entertaining expenses. If a car is provided, it will log the total mileage each week and the amount of private mileage included in that, the petrol and oil bought and any maintenance and repairs that were necessary. A separate *vehicle report form* is sometimes used.

Another important control activity is *journey planning.* The aim here is to ensure that salespersons take the most advantageous and economical routes on their calls, dependent on the location of the customers, the base from which the salesperson operate, traffic and road conditions and traffic congestion areas. The last means that the shortest route may not be the least time consuming. Good journey planning means that salespersons spend more time selling and are not fatigued by travelling unnecessary distances. Time wasting is also reduced.

Other sales control documents can include special reports when new accounts have been opened or lost ones regained and reports on competitive activities. The sales office will also maintain sales record sheets which may be based on area, type of customer, individual major customers and each salesperson, or any combination of these. Finally, it is usual to maintain some form of customer records (on cards or computer tape) which show the name and address, the location of buying points, who makes buying decisions, points for delivery, the products bought and the value and units of each that are bought. These form a useful starting point for the performance review stage of sales and marketing planning.

7.10 ESTIMATING THE SIZE OF THE SALES FORCE

When estimating the size of the sales force, consideration is given to the number of customers to be serviced, the size of their demand for the firm's products and so the frequency of calling, with finally, the number of 'selling days' available. The last is *not* 365 days! Deductions must be made for 'non-selling' days such as weekends (104 days); annual holidays (if three weeks deduct 15 days); public holidays (about nine in the UK); time spent in the office; any sales or other conferences; and preferably, an allowance for illness. Normally there are only about 200 to 220 'selling days' in a year. From this theoretical estimate, the money that can be spent on the sales force (the personal selling budget) is considered. Usually this means that only a smaller force is possible. This calls for adjustments to selling methods (for example, use of agents, franchisees, direct mail, etc.) or at worst a revision of marketing objectives and targets.

7.11 CASE ILLUSTRATIONS

In 1980, Birds, the British custard makers, replaced their cartons of Angel Delight with sachet packs and promoted this change with a £250,000 campaign in the women's press. Consumer research has shown that 72 per cent of housewives in Britain felt their needs would be met by a sachet and that a carton was wasteful. A further 12 per cent felt that a single sachet met their requirements. In-store tests confirmed this with higher sales for sachets compared with cartons. The press campaign was supported by an on-pack promotion offer.

Finally, another sad tale. A major manufacturer, finding home demand was declining, decided to open up some new overseas markets in developing countries where sufficient industrialisation had taken place to indicate likely demand for the products in mind. However, they found that thorough market and customer research were not possible as the basic information did not exist and there were no research organisations that could undertake the fundamental work. The firm selected their best home salesman and sent him out to the countries concerned to 'see what the demand would be'. The salesman also had little or no knowledge of the countries visited and only very limited experience in 'exporting'. Further, he found the climate and conditions irksome and, without realising it, failed to hit it off with the local nationals. His report proved later to have been superficial and based on plain guesses rather than hard facts.

The decision to go ahead was taken and the same salesman was given the task of finding and appointing sales agents in the countries selected. He had had no experience of this and was not properly briefed. Needless to say the agents appointed were unsuitable for many reasons, including lack of experience of the products, few contacts with potential users and inability or unwillingness to hold sufficient stocks. In addition the economy was not yet at a stage to afford or need the products concerned. The firm did not provide any other back-up services, the right technical people being too busy in Europe. Sales failed to take off, the projects had to be terminated and substantial losses were incurred. (A few years later another firm went in with the same products but mounted a well-qualified team to do the initial studies and to launch the project. By then the economies of the countries concerned had advanced spectacularly. The project proved successful and was made fully viable on a long-term basis by development of a joint venture with a local manufacturer. The latter was also given the task of developing the necessary communications network, including the appointment of sales agents, with expert advice and help from the originating company.)

ASSIGNMENTS

1 Your company has given you the job of developing a fully integrated 'communications mix' from selling and promotional activities that had, previously, been carried out independently but within the broad requirements of the marketing plan. Show how you would link all these activities together and how they interrelate and support each other, what objectives you would set for the 'mix' and how decisions on the components of the mix, the markets and products selected would affect decisions on these objectives.

2 A firm is considering diversification from consumer goods into industrial products and services (e.g. tourism and travel). The marketing director has been asked to review the changes that would be needed in the company's communications mix. What points should the director highlight and what major recommendations should be made? He decides also to outline the review that might be necessary on media selection. You are asked by the director to prepare a draft paper.

3 You have taken up a position as General Sales Manager for a large company manufacturing both consumer goods (specify your choice) and technical products sold to industry and are responsible to the Marketing Director for both activities. You are not satisfied that the sales force is as effective as it could be. What recommendations would you make on the size, composition, nature and location of your salespersons? How would you redefine their responsibilities and activities? You feel also that their sales interview techniques are unsatisfactory. What points would you feature in a sales training programme?

4 Your brother has taken up a similar position with a major tour and travel group marketing mass and popular tours in the United Kingdom and other EEC countries (specify his choice). It also wishes to develop its business travel activities. How would your brother's views and recommendations vary from yours?

5 Having made a success of Assignment 3 you are further promoted to the post of International Sales Manager. The company's activities here need boosting. What aspects of the international sales business would you consider important and need investigation? How does international selling vary from selling in the home market? Why is the appointment of sales agents or other overseas associations so important? Prepare a paper for submission to the Marketing Director.

CHAPTER 8

PHYSICAL

DISTRIBUTION

As mentioned in Chapter 1, for marketing activities to be succesful detailed and careful attention must be given to the 'four Ps' – product, price, promotion and place. 'Place' refers to the markets in which the company has decided to operate, where potential customers normally like to purchase the products.

Physical distribution is responsible for getting the right products to the right places, at the right time, in the correct quantities and proper condition expected by customers. This must be done while, at the same time, distribution costs are held down to the lowest level consistent with the quality of service expected by customers. In practice it is never possible to maximise the quality and efficiency of the service and minimise costs. Some compromise is necessary (see Section 8.2).

8.1 ROLE AND FUNCTIONS

Readers should appreciate by now that marketing is concerned with optimising the value of a product while trying to minimise the cost of doing that. It attempts to add value to the product through every stage of the exchange process. Value can be added in many ways.

It can be done by changing the form of the item as when raw materials are processed into a finished product. It can be achieved by breaking bulk, for example, when coal is taken from a large stockpile and packed into bags or sacks so that it can be conveniently handled and used by consumers. Value is also added by packaging, for example placing toiletry products into smaller, easily handled and attractive containers that attract the interest of potential customers and are also easy to use or handle. Value may also be added by a change of time, as, for instance, when vegetables are canned or frozen at times of abundance (harvest) so that they will be available at times of scarcity (winter). Or value is added by a change of place; that is, by transporting goods from their place of manufacture or harvesting to the points of sale or purchase. Physical distribution (also referred to as *marketing logistics*), in making products available at the right places at the right times, is said to provide the utilities of place and time. That is, to have value a product must not only be available where it is wanted, but also when it is needed.

(a) Role
Thus the role of physical distribution (PD) is to optimise the value of a product by making it available as described, at the various retail outlets where customers normally expect to be able to avail themselves of it. The activities or responsibilities involved in doing this are summarised in Table 8.1. Note that these do not include the purchasing function. Physical Distribution. Management (PDM) may also be called upon to advise on the location of manufacturing units, especially for large operations involving many products sold nationally (for example, mass-market consumer goods). The aim is to achieve an efficient system that provides an acceptable level of customer service that does not involve the firm in prohibitive distribution costs.

(b) Functions
The popular or traditional concept of PD is that it is concerned with the efficient movement of the finished item to the customer. However, a totally integrated system takes responsibility for the movement into the factory of all bought-in items, their storage and inventories and movement through the factory in the course of processing them into the finished product. Then PDM is also responsible for the storage of work-in-progress (w-i-p) as it waits the next stage of manufacture and the control and supervision of w-i-p stores. Figure 8.1 illustrates the two concepts, where 'A' represents the conventional and 'B' the total system views.

PD is no longer seen as just another cost centre that can erode profits if it is not properly managed. It is now appreciated as an activity having an important role to play in the marketing mix. Thus increasing emphasis is being given to the evolution of integrated distribution strategies in the context of total marketing systems. Efficiently carried out, PD provides another important, critical and competitive edge to marketing effort.

(c) Distribution channels
A channel of distribution (sometimes called a *trade channel*) is the path products take as they move from the producer to the ultimate consumer or industrial customer. There are six basic channels.

 (i) From producer direct to consumer (consumer goods) or industrial customer (e.g. capital equipment).

Table 8.1 physical distribution – responsibilities

Depots/warehouses (in-plant and distribution or in-field)
Decisions on size, location, whether owned or leased; facilities and layout; management of; methods of handling goods.

Inventories/inventory control
Decisions on inventory policies; max., min. and reordering stock levels; control procedures, cost of.

Transportation
Decisions on mode to be used (road, rail, water, air); whether transport owned, leased, arranged on annual contract, casual hire, load and journey planning; handling special goods.

Channels of distribution
Decisions on distribution channels to be used (see Figure 8.2).

Delivery patterns
Decisions on delivery times, service levels for customers.

Processing
Drop size/cost analysis; order processing; load building.

Costs
Cost control and allocations; customer account profitability; backhaul waste capacity; labour incentives; refusals and returns; insurance cover as needed.

Administration
Management of PD operations; selection and control of administrative systems and all associated paperwork; correcting errors in dispatch and in order-taking; packing and dispatch, issuing of dispatch notes, shipping documents etc., staffing. Quality check on all items into stores.

(All decisions are taken in consultation with appropriate colleagues from other departments of the Marketing Division, Manufacturing and Finance Divisions and Personnel.)

(*continued from page 249*)

(ii) From producer through an agent to industrial user (e.g. industrial products with high technological content).

(iii) From producer to retailer to ultimate consumer (e.g. via large departmental stores).

(iv) From producer to wholesaler to industrial customer (e.g. most industrial products).

(v) From producer to wholesaler to retailer to ultimate consumer (e.g. most consumer goods).

(vi) From producer to sole agent (usually for a prescribed territory) to wholesaler and/or retailer to ultimate consumer and sometimes, to the industrial customer.

The last is often the starting-point for direct exports to overseas countries.

Fig 8.1 *physical distribution – movement of goods*

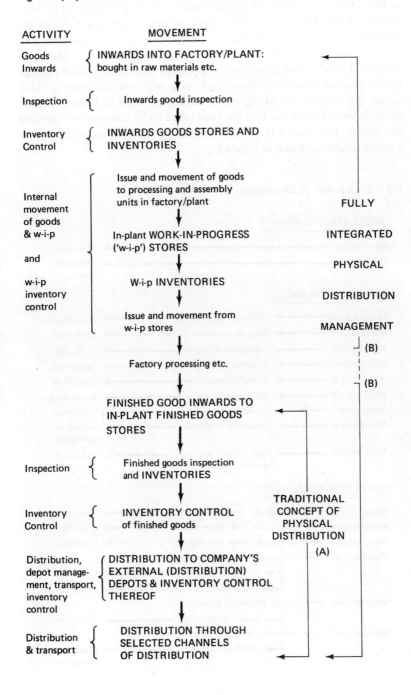

ACTIVITY   MOVEMENT

Goods Inwards — INWARDS INTO FACTORY/PLANT: bought in raw materials etc.

Inspection — Inwards goods inspection

Inventory Control — INWARDS GOODS STORES AND INVENTORIES

Internal movement of goods & w-i-p

and

w-i-p inventory control

— Issue and movement of goods to processing and assembly units in factory/plant

In-plant WORK-IN-PROGRESS ('w-i-p') STORES

W-i-p INVENTORIES

Issue and movement from w-i-p stores

FULLY INTEGRATED PHYSICAL DISTRIBUTION MANAGEMENT (B)

Factory processing etc. (B)

FINISHED GOOD INWARDS TO IN-PLANT FINISHED GOODS STORES

Inspection — Finished goods inspection and INVENTORIES

Inventory Control — INVENTORY CONTROL of finished goods

TRADITIONAL CONCEPT OF PHYSICAL DISTRIBUTION (A)

Distribution, depot management, transport, inventory control — DISTRIBUTION TO COMPANY'S EXTERNAL (DISTRIBUTION) DEPOTS & INVENTORY CONTROL THEREOF

Distribution & transport — DISTRIBUTION THROUGH SELECTED CHANNELS OF DISTRIBUTION

However, in the last two decades there have been many developments in the retailing of consumer goods. Greater use is now made of factors, brokers or franchise holders. The growth of large supermarket chains, department store groups, voluntary wholesale and retail groups have also added to the distribution dimension. The voluntary groups (e.g. Mace) are attempts by individual shops to centralise their purchasing so that through greater bulk purchases from manufacturers these groups obtain prices which match the massive purchasing power of supermarkets and large corporations. In recent years the idea has been taken up by independent chemists and others. The result has been to increase the choice of channels open to a manufacturer as shown in Figure 8.2.

Fig 8.2 *channels of distribution*

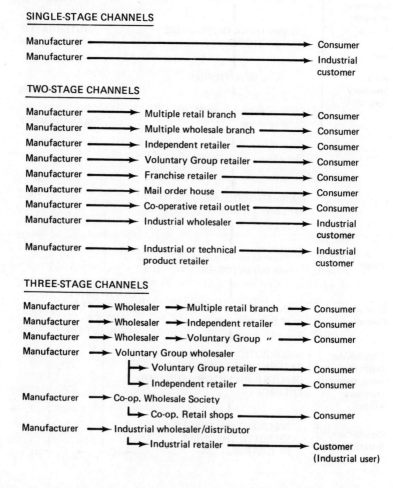

SINGLE-STAGE CHANNELS

| Manufacturer | ⟶ | Consumer |
| Manufacturer | ⟶ | Industrial customer |

TWO-STAGE CHANNELS

Manufacturer ⟶ Multiple retail branch ⟶ Consumer
Manufacturer ⟶ Multiple wholesale branch ⟶ Consumer
Manufacturer ⟶ Independent retailer ⟶ Consumer
Manufacturer ⟶ Voluntary Group retailer ⟶ Consumer
Manufacturer ⟶ Franchise retailer ⟶ Consumer
Manufacturer ⟶ Mail order house ⟶ Consumer
Manufacturer ⟶ Co-operative retail outlet ⟶ Consumer
Manufacturer ⟶ Industrial wholesaler ⟶ Industrial customer
Manufacturer ⟶ Industrial or technical product retailer ⟶ Industrial customer

THREE-STAGE CHANNELS

Manufacturer ⟶ Wholesaler ⟶ Multiple retail branch ⟶ Consumer
Manufacturer ⟶ Wholesaler ⟶ Independent retailer ⟶ Consumer
Manufacturer ⟶ Wholesaler ⟶ Voluntary Group " ⟶ Consumer
Manufacturer ⟶ Voluntary Group wholesaler
     ⟶ Voluntary Group retailer ⟶ Consumer
     ⟶ Independent retailer ⟶ Consumer
Manufacturer ⟶ Co-op. Wholesale Society
     ⟶ Co-op. Retail shops ⟶ Consumer
Manufacturer ⟶ Industrial wholesaler/distributor
     ⟶ Industrial retailer ⟶ Customer (Industrial user)

FOUR-STAGE CHANNELS

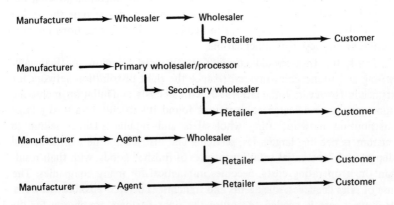

1 In these four-stage channels, the type of wholesaler and retailer involved can be as varied as shown in the two- and three-stage systems.
2 In the first example of the four-stage channel, there is considerable trading between wholesalers to avoid the risk of over- or under-stocking.
3 The two examples with 'Agent' are used when exclusive agents have been appointed for given areas. This is usual where direct exports to overseas markets are involved.
4 These examples can apply to consumer goods and industrial products. In the second example, further processing, including breaking bulk packs, may be necessary, and this is done by the first, or primary, wholesaler.

(d) Implications for marketing

In selecting channels, several points have to be considered. First, there is the size and complexity of the producer's operations. Where a substantial number of products are made in large quantities and these are sold on a wide basis nationally, the firm requires a substantial distribution network. In this case, to keep costs down the company would usually prefer to work through wholesalers and retailers. However, some special items may be sold direct to retailers, a franchise holder or to some (large or important) users.

Second, there is the degree of control the firm wishes to exert on the sale and distribution of its products and prices. Going through the 'normal' trade network means that the company can keep some control of the operations. However, the greater the rank or independence of the intermediary, the less control will a manufacturer have over the distribution channel. The company may not be able to dictate the level of stocks to be held or when and how the intermediary promotes or even sells the product. With the abolition of Resale Price Maintenance in Britain, manufacturers can no longer control the selling prices used. They can only recommend what the retail prices (RRP) should be. In some cases these do become the selling prices offered to customers, but in highly competitive situations retailers deviate from these recommendations.

Third, the firm should consider its financial strength. A financially strong and sound company can finance the right distribution network for its needs. However, in the late 1970s with all costs, and inflation, increasing substantially, even large corporations found it difficult to afford a large distribution network using wholesalers and retailers. Direct selling to customers needing large sales, servicing and distribution networks, several depots and substantial total inventories of finished goods, with their resultant high operating costs, becomes impractical for many companies. The use of sales licencees, sole agents and franchisees offered possible solutions. However, care is needed to ensure the right partners are chosen for the products and work involved. Hasty or incorrect decisions can adversely affect the whole business. The manufacturer may regret the decisions, especially if the terms of the agreement make it difficult or expensive to rectify the mistake speedily.

The fourth point to consider is the nature of the markets. If there are only a few major customers direct distribution may be possible and advisable, especially if they have special needs. If there are many potential customers, widely spread in any geographical area, middlemen (whether wholesalers and/or retailers) will be necessary. Sometimes recourse to direct mail methods can be used but again, as postal and other charges increase, direct mail costs can rise to prohibitive levels. Allied to this is the fifth point, the length of the distribution channel to the ultimate customer and the complexity of it. The help of distribution intermediaries is then unavoidable, since it would be too costly for the firm to become deeply involved in the substantial problems posed in this case.

Finally, the nature of the product has to be considered. For example, perishable foodstuffs need fast-acting marketing and distribution operations using expert wholesalers geared to the fast-moving selling that is essential (as with fish, meat and vegetables, for example). In addition, the completeness of the product line should be taken into account. If a firm is not producing a complete line, selecting a distributor who handles the missing items, even if made by a competitor, should mean that both manufacturers should benefit from the middleman's ability to offer a complete set to customers.

Thus decisions on which channels of distribution to use rest upon how much the manufacturer wishes to be involved in the problems and risks inherent in the work and how well the firm knows its markets and their distribution needs. In theory, the elimination of the intermediaries improves the firm's profitability because it no longer has to pay the necessary trade discounts. However, in practice, the more extensive sales and after-sales services, the larger inventories and greater number of depots required will lead to increased operating costs, the increase often being larger than any savings made on trade discounts. The use of intermediaries also shifts some of the costs and problems off the shoulders of the manufacturer. Further, as the middlemen collectively are in detailed, effective contact with markets and potential customers, market intelligence obtained through them can be more comprehensive than if the firm tried to go it alone. The implications for marketing of choosing the right channels and methods of distribution are considerable.

(e) Impact of marketing on PD

The developments that have taken place in the methods and techniques of marketing have also had an impact on PD. The growth in the number of wholesale and retail outlets, as shown in Figure 8.2, has lead to an increase in PD methods that can be used. Also, economic developments forced marketing executives to develop new approaches (direct mail, franchising etc.) but escalating costs have in turn forced the abandonment of some new and old, tried methods of distribution.

The market-place and its economic, legal, political, social and technological environments are dynamic (subject to change). Marketing and PD approaches need to change to keep pace with these developments if the basic concept of more efficient and profitable marketing is to be maintained. Therefore it is necessary for executives to re-examine, from time to time, the rationale on which their distribution systems are based. Otherwise they will become out-of-date and inefficient. In current situations the starting point is the essentiality of having a cost-conscious approach to distribution, the largest single item of cost in the whole marketing operation.

(f) Physical distribution systems

In selecting and designing these systems, firms must consider the points mentioned in Sections 8(d) and 8(e) above. In practice this means taking note of the markets or market segments to be serviced, the location of manufacturing and distribution systems, the size and nature of the depots required, the availability and location of middlemen and the transportation facilities (roads, railways, sea and waterways, air-freight routes, airports and other termini). The system design will also be influenced by estimates of product flows (total quantities, loads or shipment sizes, size of 'drops'), the personal selling methods used and the delivery times expected by customers. In addition, the distances between pick-up and dropping-off points, whether bulk shipments are required and the perishability of the goods, feature in the system design. Other materials handling aspects to be considered include how the products will be packed (do they need stout packing to prevent damage or deterioration in transit?), whether containers or pallets will be used and the mechanical handling equipment that is available or will be needed. All, in turn, will be constrained by the costs which can be afforded.

In addition the system must possess flexibility so that it can be modified easily when changed circumstances make this necessary. Thus there must be awareness of possible future market developments. Changes in markets, raw materials used, manufacturing locations and distribution and storage technology can demand alterations to the system. For example a major change of recent times has been the greater use of containers and pallets. This led to improvement in the packing and handling of goods with faster transportation times. The development of container ships and ports with the necessary handling equipment speeded up distribution to overseas markets while reducing the problems of damage or loss in transit. The choice of system can have significant impact on product design, plant location and design as well as market selection and the communications mix used.

An effective distribution system can be a powerful element in a firm's marketing mix and plays an important part in earning revenue. However, the traditional view of management is that the work is made up of several discrete operations (purchasing, manufacturing, marketing, warehousing, transportation etc.). The management procedures and techniques have, as a result, been devised to ensure that each activity is conducted to maximum levels of efficiency and cost-effectiveness. It was some time before it was accepted that in closely interrelated activities, attempts to maximise the efficiency of any one part, without regard to the system as a whole, only leads to sub-optimisation of the whole.

It is now appreciated that if firms are to minimise total operating costs and optimise revenue, there must be a correct balance between all activity centres. The nature of this balance will vary from industry to industry, even company to company, depending on how firms work best. Distribution is a system comprised of a series of sub-systems. Proposed changes in one sub-system must be checked for their effect on other parts of the system. Indeed the interrelationships and interactions between the different activity centres of the system must be known.

For example offering a peak service involves a complex and substantial distribution system which will be costly. On the other hand, a low-cost system will necessitate holding limited inventories, using limited transportation and a reduced number of depots. This will result in longer delivery times and give customers a very restricted service. Or using rail instead of air freight will reduce freighting costs, but because of slower transit times capital will be tied up longer since customers' payments will be delayed.

This could affect cash flow adversely. Then delivery delays may force customers to switch their orders to competitors. Or the use of cheap containers may reduce shipping costs but if this leads to more damage and losses in transit, the monetary loss may be greater than the initial saving. If customer goodwill is lost the total losses will be substantial and permanent. Or if a decision is taken to hold lower inventories, to reduce inventory costs, without consideration of the demand pattern and product flows through the system, it will mean more 'stockout' positions, inability to deliver on time, special production runs and so on. The cost of all this will exceed savings in inventory costs.

8.2 COSTS AND BENEFITS

It has been stated that PD costs form a substantial element of total marketing costs. In the 1970s the average was 30–33 per cent. With the effect of inflation, by the end of the decade the average was estimated variously as being 35–45 per cent, depending on the type and nature of the business.

PD costs measured as a percentage of sales price are shown in Table 8.2. While the figure in 1969 averaged 16 per cent, by 1979 it was 24.4 per

Table 8.2 **average breakdown of distribution costs measured as percentage of sales price**

Item	1969		1979	
Administration		2.0		2.5
Transport				
Inbound	1.5		2.0	
Outbound	4.0	5.5	5.3	7.3
Receiving and dispatch		0.5		1.0
Packaging and packing		2.0		3.0
Warehousing				
At factories	1.0		1.8	
Distribution depots	1.5	2.5	3.0	4.8
Inventories (stockholding)				
Interest on investment	2.0		3.0	
Taxes, insurance etc.	1.0	3.0	1.8	4.8
Order processing		0.5		1.0
Total		16.0		24.4

Source: 1969: International Commercial Techniques Ltd.
    1979: Planning for Growth Ltd, London.

Note: The sample used in 1979 was smaller than that of 1969.

cent. (As petrol prices rise so will PD costs.) The need for good cost control and for executives to be very cost conscious is clear, especially when the cost of oil and transportation are rising steadily.

(a) Costs

The aim of better PD control is to reduce costs within clearly defined marketing constraints. The marketing–PD interactions mentioned in the preceding sections need careful consideration. Thus cost control of PD is a complex subject. Yet it is worth doing since good PD represents a marketing value which can be merchandised to customers and so improve the firm's image in their eyes. The important questions that have to be answered are listed in Table 8.3.

Table 8.3　**PD costs – key questions**

COSTS
What are the *transport costs* for:

> Firm's own fleet; rail freight; road transport; air freight; sea/water transport; postal charges; forwarding agents fees, etc.?

What are the *warehousing costs* for:

> Inventories; handling goods received; locating, retrieving and order picking; insurance, heating etc.?

What are the *materials handling costs*?
What are the *packaging* and *packing costs*?
What *other PD costs* are involved?
Are PD costs broken down for home and export markets?

SERVICE REQUIREMENTS
What level of service is expected by customers?
How will this affect inventory levels?
What delivery service is being offered by competitors?
What are the PD and marketing implications of the proposed service?

ORGANISATION
Who is responsible for laying down policies and making decisions on:

> forecasts of customer needs; inventory levels; production programmes; number, location and size of depots; selecting modes of transport; order processing procedures; mechanical handling systems; packing and packaging requirements?

Does the organisation structure permit close co-ordination of PD with marketing and manufacturing operations?
What revision of the structure will improve this coordination and integration?

(b) Total cost concept

Applying the total cost concept is easy to explain academically and illustrate as in Figure 8.3. This shows how the number of depots needed for an optimum cost-effective system can be deduced. The sum of curves A, B, C and D gives curve E for a specified level of service. Where E is at a minimum, the number of depots needed can be read off. In practice it is not quite so easy to do!

The first hurdle is the determination of customer response to, or acceptance of, different levels of service. Must all orders be delivered in x days, or would 98 or 95 per cent be acceptable? What value should x have, 2, 3, 4 or more days? The answers are crucial to the PD costs that would result. Then there is the nature of demand for different products. What quantities are required, what 'drops' (amount delivered at any one time) are essential and what time-intervals are involved? What trade-offs between individual cost items are possible without leading to poor service and high costs?

Figure 8.4 illustrates the problem. The various cost curves are taken from an actual case for non-edible consumer goods in demand throughout the United Kingdom. It has been determined that 92 per cent of all orders

Fig 8.3 *physical distribution system costs*

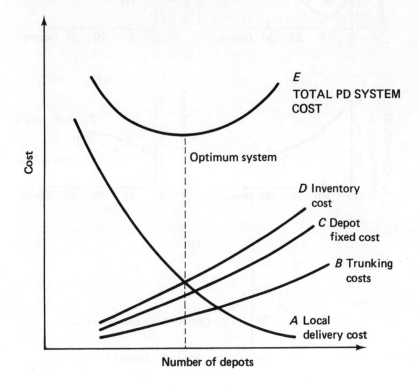

260

Fig 8.4 *total cost concept for PD systems*

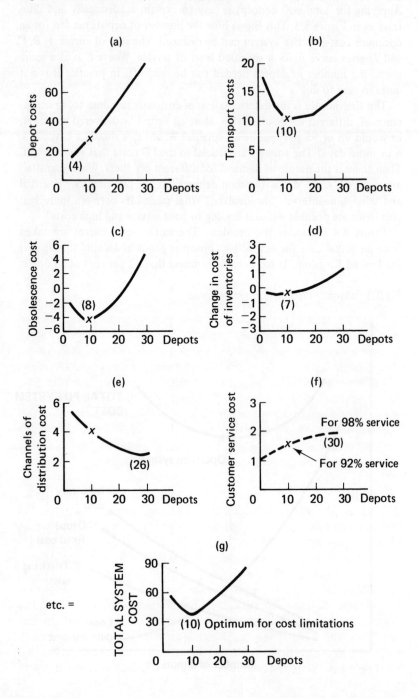

had to be delivered within 72 hours of orders being placed. This was the level of customer service found to be necessary and, taking the locations of the main markets into account, decisions were needed on the number of depots required and their locations. If minimising depot costs (a) was the sole criterion, only four depots were permitted but transport costs would be high. If the latter were to be minimised (b), without regard to other factors, ten or eleven depots were required. However if the obsolescence costs (c) of inventories was the only criterion then eight depots were advisable.

However, when inventory costs (d) were the only consideration, seven depots were indicated. If the main aim was to minimise the channel of distribution costs (e) ten depots would be needed. This number would also be sufficient to give the required service level (92 per cent) (f). Note however if the level of service was increased to 98 per cent some thirty depots would be required. That is for an improvement of only 6 per cent the number of depots needed would be trebled. When the total systems costs were taken into account (g), ten depots were needed and this number was selected. The depot costs for ten depots is shown on curves (a) to (f) by the mark x.

In practice the customer service level achieved was around 95 per cent so that the service provided was better than planned. The increased customer goodwill justified keeping the service at this level especially as the long-term leases on the depots did not permit an early change in the system. With present-day economic conditions and steeply rising operational costs and in 1979 the drop in demand for all products, the firm cut back to 8 depots as soon as leases permitted. This required adjustments to inventory levels, transportation and routing and after six months the customer service level was down to 91 per cent. However, in the conditions prevailing during 1980/82 there was no adverse effect on customer goodwill. The big savings in PD costs that this approach achieved were still worthwhile.

(c) Benefits
Apart from the benefits mentioned earlier, an efficient, integrated PD system offers other benefits. Profitability can be improved not only because of cost savings but also because the detailed study of all facets of PD will show when it is advantageous to switch expenditure from one item to another, or when to change a method, for example the mode of transport used. While air freight is more expensive per unit than surface transport, for instance, the faster deliveries, lower inventories and inventory costs, less damage and loss in transit and maintained delivery promises will provide customers with a better service. This may persuade customers to put more business (larger quantities and orders for other items not hitherto bought) the firm's way. Thus PDM represents a 'value' which companies can use to

enhance the attractiveness of their operations to potential customers. Higher levels of service can be maintained while keeping costs under control and at reasonable levels.

8.3 DEVELOPMENTS IN PD

Many developments in retailing have led to the need for more efficient PD. The growth of large organisations, such as supermarkets, and the intensification of competition between them, with the need to keep prices down, led to the development of own or house brands. Manufacturers' sales staff became more concerned with account management than simply selling. The immense purchasing power of these organisations also demanded efficient service. Old, slipshod distribution methods were no longer acceptable and business went to producers who could guarantee efficient delivery.

Scrambled merchandising (retailers carrying an ever-increasing range of goods and not just their traditional items, e.g. in Britain note the range of products now sold by W. H. Smith – originally stationers and book and magazine sellers – and Boots the Chemist) increased. It became difficult to classify retailers accurately. Delivery problems (because of the variety of products to be dropped at any one delivery point and the varying quantities involved) became more complicated. For example the assortment of food and non-food goods required by supermarkets, the items sold by large chemists (ranging from medicines and chemist sundries to photographic equipment, toiletries and household goods) and the goods on sale in departmental stores (practically every item a consumer could require), have seen product ranges extended far beyond traditional practice.

In difficult economic conditions with demand for any one item declining, such proliferation might continue. On the other hand, if operating costs continue to rise at staggering rates, some outlets may be forced to cut back on their range of goods. This may simplify distribution problems but could just as well complicate them for systems designed for current, complex retailing methods. Further, the use of franchisees has increased. This may continue as a growth area as producers are forced to withdraw from as much of the distribution channel and work as is possible.

Developments in wholesaling include the use of more sophisticated management techniques, especially inventory control, resulting in improved efficiency and reduced operating costs. When wholesalers reduce their inventories, the onus is on the producers to provide a fast, efficient service in the delivery of replacement stocks. Wholesalers have attempted to move back to the producers the burden of carrying some of the stock needed in the distribution network. If the recession of 1979 and the early 1980s continues, this trend may continue.

With industrial products there has been a reduction in the lines carried by wholesalers and retailers. Some now specialise in very limited fields. Further, new technological developments (for example in electronic components, equipment, computer hardware and software) have resulted in the emergence of many specialist handling lines not adequately serviced by traditional middlemen. While this trend has simplified delivery to any one distributor, the multiplicity of distributors with their various specialised needs has complicated the PD system required for some industrial products.

Other developments arise from the need to provide a good PD service as an essential part of the marketing operation. Good control is needed of the service but this cannot be achieved without knowledge of the workings of other members of the network. Active participation in and support of the agreed system by all members of the network are essential. There must be better co-operation with appropriate inter-organisational information flows, not just product flows.

Also, assuming that the big retail chains will maintain their dominant position for many products in the marketing channel, despite economic difficulties, the heterogeneity of physical processing (as with pack sizes, delivery procedures and so on) on manufacturers will increase. Suppliers will have to try to achieve agreement on a wide range of points, from standard packs to mutually acceptable distribution and marketing policies.

Distribution is technologically orientated and the computer and modern mechanical handling equipment have played a big role in the development of PD systems. However, in the future it seems that the emphasis must be on service as the dominating goal. This will be coupled with more efficient overall control (not just of costs) of the system. Manufacturers will have to reach out beyond their own needs to obtain a properly integrated and co-operative network or system, otherwise effective system performance will be unlikely.

8.4 DISTRIBUTION IN THE EUROPEAN ECONOMIC COMMUNITY (EEC)

The European Economic Community is an important market for British goods, now part of the country's 'home' market since Britain joined the EEC. Firms must consider the PD networks that exist in partner nations. The variations are considerable and warrant study.

Since the formation of the Community, improved standards of living, greater use of cars, changes in consumer needs, increasing volume of business and rising cost of lands and buildings have led to fundamental changes in the distribution networks (wholesale and retail) in all member nations. The greatest growth has been in self-service stores selling high-volume goods at low margins. However, more recently, consumers have shown greater interest in specialised outlets in the commercial centres of urban areas. By the end of the 1970s there were indications that preference was being given to neighbourhood services rather than costly out-of-town shopping centres. The rising cost of fuel, which increased distribution costs and those of private motorists, may also favour this trend.

A report in 1979 (*Continental Retailing Groups*) by Management Horizons Ltd, exploded the myth that only in the United Kingdom is retailing power concentrated in a few firms. Table 8.4 shows the percentage share of total retail sales by multiples in the different countries covered by the report. The 25 largest groups (excluding symbol or buying groups) achieved sales of about £41 billion in 1978. There were also favourable comparisons with Britain on retail sales per square metre (£3000 or £280 per square yard) and sales per employee (£100,000) for the top 15 companies studied.

Table 8.4 **multiple traders' share of retail sales in Europe**

Country	% of national retail sales
Finland	57
Switzerland	46
West Germany	33
Sweden	30
Holland	29
France	27
Austria	20
Denmark	19
Belgium	16
Norway	15

EEC countries shown in italics

Source: Report: *Continental Retailing Groups* (Management Horizons Ltd, 1979).

Some general observations are possible. For the most part British distributive firms are larger than their European counterparts at both wholesale and retail levels. They are backed up by the manufacture of most consumer goods on a much larger scale than in other countries, except perhaps Germany. The larger British retailers tend to be more profitable than their counterparts in Europe due to the larger scale of their operations and greater efficiency, rather than higher gross margins. Also, they have greater experience in large-scale mass distribution and in centralised buying of consumer goods. On the other hand, they do not use space as intensively as their Community counterparts as a matter of policy based on consumer preference.

(a) Wholesaling

The number of wholesaling establishments in the EEC is about 400,000, but these include businesses handling livestock, grain, petroleum, skins, building materials, machinery, other raw materials as well as finished consumer goods. This figure also includes firms engaged in importing and exporting and those who sell products to industrial users and other wholesalers as well as to retailers. Allowing for the difference in definition, the wholesaling business is much larger in Britain than other EEC countries. Yet wholesaling plays a smaller role, relative to retailing, in Britain than in her partner nations. For every person employed in wholesaling about six are in retailing, whereas in the rest of Europe, excluding Ireland and Italy, the ratio is 1:2.5.

However, statistics reveal that wholesaling business in consumer goods trades are on average much larger in Britain than in other EEC countries, though wholesalers play a more important role in the distribution of food and textiles in other EEC nations than in Britain. For example in Britain about 40 per cent of all foodstuffs pass through wholesaling channels but in Germany the proportion is over 50 per cent and in France it is 60 per cent. A similar situation exists in the clothing and textile trades.

The relatively greater importance of wholesaling in other EEC countries is a reflection of the large share of the market held by large-scale retailers in Britain who deal directly with their sources of supply. The more fragmented nature of retailing on the Continent is another reason, as is the generally smaller scale of production and marketing. All these factors place greater dependence on wholesaling. The greater distances involved, smaller manufacturing units and fragmented retailing also limit the possibility of direct sales from producers to retailers. In consumer goods the importance of wholesalers is also influenced by the share of total trade held by voluntary wholesale chains, which is much higher in the other EEC countries than in Britain.

To summarise, the whole distribution network plays a more important role throughout Continental Europe than in Britain. Further, British wholesalers operate on a larger scale than their counterparts in the EEC. Finally, as a result of joining the EEC the importance of the British wholesaling trade has increased further.

(b) Retailing

There are a number of similarities in the pattern of retailing in EEC countries and these are greater than the dissimilarities. While in practice it is better to concentrate on the trends towards a pattern that is familiar rather than on the differences that exist currently, a summary of the major differences in each country is necessary for the purpose of this book.

France is a country of contrasts. It has the largest departmental stores and superstores and the largest regional shopping centres of the whole EEC. However, it has also a very large number of traditional shops often using methods of the nineteenth century. It has too a network of open and covered markets. A third of the shops employ only one person. A third of all poultry purchases and a quarter of purchases of fruit and vegetables are made in a market or at a farm. The retailing system is thus more fragmented than in Germany or Britain and resembles that of the Netherlands. This is in part due to the low density of population making mass marketing difficult to achieve.

The conservative nature of the distribution system is due to greater specialisation and more extensive, traditional processing by retailers. For example, the function of the *patisserie* (cakes and pastries) and the *boulangerie* (bread) are fulfilled in Britain by bakers.

The French consumers prefer products and services adapted to individual needs. They do not readily accept mass-produced goods, though this reluctance has been reduced in recent years. While recent trends have been away from the small shopkeeper, the development of low-cost retailing techniques has been slower than in Britain. Most retailers still prefer high margins rather than high volume for their profits. To exercise the same control or influence over distribution channels is more expensive than in Britain. Selling and distribution costs are higher because of the large number of intermediaries at each stage.

The main development of the 1970s was the creation of hypermarkets (mass merchandisers) often on green-field sites. This spontaneous proliferation was the result of rapid and haphazard urban development with poor shopping facilities. Run on similar lines to American discount houses, they had an immediate impact on sales of a wide range of non-food items. In 1953 the State, motivated by the desire to regularise transactions, helped to establish markets of national importance responsible for marketing perishable foodstuffs, especially fruit and vegetables. By the mid-1970s twenty such markets were in operation handling 4 million tonnes of goods. The big Paris-Rungis market along handled 1.4 million tonnes. Private enterprise, encouraged by attractive credit terms, established 24 wholesale distribution centres handling a wide range of industrial products.

In *Germany* the development of modern PD systems outstripped those in Britain. The application of the low margin, high turnover principle is long established. Self-service and supermarket stores of all kinds abound, many handling a wide range of food and non-food lines. However, unlike Britain, there are fewer food stores than non-food ones. However, a third of the retail trade is accounted for by food stores.

Discount houses have also been developed more rapidly and mail order is well established. However, the distribution structure is said to be more fragmented in that there are fewer very large multiples, probably because of the long-established strength of independent retailers (and wholesalers). The most important are the retailer co-operatives which are retailer organised. The combined share of total sales by the large-scale retailers exceeds 70 per cent, higher than in any other EEC country. Over 500 superstores have been opened but there has been a decline in the total number of retail units.

Italy, despite industrial growth, still has a distribution system that largely is appropriate to a low-level economy. It still has a large number of small, independent outlets. Many seem scarcely viable but survive because of the system of local licensing. The average size is small (2 employees per outlet) and some 40 per cent of fixed shops are less than 250 square feet in size. In contrast the variety chains, Standa (Montedison) and La Rinascente-Upim are large by any European standards.

Since Italians prefer individualised merchandise and services, the middlemen are partial processors and finishers of many goods. Commercial co-operation has been less eagerly adopted partly because individual retailers have less need for defensive coalitions. Despite this, multiple shops operating supermarkets have increased. However, the absence of really strong multiple shop competition has allowed the consumer co-operative movement, retail buying groups and voluntary wholesale chains to expand, if slowly.

The effect of the inadequacies of the system is to keep distribution costs high. This is not only due to trade margins being high but also because selling and distribution costs are heavy, since a large number of distributors have to be reached. For example, in the grocery trade, manufacturers' sales forces can number 500 or more! Thus many manufacturers avoid traditional distribution channels and prefer vertical integration.

By contrast, *Belgium* has one of the highest densities of retail outlets in proportion to its population, with resultant low throughput per outlet (second only to Italy). However, the three largest firms (Inno-BM, Sarma and GB Enterprises) account for more than 15 per cent of retail sales, the highest concentration in Europe. However, retailing is still a family business though since the 1960s some 30 per cent of grocery outlets have closed and voluntary chains have been developed. In relation to its population and area the country is a leader in the development of large closed-mall shopping centres and superstores. Belgium has experienced considerable penetration by American firms. For example, the third and sixth largest retailers, Sarma and Galeries Anspach, are owned by J. C. Penney and Sears respectively.

Multiple shops in the food trades have increased since the 1960s but the number of outlets have been reduced. In the non-food trades the number of multiple shops is limited and few have full national coverage. Their total share of the trade is low. Multiples have been hampered in their development by their associated chains of franchised retailers. These were originally set up to circumvent legislation which, until the 1960s, prohibited the *grands magasins* from expanding beyond their 1937 positions. However, in the last two decades, self-service stores have been expanded and the highest rate of conversion, as in Britain, has been in food stores. There has also been expansion of superstores and supermarkets and multiple shop retailing in the non-food trades. Specialised non-food outlets have also been increased.

The general system in *Luxembourg* is similar to that of Belgium except that large-scale retailers and very large shops do not exist. In 1932 laws were passed that effectively prohibited departmental stores and the creation of new multiple shop organisations. Existing ones were also prohibited from opening new branches, while consumer co-operative societies came under this legislation also. This prevented all but limited growth in new forms of trading. In 1962 these laws were confirmed. However, recently, the restriction of retailers to only one line of merchandise has been interpreted more liberally.

The *Netherlands* has well-organised retailers of all sizes. The bigger firms have large-scale operations and account for over 15 per cent of total sales. Thus the country has a low density of retail outlets for its population and less than 5 per cent of the outlets are not affiliated to a retail co-operative, voluntary chain, consumer co-operative or multiple chain. The voluntary chain is by far the most important and its strength is due to early acceptance by consumers and the rapid development of self-service trading. The last accounts for 75 per cent of total retail outlets.

There are fewer food stores than non-food ones and the use of private labels has lagged behind the development of self-service trading. Retailers are reluctant to lose the benefits of advertising by manufacturers and the usually higher margins available on nationally branded lines.

Medium and small-size retailers are strongly organised in buying groups and voluntary chains of all kinds. The latter are usually associations of wholesalers and retailers who use a group name and possess a central co-ordinating body. Many of the smaller groups are regional rather than national.

Since 1945 the main concern was to integrate retail trading into an urban framework. Facilities were relocated within reach of consumers living in the new residential areas of expanding towns, in consumer centres containing other collective facilities. The policy of keeping urban areas alive and economically sound is the reason for opposition to the development of green-field sites for distributive purposes.

In the *Republic of Ireland (Eire)*, hypermarkets are not a substantial, characteristic feature of retailing because of the low urban concentration. However, town centre renewal programmes have resulted in the construction of shopping centres. Itinerant, motorised traders continue to be of great importance. As with Britain, Germany, the Netherlands and Denmark there are no specific regulations on the opening of commercial outlets.

Nearly 50 per cent of all retail trade takes place in the city of Dublin and its suburbs. The sales per retail outlet in Dublin is about three times greater than that in the rest of the country. Dublin has departmental stores, supermarkets, shopping centres and variety stores while the rest of the country has general stores and public houses selling grocery goods and other items. In the country, purchases from farms are not recorded in official statistics of retail sales.

Multiple-shop trading in non-food items is relatively under-developed. In both the food and non-food trades British multiple-shop organisations have long operated a limited number of branches in Eire. However, in recent years there have been developments of large retailing units, super-markets and shopping centres in Dublin, Limerick, Cork and some other towns.

In *Denmark* retailing is dominated by the importance of the Copenhagen market, some 40 per cent of total sales taking place there. However, the main growth has been in suburban shopping centres of the city rather than in the central commercial zone. Departmental stores are well established but outside Copenhagen only three towns are large enough to support medium-sized stores. Variety stores have also been developed and the co-operative movement accounts for over 15 per cent of total sales. The latter and private trade, inspired by Swedish firms, have played a major role in the growth of retail sales.

Multiple-shop trading and chains of variety stores have been slow to develop because of a law which limited the number of branches that could be operated by a retailer in one commune, unless the retailer was also a producer. This produced a distorted pattern of multiple-shop organisations, most of which were integrated with production. However, the repeal of this law permitted more normal development but the geographical charac-ter of the country presents problems of control for any firm seeking national coverage.

The consumer co-operative movement has been very active. In 1973 the individual societies merged into a single one covering the whole country. It is the biggest single force in the food trades. Growth in the number of supermarkets and variety stores has been accompanied by a reduction in the number of individual food establishments. Multiple-shop organisations, influenced by Swedish and British experience, have developed well in non-food trades but the retail buying groups offer strong competition to them. Traditional departmental stores have limited opportunities for expansion except in new shopping centres.

Greece joined the EEC on 1 January 1981. The distribution network and problems are very similar to those found in the Republic of Ireland, Denmark and Italy. Over a third of the population is located in Attica, in and around Athens. If Thessalonika is taken into consideration, over 50 per cent of the population is in these two areas. Four-fifths of the country is mountainous and very sparsely populated. Road and rail communications are limited and the sea still forms the major means of communication, no townships being more than 100 kilometres from the sea.

While Athens has supermarkets and departmental stores, most of the distributors (wholesalers and retailers) are small family operations serving the local community, similar to the Italian pattern. However, because of the concentration of the population, consumer goods sales forces do not need to be as large as those in Italy. While there has been considerable industrial development, the economy is still relatively precarious. Agriculture has lagged behind industrial production despite growth of the working population in the farm sector (31 per cent). Mainly small farmers working under difficult conditions, they make only a small contribution to the GDP. Industrial growth has been concentrated around Athens and Thessalonika and not all sectors have been as successful as engineering, textiles and petrochemicals. Greece has one of the world's largest shipping fleets.

The country has a growing trade deficit because of its dependence on imported capital goods. This is partially offset by foreign currency earned by tourism and shipping. Inflation has been higher than in any other Western country.

The meaning normally ascribed to the different types of organisations in the EEC are shown in Table 8.5.

ASSIGNMENTS

1 Your company's distribution activities have been run on the traditional fragmented basis. A junior production executive has been in control of inventories and depots while Marketing has specified and selected the channels of distribution and methods of transportation used. This has proved expensive and inefficient. The firm has decided to introduce the concept of physical distribution management and you have been appointed PD Manager. Because of the hostility to this move you have decided that you will produce a paper showing the role of PD, the impact it has on more profitable and efficient marketing and the importance of an integrated system, for circulation to all executives. Prepare such a paper.

2 Subsequently you find it necessary to show why it is necessary to select channels of distribution carefully in relation to the firm's products and markets and why the total cost concept is also vital. How would you go about demonstrating this to colleagues? Prepare a paper.

Table 8.5   some EEC definitions of distributive organisations

Consumer co-operative societies	Organisations engaged in retail trade that operate on co-operative principles.
Departmental store	A large retail establishment with at least 2500 square metres of selling space, selling at least 5 different groups of merchandise (of which one must be women's apparel), in separate departments.
Multiple shop organisations	Organisations operating 10 or more retail establishments. (Does not include consumer co-operatives, departmental and variety stores).
Retail buying group	Sometimes called a retail co-operative, is a group of retailers who have agreed to purchase some of their supplies in common and to participate in other joint activities.
Supermarkets	Retail establishments selling mainly foodstuffs by self-service, with a minimum of 400 square metres of selling space.
Superstore or Hypermarket	Retail organisation with at least 2500 square metres of selling space, selling by self-service a wide range of goods, of which half is food. Parking spaces are provided for customers' cars and the stores are located at the edge of towns or outside of towns.
Variety chain stores	Operate 10 or more establishments and sell a wide range of goods.
Voluntary wholesale chains	Where a single wholesaler (or a group of wholesalers) operates with retail members in both buying and retailing activities.
Wholesale buying group	An arrangement whereby wholesalers in the same trade co-operate for the purpose of buying and other joint activities.

3 Some years later the company decides to expand its sales to EEC countries. Initially this will be confined to consumer goods. Prepare a report for the Board outlining the differences that will be encountered and how these may require modifications to the company's PD system as used for sales in Britain.

4 You are then asked if the PD system as used is applicable to other overseas markets. What would be your reaction for (a) major developed countries and (b) developing nations?

CHAPTER 9

SOME OTHER ASPECTS
OF MARKETING

This chapter will cover other major points of marketing.

9.1 OTHER COMPONENTS OF THE MARKETING MIX

Executives often believe that the task of marketing has been completed when the finished product (or service) has been promoted, sold and delivered to the ultimate customer. This is indeed not so.

(a) After-sales service (or 'product service')

For most products and services there is need for some kind of after-sales service (often called 'product services') to customers, even if at first they do not realise that they have such a requirement. After-sales services are needed by industry and the consumer. They range from expert opinion, advice and assistance on the use or application of the product and maintenance and repair in the case of household appliances, manufacturing plant and other equipment. The work includes advice on, and assistance with, modifications to plant, on site, to improve the efficiency of its operation. These product services should not be confused with what are called 'service industries' (discussed in Section 9.4).

After-sales services are required, for example, when household appliances (refrigerators, cookers, washing-machines, vacuum cleaners, other gadgets) require regular maintenance and repairs. They are needed for the same reasons for television sets, radios, tape-recorders, video-tape machines, cars, motor-cycles and lawn-mowers. In industry, maintenance and repairs have to be done on all machinery (drills, lathes, millers, cranes, furnaces and other equipment), trucks (goods and fork-lift) and anything else that is subjected to normal wear and tear.

Then there are the product services required for specialised items. For example, computer users, besides needing normal maintenance and repair services, also require the assistance of systems analysts. They trace the flow of information, decisions and organisation inputs and outputs of clients. They can then make recommendations on how their computers and software should be used to give customers appropriate and efficient systems. Thus computer manufacturers ensure that not only are customer satisfactions achieved, but also that they create a successful business for themselves. Similarly firms need advice and help on the use of office equipment such as photocopiers, typewriters and word processors.

Finally, with bought-in items (metals, plastics, resins, lubricants, fuels and other consumables) users need advice and assistance on their efficient use. This can range from help on how to use expensive fuels and materials economically (vital in times of scarcity and high costs) to highly technical aspects concerning how bought-in goods may be best incorporated into the customer's finished products. For example, paint manufacturers may need advice on which resins to use to improve the corrosion-resistance of their paints. Other manufacturers may need advice on how best to use plastic granules when extrusion or blow-moulding of their products are involved.

The consumer also requires assistance in areas other than to do with household machinery. For women this can range from advice on how to make the best use of a sewing-machine, to fabric care in cleaning and the correct choice and use of cosmetics. For men, advice may be needed on the use of hand and mechanised tools in 'do-it-yourself' work, on correct maintenance of the home, on electrical safety measures and car maintenance. All offer opportunities for after-sales services that boost the sales of goods and the reputation of the firms providing them.

Thus after-sales services play a major role in the marketing mix by enhancing the saleability of products, ensuring repeat buys by satisfied customers not only of the items concerned, but also of the firm's other products and in establishing and sustaining market leadership status. However, all these services cost money and costs can be high. While for maintenance and repair services it is normal to charge for the work, in other forms of assistance this cannot always be done (for example, home advice on the use of cosmetics). In such instances the cost is allowed for, to some extent, in the sale prices of the product, but if competition is strong there is a limit to how much can be 'built into' the unit price. Then the service provided must aim at securing greater sales than would be possible without it, to justify the cost of the service.

(b) Warranties and guarantees

The usual form of product warranty assures the purchaser that the item will be replaced, or repaired free of labour costs, or there will be refund of the purchase price should the product prove defective within a specified time. With cars, warranties are normally couched in terms of time (a number of years) and mileage, whichever is the longer. Warranties increase the confidence customers have in the product and its manufacturer and can stimulate demand. The warranty is described as a subsidiary promise or collateral agreement, a breach of which allows the buyer to make certain claims (for damage or restitution of loss etc.) against the vendor. The warranty may be 'express' (deriving from a specific agreement) or 'implied' (deriving from the operation of law).

A guarantee is an assurance (express or implied) of the quality of the goods supplied (or that the price asked is the lowest on the market etc.). There is usually a promise of a refund in the event of poor performance, or if the goods are not as described. It is used as a sales aid, especially for mail-order business. In this case the goods cannot be inspected before purchase and the guarantee is to assure customers of the good standing and reputation of the vendor and the products offered.

So warranties and guarantees are also important components of the marketing mix. When the marketing mix is being planned, the nature, content and extent of the warranties and guarantees to be offered should also be considered. They are particularly effective when the product price is high, or when it is bought infrequently, or the product is seen as a complex one with considerable technical content. They are also important when the firm's market share is small. It is now common practice to give warranties for all major items purchased, though guarantees are given when it would be inappropriate to give a warranty, or when it could not be enforced. Guarantees would be given for raw materials and other consumables incorporated into other goods and for home use items such as soaps, detergents, cleaning fluids, cosmetics and toiletry items, especially when the items are highly essential or important to the customer or when health and safety in home or work-place are concerned.

Finally, there is the question of misleading warranties and guarantees. Theoretically a warranty offers two-way protection. First, it protects the customer against losses due to the purchase of defective goods. Second, it limits the vendors' liabilities for repair and replacement. However, extensive use of 'legalese' can cause confusion. Laymen may find it difficult, or impossible, to decipher the true terms of the warranty and thus fail to make proper use of it for their protection. In other cases the terms may be deliberately misleading, purporting to offer security when legal interpretation shows that no real protection exists. It may not be possible to meet the conditions of the 'warranty'. Such misleading warranties and guarantees are eventually harmful not only to the offending firm, but possible also, in the end, to the whole industry.

(c) Codes of practice

Marketing, like other management techniques, has been subjected to misuse and abuse. The activities of 'dirty tricks' groups can fool many customers into making bad purchases (either buying the wrong item or one they do not need or simply a faulty product). This results in intense customer dissatisfaction. In recent years codes of practice for marketing and other business activities (e.g. banking, insurance, car and other maintenance) have been devised, often by government initiative and participation. These codes call for the development of, and adherence to, some 'professional ethic' based on the concepts of dignified professionalism and decent behaviour. These are supposed to transcend organisational and individual goals and ethics (or lack of them!) and the relentless drive for higher profits, come what may. They require the existence of a peer organisation that can exercise sanctions against offenders (e.g. the professional associations or institutes of accountants, lawyers, engineers, dentists, doctors, stockbrokers and company directors). Table 9.1 summarises the points covered by the codes for marketing in Britain and the United States of America.

Table 9.1 marketing codes of practice

1 *Britain*
All members of the Institute of Marketing are answerable to its Council for conduct which, in the opinion of the Council is in breach of its Code of Practice. The Council may take disciplinary action against any offending member. The Code covers the following points of professional conduct:

honesty; professional competence; conflict of interest; securing and developing business; confidentiality of information; adherence to other relevant codes (advertising, sales promotion, public relations, market research); procedures for handling complaints; misuse of the Code; etc.

2 *United States of America*
The American Marketing Association's Code of Ethics states:

As a member of the A.M.A., I recognise the significance of my professional conduct and my responsibilities to society and to other members of my profession:

1. By acknowledging my accountability to society as a whole as well as to the organisation for which I work.
2. By pledging my efforts to assure that all presentation of goods, services and concepts to be made honestly and clearly.
3. By striving to improve marketing knowledge and practice in order to better serve society.
4. By supporting free consumer choice in circumstances that are legal and are consistent with generally accepted community standards.
5. By pledging to use the highest professional standards in my work and in competitive activity.
6. By acknowledging the right of the A.M.A., through established procedure, to withdraw my membership if I am found to be in violation of ethical standards of professional conduct.

Such codes are also important elements of the marketing mix in that they set the tone and standard of marketing conduct, assuring customers of the firm's integrity. Thus they can enhance demand for its products or services. The codes are not immediately apparent to customers except in the manner and conduct of the firm and its staff. They become more apparent when complaints arise. How quickly and well the firm responds to them sets the tone for future business. In times of increasing 'consumerism' (see Section 9.3(b)) the existence of, and adherence to, codes of practice becomes even more important for all marketing operations.

9.2 MARKETING PLANNING AND MARKETING PLANS

Marketing planning may be done formally or informally, in simple or sophisticated manner. However it is done, planning these days is inevitable when economic and other market conditions pose a choice of alternative courses of action. For example, which factors are important in any analysis of market conditions? Should the marketing be centralised or decentralised for administrative or operational purposes? What should be the firm's marketing goals and social concern or responsibility? Should it be operational- or product-orientated or geographically based? What resources are needed and how can they be obtained? What methods of control and evaluation would be best? How should the various components of the marketing mix be combined and what costs are permitted?

These and other points have made it advisable for there to be formal marketing planning. Whether it is simple or complex in nature depends on the tasks to be done, the problems to be overcome and the sophistication of the staff and how they operate most efficiently. The dynamic nature of markets, their increasing complexity and fierceness of competition have forced executives to give more attention to formal and scientific methods of marketing planning as explained earlier in this book.

The chief marketing executive (marketing director or manager) is responsible for the planning of the goals, product-market offerings, price, organisation and resources in general for the marketing department. These are co-ordinated with the plans of the other divisions (manufacturing, finance, personnel). In fact the planning process starts in each department or sub-department with staff reviewing past performance and identifying the reasons for successes and failure, how the former could be developed and the latter overcome. They can then indicate what performance would be possible in the next planning period, given the status quo and given specified additional resources or changes. In co-operative communications with colleagues from other departments, in the marketing division and with appropriate departments of other divisions, agreement is reached on the overall marketing plans that should be implemented in the next operational period.

Communications in the planning work are both vertical (throughout the marketing division) and lateral (between marketing and other divisions). The work is guided by the corporate objectives indicated as desirable by the board and the need to be realistic. Objectives that cannot be evaluated or achieved and strategies and tactics beyond the firm's capabilities have no part to play here. Attempts to incorporate them into the plan can lead only to problems and impede effective action programmes.

Plans are expressed in detail for about the first two years of the planning period and then in progressive outline for later years. Performance is reviewed at the end of every sales period (week, fortnight or month) but not revised until two or three sales periods have passed. This makes sure that response is made only when changes can be judged to be reasonably permanent. That is, no adjustments are made for what may turn out to be just momentary deviations. At the revision stage, a further time period equivalent to the length of the review one is brought into the total plan. Thus the total plan always covers the full number of years for which planning was done in the first instance. This is known as the 'rolling plan' approach. Marketing planning is a continuous process, as shown by Figure 9.1. Note the two-way flow of information as represented by the double arrows.

(a) Marketing objectives

The objectives, or goals, or targets normally used are:

profit (£s)
return on investment (%)
sales (in units) and turnover or revenue (£s)
market shares (%)
profit to sales and other relevant control ratios (%)
annual rates of growth (%) for all the above

They are the means whereby performance can be measured and actions controlled. These goals should be broken down into separate sets of targets where firms operate in more than one technology or industry and where market or customer factors indicate this to be advisable. They become a focus for individual motivation besides being the basis for co-ordination and planning in the marketing division and throughout the enterprise.

The profit target is important since, for any given pricing situation, until it has been established decisions on permitted costs cannot be made. It sets the parameters for the pricing policies to be followed. Further, the profit earned determines how well employees may be remunerated and financiers rewarded for the capital they have placed in trust with the company. The return on investment target judges how well the firm is

278

Fig 9.1 *marketing planning*

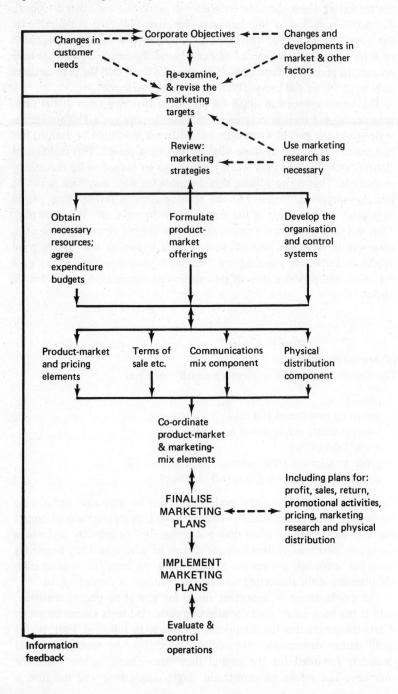

utilising the assets (capital) invested in it. These two are used by investors to judge if the company is well managed.

The sales and turnover targets indicate what has to be achieved to realise the profit and return goals and what manufacturing, personnel and financial resources are required. Market share targets indicate the competitive abilities of the company and the market positions the firm must achieve to contain or overcome competition. Too small a market share makes the firm vulnerable to larger competitiors. Too large a share may invite attacks on its markets by smaller competitors. Annual rates of growth targets offer a reasonable challenge to executives to do better each year and so build the firm's financial and economic strengths for future growth and development.

(b) The marketing plan

The marketing plan is the principal operational and control document of the marketing department. It specifies what has to be done, when it is to be done, who does what, how it will be done and the targets to be achieved. It will also set out the expenditure budgets permitted for each activity and the return these must obtain. The plan gives firm direction to the operation and helps to co-ordinate the work of all divisions of the firm while motivating staff to achieve ever-improving results. It provides a systematic written approach to planning and action and sets the standards against which progress will be measured.

It provides a record of the reasoning behind marketing decisions that have been taken. It also identifies areas of strengths and weaknesses so that the firm may exploit the first and avoid or eliminate the second. The plan examines and suggests the alternative courses of action by which targets may be achieved. It presents recommendations to senior management in such a way as to be easily understood, permitting correct decisions to be taken quickly.

The purpose of the marketing plan is to show where the firm has got to at a given date and where it is going if no changes are made. In addition, it must show where the firm should be going in the light of market and other changes, how it will get to its new position and the date, a few years hence, when it should get there. The plan will also show the estimated costs and benefits and what changes in the organisation are necessary. It should also define the alternative courses of action that should be taken if less likely, forecasted events do occur. That is, the plan must have in-built flexibility.

There are many ways a marketing plan may be written. Each firm must decide what is the best for its purpose and method of operation. However, the plan should be long on figures and statistics and short on words. There should be sufficient of the latter only to give meaning to the former and explain the rationale. If long reports on past performance, history, competition, some research and so on are necessary, these should be put in as appendices for those who must read them. The main points that should be covered by the plan are listed in Table 9.2. The questions that have to be considered are shown in Table 9.3.

9.3 MARKETING AND SOCIETY

Readers' attention is drawn to the comments in Section 2.1 ('Business and Society'). Consideration will be given in this section to marketing's involvement in, and responsibilities to, society.

The traditional concept of business responsibility concerns executives' accountability to customers, investors and employees. With customers, executives are required to provide quality products or services at reasonable prices. With investors, it is a question of securing acceptable return for the funds entrusted to the firm. Finally, with employees it is a question of providing employment at adequate remuneration which is seen to be fair. However, business and marketing's responsibilities are now seen to extend to society at large. It is no longer sufficient to meet only the three points mentioned above. On their own they are not considered socially responsible objectives.

Socially responsible marketing decisions must take into account the eventual long-term consequences of the actions taken. Future generations, as well as existing ones, must be taken into consideration. For example marketing decisions should show regard for the problems facing people in low income areas. As things are, urban and rural poor tend to pay more for their merchandise than the better-off living in the suburbs. This is not due to any deliberate policy decisions but rather to the realities (costs, etc.) of the service and quality that can be offered to markets with limited demand. Should this continue? Or should firms devise marketing policies that permit eradication of this inequality, even if it means sacrifice of some part of their profit?

There are other aspects of social responsibility. One is the relationship that should exist between this responsibility and the profit motive. In simple theory, it may be justified to strive for optimal levels of profit and to follow appropriate pricing policies. However, if it causes deprivation for the less affluent and poor, is it justified, especially in the long term?

Next, there are the associated pricing decisions. Is it right to charge more than a product's value, even in times of scarcity? But what 'value' has a product? This depends on the contribution it makes to customers' needs and the degree of essentiality or desirability as perceived by users. Much of what is judged to be 'value' is really in the imaginations of customers and may not be factually correct. For example a Rolls-Royce car has no greater utility value than any other car but the prestige of

Table 9.2   **marketing plan – contents**

1	*Subject*	Brief statement of the product groups or activities covered by the plan.
2	*Period*	Specifies the length of time covered by the plan and the starting date.
3	*Products*	Defines the products in detail.
4	*Targets*	Specifies the quantities to be achieved in each year of the plan for the objectives listed in Section 9.2(a) of the text.
5	*Basic campaign plan*	Indicates in general terms what has to be done to achieve targets.
6	*Sales targets*	Chiefly a set of tables setting out the sales to be achieved for each product, territory and salesperson and sometimes of customer groups or large customers.
7	*Market shares*	Another set of tables showing the market shares to be achieved by each product (or product group) and sales territory.
8	*Profit plans*	A further set of tables showing the profit to be earned by each product group, sales territory and salesperson (if possible also, the return on investment).
9	*Product plans*	Details the product modifications and rationalisations that will be needed.
10	*New products*	Because of the detailed work involved, usually best for this to be shown separately from (9) above.
11	*Pricing plans*	Details the pricing strategy, policy and unit prices, discounts etc. to be followed.
12	*Sales campaign*	Full details of summary given in (5) above.
13	*Promotions plan*	Specifies the advertising, sales promotions and public relations campaigns to be followed. Should include media schedules.
14	*Competition*	Details the competition to be overcome.
15	*Distribution*	Specifies all aspects of physical distribution, including channels and methods, transportation, inventories, depots to be used.
16	*R and D*	Sets out the research and development work: marketing dept. see as necessary if the targets and long-term development are to be achieved.
17	*Finance*	All sections above incurring expenditure will have their budgets stated. Here these are collated and shown against the targets (profit and return) to be achieved.
18	*Organisation*	A statement of the organisation needed.
19	*Training*	States the training needs of the dept.

(For consumer goods there would also be sections dealing with merchandising, packaging and point-of-sale needs).

Table 9.3 **marketing planning - key questions**

Markets
What markets do we serve? Why? What market shares do we have? What are the volume trends? What factors are affecting this? Who are our competitors and what are their market shares? How are these changing? What markets should we be in? What are the ruling prices? How are these likely to change with cost and other changes?

Products
What products are we making? Why? What products are we selling? Why and how? What products are competitors offering? How do they compete? Where and why do they compete with us? What new activities and products are they planning? What product modification, rationalisation and new product development will we need? Over what time-scale? At what cost? How will this affect our prices, profits and return on investment?

Distribution
Which channels and what methods are we using? Why? Which are being used by competitors? Are customers getting the service they need? Any improvements possible? Any cost savings possible? What discounts are offered? Why?

Resources
What financial, plant and manpower resources are we using? What are our managerial and labour skills? How will all this have to be changed for the future? Availability? Costs?

Environment
How are economic, technological, legal, political, social and ethical aspects changing? How will this affect future business? How do population growth and movement affect demand? What is the firm's relationships with customers and society at large? Also with competitors? What other considerations (pollution, consumerism etc.) have to be taken into account?

owning one adds greatly to the concept of 'value' to those who can afford to buy it.

Then there are the unethical or illegal pricing practices, such as unfair pricing, price discrimination and collusion between manufacturers on the market prices that will be charged. While many nations have various price-control regulations, these practices still emerge from time to time. Further, there is the obligation of executives to their customers to warn them of impending changes in prices, discounts and related matters. Should they? They do not give advance warning of price reductions for fear that there will be a drop in sales and distributors will be left with stocks of more expensive items, as customers await the lower prices or better terms. However, they do sometimes give warning of pending price increases to influence customers to buy before prices go up. They can use this device to increase sales when they want this. Is this ethical? Should this double standard be maintained?

Product management is not immune from ethical questions. The points to consider here are planned obsolescence, product quality, packaging and brand similarity. Obsolesence is built into the product to make sure it does not last too long and so boost total sales by more frequent repurchases than would otherwise be necessary. Sometimes offering an item of lower quality will also assist this aim. Then by putting, for example, expensive toiletries into containers with a thick base they may fool the unwary into thinking they are getting more for their money than is the fact. Running very similar brands can help to sell inferior products on the strength of the reputation of better products with similar names. Note also that when a longer-lasting product is introduced (e.g. the everlasting match) bigger competitors usually buy its manufacturing rights and do not introduce it on the market. It would damage the sales of their existing, shorter-life products.

Competitive pressures have forced some manufacturers to follow deceptive packaging methods. First, they use larger packets than necessary and so can give the impression they are offering more of the product than competitors at the same price. Or they use odd-size packs that make it difficult to compare prices. Further, bottles with concave bottoms can mislead on the actual quantity offered. Laws exist to make manufacturers show on the containers what net weight or volume is contained in them, but when a variety of sizes is involved it is not easy for the customer to make accurate assessments of unit prices.

However, the largest number of ethical questions arise with the promotional elements of the marketing mix. In advertisements are the messages conveyed accurate? Is an unfair sales advantage being obtained by slanting campaigns to children, women or ethnic groups? Do the advertisements play unnecessarily strongly on customers' desires, fears, prejudices or susceptibilities? Is the consumer given sufficient information to make sound buying decisions? Is the play on sexual connotations ethical? It may be acceptable in a modern permissive society, but is it fair? Is it right for advertisements of cosmetics to hint that they will turn every woman into a beautiful, glamorous creature when, in many instances, it would be a miracle if they did?

Similar problems arise with sales promotions. Do they give real value? Are all price offers real savings for what is supplied? How ethical or fair are direct-mail offerings? Could the identical item be obtained at the same or lower prices from normal retail outlets? Do the cheaper products offered represent as good value as the more expensive items obtained through normal channels? What is the real worth or utility of 'free gifts'? With public relations, how true is the information provided? Is sufficient information provided for readers to make correct assessments on the subject? (Here it is worth reminding the reader of the ethical standards set by the American Marketing Association as set out in Table 9.1.)

Next come the questions of pollution and destruction of the environment or ecology. Should firms continue to sell profitable products that users want if their use will pollute or destroy the environment? Should plant that gives noxious or dangerous effluents continue to be sold and used? Should dangerous additives (in food, cleaners, paints, clothing) continue to be used? Should items which create dangerous waste disposal problems continue to be sold? These are just some of the questions which have to be resolved if a firm's marketing ethics and social responsibility are to be of an high order. If acted upon correctly they could lead to loss of revenue and profit. Finding alternatives could be expensive.

Yet even when harm-free alternatives are available they are not used. Should whales continue to be slaughtered to provide the oils needed in cosmetics and for other uses? Should the only two remaining rain forests of the world be destroyed to allow increased mineral extraction when synthetics are available? Does the world need to be so profligate in the use of scarce minerals? Should the beauty of the countryside be ruined by opencast mining of coal, iron ore and gold to satisfy the apparently insatiable appetites of consumers? Should wildlife habitats and the wildlife itself be destroyed for the same reasons? The problems posed do not have easy solutions, but if the standard of life is not to be destroyed much more consideration of them, and resultant action, is needed.

(a) Consumer protection

The growing interest in this subject, plus the activities of a few unscrupulous 'businessmen', has led to increased legislation. These regulations were intended to give the consumer (and to a lesser extent industrial customers) more protection. In Britain the laws on the statute-book include those shown in Table 7.9. Of these, the ones most concerned with consumer protection are the *Consumer Credit Act, Fair Trading Act, Hire Purchase Acts, Resale Prices Act, Sale of Goods Act, Trade Descriptions Act,* and *Unsolicited Goods and Services Act* (see Table 7.9 for the relevant dates).

It is arguable that some of these laws do not in fact help or protect the consumer as was intended. For example, the *Resale Prices Act*, which ended manufacturers' right to fix resale prices, was meant to ensure that consumers would obtain products at fair prices and not at ones inflated by considerations other than the true economic levels. Alas, since sellers are free to sell goods at any price, there is no longer any guarantee that the price in one shop is the same as in all other outlets. Often the consumer may find later that other shops are selling the item at lower prices.

Thus the consumer would have to visit every shop to check prices (and, with pack variations, the net weights offered) to find out which shop has the best price. Even then this takes no account of price variations in other towns. The brunt of this perambulation falls heaviest on the overworked housewife. In most instances they just do not have the spare time or energy to inspect merchandise at several shops. They buy from their usual retail outlet whose advertising campaign may plug their claim that they offer the best value for money (interpreted by consumers as involving the cheapest price - which may be far from the truth). Thus a high percentage of shoppers are probably paying more than the most competitive prices.

Again the *Trades Description Act* was meant to prevent traders from using misleading descriptions of the goods offered, whether in terms of their properties, value, life and so on. In practice it has proved difficult to obtain sufficient evidence that would stand up in court and so achieve judgment in favour of the aggrieved customer. For example, there was the case of the tour operator who was taken to court because a picture in the company's brochure, of a beach barbecue dinner, was found to be of a different hotel, beach and resort from the ones implied by its location in their publication. The facilities complained about were inferior in all respects. The company won its case. The court accepted that the picture was meant *only to give a general indication* of the event and *not intended to be an exact presentation* of what customers would in fact experience! There have been several cases of a similar nature, on a wide range of goods and services, which obtained similar judgements. Though this interpretation may be acceptable in law, is it ethical and does the Act really protect consumers?

(b) Consumerism

Consumerism is described as the demand that firms give greater attention to consumer desires, not only with regard to product offerings, but also their standard of life and the long-term effects of the firm's actions. It is a protest against malpractice and abuses, some of which have been mentioned in the opening paragraphs of this section. It is an important part of the drive for greater social responsibility by firms. While creating short-term problems, it could offer new opportunities and challenges to marketing executives.

For example, the regulations governing the minimum depth of tyre tread permitted on cars, for road-safety considerations, present problems for the consumer who must buy new tyres more frequently. However, if some manufacturers can improve the working life of their tyres to give longer tread wear, they could obtain a bigger share of the market at the expense of those who do nothing about this. Regulations requiring cars to be safer will pose problems for the manufacturers who do not comply quickly enough. Those who can modify their products in a short time would again achieve increase in sales and market shares. However, until consumers are better educated on all related subjects, and thus become more knowledgeable, the claimed benefits of consumerism are not likely to be fully realised.

None the less the present consumer movement seems to be stronger and longer lasting than earlier attempts. It thrives in all EEC countries, Australia, Scandinavia and some others. Its demands are no longer just about consumption aspects but includes assessment of changes in technology, life-styles, public attitudes, affluence and the media. This is due to growing concern about the quality of life as incomes, standards of living and education improve. Another factor is the increased complexity of technology and marketing putting the buyer at an ever-growing disadvantage in relation to the seller. Then there are the stresses and strains developing in the economic and political systems, inflation, pollution, the population explosion, loss of faith in politicians and their institutions. Finally, there is the 'impersonality' due to the increasing size of firms and institutions, aggravated by computerisation and automation. The last two, consumers feel, are causing them to lose identity and just become numbers or cogs in the business and state machines.

On the other hand, not all protests on behalf of consumers are well founded. Many individuals and some organisations are misguided and badly informed. There is the unfortunate but true fact, also, that to the media bad practice is 'news' and good ones generally are not. So the public often gets a distorted view of the real position. Thus care is needed in evaluating the true value of any protest both as regards its source and its significance in the total context. Often protests just represent the personal views of the persons making them and are somewhat removed from those of society at large.

There is substantial agreement by business people and consumer organisations that the basic objectives of marketing and consumerism are not in conflict. There has been increasing acceptance of an 'environmental' view by many firms. Marketing is no longer concerned with only profit making (described as 'micro-profit applications') at the exclusion of all else. Company and industry self-regulation is developing, if slowly. Some firms have established consumer affairs departments. They do not deal just with complaints but study the total implications of company policies and actions. Some have produced codes of practice. These changes stress the dynamic nature of the marketing environment. Thus executives must keep themselves alert and informed on these subjects.

9.4 MARKETING OF SERVICES

The basic marketing concept applies to service industries as much as to manufacturing. The techniques may need to be modified to suit the special characteristics of the 'products' of servicing industries. The nature of services and their characteristics were discussed in Section 5.2(b) and listed in Table 5.2. Here the marketing of these services will be discussed.

Service industries span a wide range of activities and form one of the faster growing sectors of the economy of most countries, especially Western developed nations. They range from professional services (accountants, lawyers, doctors, dentists, management consultants, architects etc.) to more general services (post and telecommunications, transport, holiday and travel facilities, tourism, hotels, government departments and agencies such as defence, laundry, education, domestic help, design, research facilities and investment services) and the usual maintenance and repair services. There is also the provision of technical advice and assistance by product manufacturers. They are all required at some time by individual consumers and industrial and commercial enterprises though the last two are the largest users of many of these services.

The basic marketing approach is similar to that for manufactured goods. The service company must identify profitable market segments from the universe of potential users who have need for its services. It should forecast the size and nature of demand, the ruling market prices and the strength and nature of competition. The needs of the selected potential customers should be analysed to see if the services to be offered really meet their requirements. Forecasts have to be made of market shares, the prices to be used, the estimated profit and return on investment. Decisions have to be made on the resources that would be needed. Then decisions on how the services should be sold and promoted can be finalised. So too can decisions be taken on the organisation needed and the methods of control and supervision which will be used.

The above may prove more difficult to do in practice then to discuss academically, for various reasons. For example, in some professional services (doctors, lawyers, accountants) in some countries, self-imposed (or 'ethical') constraints are placed on pricing and the methods of selling that can be used. Often the latter is totally banned! Then most impose restrictions on the advertising that may be used and again there may be a total embargo on such activities. (In the United State of America, however, the restrictions are much less severe, the emphasis being placed on ethical standards.) Open competition may also be forbidden (see also Section 9.4(a) on the methods of regulation used).

Then there are services providing customer benefits which may not be immediately apparent or direct in nature. An example is life insurance which becomes effective when the buyer dies and the benefits are paid to the dependants. Another is the building societies (and banks) who make loans to house purchases. Customers are free to choose, within specified loan limits, where they live, the type of dwelling they buy, while in times of inflation they will show some long-term capital gain. The marketing activities of building societies will emphasis these derived benefits rather than the product (house) itself. These and other special characteristics make it difficult to find the true answers to the points mentioned in the third paragraph of this section. In the case of manufactured goods the important factors are obvious and understood and are governed by economic relationships (e.g. costs, life of product, user needs) and technical considerations.

Another difference is the fact that the lack of a physical product reduces the need for distributors or middlemen, though insurance brokers are essential to that industry and fulfil this function. Agency systems have however emerged for various services (travel and tourism, hotels, public transport including airlines, insurance and credit facilities). Then entry is governed by the skills, knowledge and reputation of the vendors rather than by a collection of expensive equipment, buildings and substantial capital. (However, in Britain and some other countries, banks, insurance companies and investment services have to put up substantial funds to satisfy the authorities that they are sufficiently solvent for the business they intend to launch.)

In the case of government services it may not be a case of stimulating demand but rather controlling it and, in hard times, reducing demand. However, in the case of some other government services (public health) they will have to stimulate demand for services such as vaccinations and inoculations as necessities in preventative medicine. Then government departments may have to persuade firms to export more and to convert indifferent groups of consumers to accept other services. They may have to make consumers aware of hitherto unrealised needs. Thus there is a requirement for marketing here also, albeit in greatly modified forms.

For all services, people (staff) are the prime asset, or 'capital' of the firms. Their behaviour, conduct and knowledge are critical factors since customers will rate the firms according to these staff abilities. Apathetic or hostile staff will lose business for a firm, whether restaurant, hotel, travel agent, tour operator, bank or insurance company, to mention a few. A lax lawyer, or unhelpful official in a government agency, will also create customer dissatisfaction. A courier with a tour operator who does not know the country or is not interested in the people in his or her charge will give rise to customer complaints and they may not return the following year to that company. In all these cases the customers will probably transfer their business to a more efficient competitor.

Thus in service industries the 'salesforces', all who deal with customer enquiries and sell the firm's services, are more important than in manufacturing industries. Their role is more substantial even if they do not see themselves as 'salespersons'. So staff management, recruitment and training are very important parts of the planning and design of all service industries.

The pricing of services can also pose problems. The low cost of entry leads to more intensive competition. This, coupled with the inability of customers to evaluate correctly the true worth and relevance of the services they buy, results in prices being low and very slim profit margins. Manufacturing industry's traditional cost-plus pricing methods cannot be followed when staff is the major cost element. Insufficient allowance is made for other cost elements and margins are squeezed further. With some services (travel agents, for example) where their own income and revenue is obtained by a limited discount (10 per cent in the case mentioned) on the total business placed, profit margins are small.

Thus many service industries cannot generate the funds to afford expensive or sophisticated marketing operations. They have to think very carefully about which marketing activities they need and how these can be used efficiently and with minimum costs. Even marketing research may have to be done in carefully planned annual packets. With a carefully thought-out programme for several years, a service firm can build a good information bank. Thus service industries possibly need more competent and knowledgeable marketing staff than the average manufacturing company. There is little room for mistakes and unnecessary expenditure.

Greater use has to be made of market and consumer information generated by the company's business. For example people involved in selling should be advised and trained on how to watch for and collate important information. They must also be briefed on the data required. In the travel industry records should be kept of the travel or holiday enquiries placed, the quotations made and the conversion rates to sales. The company's invoices provide information on the country visited, hotel and resort used, duration and timing of the travel and where customers live. They will also show the prices that are being paid. Other needs can also be logged but it will not be possible to gauge their social or job status or their incomes.

However, for tour operators, the courier can help to uncover personal details such as these. In the course of meeting customers, couriers can guide the conversation into areas where the customer will reveal personal details such as job if not income. Also if other remarks are carefully analysed, indications of customers' social status and thus product preference may be indicated. This will add to the work of couriers but it may be worthwhile and is a way out of the difficulties posed by limited funds for research.

With government services, if marketing is not mainly interested in limiting demand, the critical factor is that of choice. Industrialists can refuse to export. Householders can refuse to insulate their homes if they are not convinced it is worth the cost or if they are planning a house move. Mothers can refuse to have their children inoculated. Marketing then has to place the emphasis on persuasion, seeking to influence consumers to reach positive decisions about better health care, better use of educational facilities, energy conservation, relocation of industry or whatever is the government's pressing need of the day.

Another big difference is that users of services have greater personal contact with the staff of service industries. While they cannot, and do not, expect to be able to contact any but the salespersons of a manufacturing enterprise, they do expect to see bank executives, insurance staff, travel agents' and tour operators' executives, investment advisers, lawyers, accountants, garage mechanics and so on, when they have need of their services. Thus staff have to be much more knowledgeable of the services they are offering or at least where to turn up the relevant information quickly and accurately. Failure here will just push the customer down the road to the nearest competitor.

(a) Regulation

Service activities, including pricing, are regulated in three basic ways. First, there is *self-regulation*. In this case the industry has a self-appointed controlling body drawn from amongst its own members. Examples include accountants, lawyers, doctors, dentists and the travel industry. They set the ethical standards for the work, the prices or fees that can be charged and what if any advertising and competition – and the nature of them – that is allowed. Usually they frown on, or ban, any obvious selling by members. In Britain, while rest homes, abortion clinics and health farms can advertise their services, doctors are still prevented from advertising their own personal services. The exception is the travel trade. They can use normal marketing activities and the controlling body is primarily interested in correct and ethical behaviour by its members. There is also a central fund to reimburse customers of firms that go into liquidation before the travel facility that has been paid for has been provided. Or other member firms take on the customers of the unfortunate company. It also sees to the safe repatriation of customers who might otherwise be stranded abroad.

The next form is *public regulation*. In this, central or local government agencies (sometimes government departments) lay down the rules and oversee adherence to them. In Britain, public utilities (electricity, gas, transport such as British Rail) and major state or nationalised industries (e.g. coalmining, steel and to a lesser extent firms such as Rolls-Royce Aeroengines, British Leyland) have to seek official approval on major policy decisions and, sometimes, pricing. The trouble with prices is that governments tend to make decisions based on public opinion (what votes they may gain or lose) rather than on the economic realities of the situation. Thus the price increase permitted may not represent the true rise in costs. Eventually economic reality has to be faced and then very large price increase are unavoidable. The effect could be disastrous for users and results in great public displeasure. *International public-regulation* is achieved by IATA (International Air Transport Association) with airlines. Since IATA takes its cue from member governments, their activities represent public regulation rather than self-regulation.

Finally, there is *demand regulation*. Here normal market factors are at play and are allowed to determine demand. Examples in service industries include hotels, restaurants, tourism and travel facilities. Even here, though, there can be government interference. In the case of hotels there are the safety and fire regulations. Or there can be dictation on the lowest prices tour operators may charge. In Britain some years ago, tour companies could not offer off-peak season holidays at total costs below that of the then normal return fare to the selected destination. It will be seen also that while the travel industry is mainly demand-regulated there is some self-regulation on ethical conduct.

(b) Non-profit-making organisation

It has taken some time for executives to realise that marketing has an important role to play in promoting the activities of non-profit-making organisations, whether publicly or privately organised. It was assumed that as they did not, or could not, make profit, the hard-nosed commercial activity known as marketing was neither necessary nor appropriate. Nothing could be further from the truth.

These organisations have to sell their services or ideas to the public. Many organisations (museums, charities, art galleries, orchestras) have to attract sufficient funds to carry on their cultural and social activities. Many educational establishments (colleges and universities) have to raise funds to endow some of their work and to attract customers (students, graduates, post-graduates) to study or do research work at their establishments. Social, sporting and other clubs have to make their existence and facilities known to attract sufficient members to allow the clubs to continue in existence. Even the police need to attract recruits, seek the support of the public they protect and improve their public image. All of these problems are marketing ones.

The approach is similar to that for other services and as set out in the third paragraph of this section (9.4). However, the selection of markets may have to be even more carefully done and the product selection is specialised and limited. Funds are limited so marketing planning and operations have to be considered carefully and carried out with even greater precision. Profligate spending is just not possible.

In some instances, these organisations may also have to limit demand for their services (or in the jargon, be involved in 'demarketing'), because of limited resources, or for other social reasons. For example, medical organisations promote health care or preventative medicine to minimise the incidence of sickness and also relieve pressure on overloaded hospital and other resources. The police seek to educate the public on crime prevention, for example safeguarding the home to prevent burglary, to reduce the incidence of crime. They are also trying to limit the demand on their resources in this area so that they are free to give more attention to serious crime (murder, terrorism and so on). So even here marketing has an important, if not critical, part to play.

9.5 INTERNATIONAL MARKETING: CONSIDERATIONS

It is now generally accepted that 'international marketing' covers all activities from direct exporting of finished products to overseas markets, to wholly or partly owned subsidiaries of all kinds, joint ventures with foreign organisations and the big multinational operations. Fundamentally there is no difference in the basic approach to marketing to overseas markets, whatever method is used. Markets have to be identified and selected according to the usual criteria. The product mix has to be decided. Other relevant components of the marketing mix have to be identified and selected for each product-market situation and then the marketing operation can be planned, launched and controlled. However, allowance must be made for the differences, some subtle, which exist in some important aspects overseas.

For example it is insufficient to study overseas prospects only from a geographical viewpoint, that is, according to national boundaries. It is necessary to consider the economic geography of regions (economic development, population, educational standards, income, etc.). Ethnic groups have also to be studied and it should be realised that they have the habit of not conforming to national boundaries drawn by politicians. This is particularly so in Africa and the Middle East. Then generally held concepts may not be correct. For example India is a (predominantly) Hindu country but it also has the largest Muslim population of any. Language, culture, attitudes to change or marketing or business, views about involvements with foreign enterprises, level of wealth, social systems in operation and the marketing and distribution infrastructures existing are other aspects that must be studied and understood. These are listed in Table 9.4 for easy reference, and will be discussed later.

Firms wishing to put their international marketing operations, of whichever kind, on to a sure footing are advised to bring the corporate planning approach to them. Overseas operations must be planned in totality, on a long-term basis and with greater precision than in home markets. The time commitments and risks are greater and more complex. Shunting off the odd order when there is spare capacity at home will not do. Potential customers will turn to other sources if they feel a supplier looks on them

Table 9.4 **international marketing: areas for study**

Economic	Standard of living Income and wealth Costs Stability and growth
Economic geography	Size of country and population Spread of population and ethnic groupings Literacy and culture Language Religion and philosophy
Marketing and physical distribution	Facilities available Sophistication and attitudes Economic relationships to marketing
Political and legal	Political attitudes Legal constraints Other regulations and controls
Social	Present state and nature of society Future trends or developments
Technology	Current state Future developments

as a convenient source of business only when times are hard at home. Overseas customers expect reasonable continuity of supplies, with quality at agreed levels and deliveries honoured to the letter.

International marketing has significance for both the economic development of countries and the profitability of firms. It is important to the economic development of developed *and* developing nations. For developing countries, economic development requires not only markets that link, effectively, urban and rural zones but also the creation of wider marketing activities to generate industrial production and stimulate diversified product-market activities. Marketing is the most important multiplier of developing, growth areas and is thus of importance to developing countries. Besides expanding markets and increasing profits, it helps to accumulate capital, balance international payments, exchange primary produce and raw materials for machinery and equipment, expand production facilities and develop economic expansion and competence. It increases incomes and purchasing power, leads eventually to mass production and distribution and the creation of a middle class whose demands stimulate continuing economic growth. All this is vital to developing countries.

(a) Economic factors
Besides attempting to measure the same economic factors as for home markets, particular attention should be given to the *standard of living*.

What is the current standard and how successfully is the government living up to its declared aim of improving it? How is the quality of life changing? Is the country poor and interested mainly in staples (foodstuffs, fertilisers, simple agricultural equipment and essential medicines) or is it able to absorb other items, including 'luxuries' and if so, which? Note that what may be a luxury in say African nations may not be so in more affluent and developed countries like Singapore and Malaysia. Yet developing countries will give priority to industrial products and equipment they consider necessary for what may be, to them, planned essential industrial development and growth. Consideration should also be given to determining whether the economy is basically sound and stable, what the overall chance of growth would be and the direction that growth might take.

The levels of income and the income structure must also be studied. They indicate the level of prosperity of the country and its ability to consume specific goods. Care must be taken to ensure the firm is comparing like with like. For example some countries, including India, pay various grants and allowance to individuals. These may not be included in official statistics on personal incomes. Thus an individual's discretionary income may be larger than indicated by basic earnings.

The tax structure of the country should also be checked. Tax takes a big bite out of the incomes of consumers in developing countries. However, some countries give employees various tax-free allowance towards rent, cost of living and so on which partly offset the effects of relatively high taxation. In India in the 1970s some allowances amounted to about 400 per cent of basic hourly earning rates. Some countries impose punitive tax increases when employees receive increases in their earnings. The additional slice of tax may be so large that the person getting the increase in earnings might find that after tax the net earnings are less than before. (This explains why promotion is often declined. The worker will be taking on more responsibility and risk for a lower after-tax income!) The 'higher earnings levels' can also be quite low by Western standards. In some instances annual salaries over £2500 (equivalent) can incur tax at 70 per cent or more.

It is also necessary to study the ruling market prices, not only of alternative or substitute products to those the firm has in mind, but also for essential commodities. In some countries essential goods produced indigenously will be less expensive than imported items. In others they can be more expensive. It depends on the availability of the right sort of labour, the right plant and essential raw materials. If the last have to be imported then cost of production may not be much cheaper than imported goods. A study of prices for these items will indicate the probable disposal incomes of consumers and their purchasing power. It will also indicate what sort of manufacturing, marketing and distribution costs will be encountered by the incoming firm. Thus decisions can be taken on whether local manufacture would be advantageous or not.

Finally, it is essential to establish the stability of demand in intended markets and what the prospects are for growth or decline. Obviously firms entering a new overseas market would want several years of economic, market and political stability. Otherwise it would not be possible to build a successful business with a long-term future.

(b) Marketing and physical distribution

It is essential for firms to have a sound knowledge of what marketing and distribution facilities exist in target overseas markets. Besides checking on the actual hardware and infrastructure available, its efficiency must be gauged. A country might have an impressive amount of refrigerated rolling stock on their railways. However, if most of it is not in working order, or works for erratic and unpredictable periods because of lack of funds for efficient and regular maintenance, goods needing these facilities would face problems. Further, what road and road transport facilities exist? If roads are poor or non-existent, transport of heavy or delicate equipment would be hazardous. If trucks break down frequently, tyres and other parts fail easily and are difficult to replace, if maintenance is unrealiable, or if the right size and type of vehicle is not available and mechanical handling is by manpower only, further distribution difficulties will arise.

Climate and weather must be known. What protection will products need, in use and transit, to minimise corrosion and contamination? Will full tropicalisation be necessary? Is there any fine dust or sand in the atmosphere? This can get everywhere and can spoil delicate equipment, leading to frequent breakdown. Does the equipment have to stand in the open under all conditions and how will the climate affect it and its operation? If maintenance facilities are lacking, climatic conditions can cause considerable problems.

The marketing infrastructure of some countries is rudimentary and activities that are standard and usual in the home country may be out of the question overseas. For example Britain is just about the only country with truly national daily and Sunday newspaper. In other countries paper tend to be local, serving a limited community. Where there are many languages or dialects, there will be a large number of papers in circulation. This creates advertising problems. If the message has to be modified to suit different dialects and ethical views, then advertising can be costly. If there is no television and no advertising on what television and radio services there are, then these media cannot be used. If there is no advertising industry of the necessary standards, expertise and competence, mounting an advertising campaign is further hampered. If there is a shortage of the necessary skilled and experienced salespeople, the selling operation will pose further problems. If those available have ethical views (or religious ones) which make them refuse to sell certain items the firm will find itself facing an insurmountable difficulty.

Then the standard of marketing possible must be established. Some executives believe that sophisticated methods can only be used in the later stages of a country's development when the necessary infrastructures are themselves sophisticated. This is not always correct. For example India has fairly sophisticated marketing despite distribution problems and the fact that nationally its standard of living is below that of southern Italy, one of the poorest areas of the EEC. This is because the minority who have the necessary purchasing power nevertheless represents a considerable number of people (several tens of millions) who are usually found in the major conurbations of Bombay, Delhi, Madras, Calcutta and other towns.

Further, the acceptance of marketing, or antagonism to it, the fashionable view on which products are desirable or 'status symbols' and ethnic and religious considerations will all determine what can be done in a country. Government views and regulations (favourable and hostile), import and financial controls and the availability of raw materials and skills will further influence the product-market offerings possible. General and official attitudes to marketing, especially in developing countries, are critical. Some see it as an invention of the devil or covert attempts by foreigners to control the economic destiny of the host country. Others (e.g. Malaysia, Singapore, Kenya, Korea, India) see it as a necessary facet of life and one that makes a substantial economic contribution to the country. Where marketing is held in suspicion and ethnic or tribal jealousies are strong, many novel operational problems may be presented. Thus good synchronisation with a country's economic development, growth plans, official and public views and acceptance of marketing is vital for the immediate and long-term success of a new overseas venture.

(c) Political and legal

In addition to the points made in the preceding sub-sections, thought must be given to the political framework of the country, the different dogma propounded by the various parties vying for power and the chances of any party obtaining and holding on to power. Often the declared public statements of policy do not always match performance. The latter can be much more severe or liberal than might be deduced from official statements. The real clues are found in what is said in private behind closed doors, the attitude to trade and whether industrial development and contributions by foreigners are seen as helping to meet the nation's objectives.

Further, decisions must be taken on whether the political system is democratic or dictatorial or a mixture of both. Then the permanency of the system must be judged. What is the likelihood of change? What effect would any change have on the economic and business situations? How permanent is any change likely to be? In other words, what is the stability of the system?

Then there is the attitude of host countries to other nations, their governments, political and economic policies. If they favour the firm's home country, prospects should be good. If the host nation detests all that the home country stands for then the firm's prospects should be nil.

The legal framework of foreign countries can be alien to the firm (e.g. for British companies, the intricacies of Napoleonic law as against British case law) and difficult to interpret and understand. Ignorance of the law is not accepted as an excuse for contraventions. So unless a firm takes steps to study the legal systems and procedures of host countries and all associated business and financial regulations and controls, costly mistakes can be made.

An important legal aspect concerns the ownership of business enterprises. Most countries (Britain seems to be the only exception these days) insist, as a minimum, that 51 per cent or more of the equity must be held by local nationals. In some countries essential industries which are capital- and skills-intensive may initially be mainly in foreign hands. However, once established and the necessary skills imparted to local nationals, then the 51 plus per cent rule is applied. Those requiring limited capital and skills which the country has must be almost entirely (c. 80 plus per cent) in local ownership. In every case expatriates are required to train their successors from amongst the ranks of local nationals working for the firm.

As already mentioned, tax laws and regulations must be obeyed. However, restrictions and laws can be imposed or withdrawn at speed and without much prior warning or explanation. It should be remembered too that in new nations politicians, the Civil Service and business people will need time to reach the degree of sophistication, competence and knowledge existing in countries that have been around for many centuries.

(d) Demographic factors

As for marketing in home countries, the size and distribution of the population must be known. Even if a country has a large population, it will pose marketing problems if this is spread over a large area in small towns and villages, or if it is mainly rural in nature. The size of market segments may be too limited. The population distribution may also be split by geographic features which may form formidable natural barriers to a free flow of trade.

Then the culture and the standards of literacy must be known for reasons stated earlier. Too many dialects hamper promotional and research activities. Methods standard in the home country may be impossible to apply. If there are no competent, local, marketing research facilities it will be very difficult and expensive to do any research. Teams from the home country may be needed and then there will be problems associated with lack of knowledge of the country, its various viewpoints on relevant matters and the many taboos which may exist.

(e) Technology
The level of technological development and chances of further advances also affect product-market possibilities. In developing countries where technology is at a rudimentary stage, standard sophisticated products of the home market would be inappropriate. Simple products may have to be devised or those involving 'intermediate technology' may be all that is possible. It may be necessary to carry out considerable modifications of standard products. The costs may be prohibitive in the light of limited potential demand.

Thus there are many potential problems facing those firms interested in developing international operations. The more common pitfalls are summarised in Table 9.5 (see also Section 7.9(d)).

Table 9.5 **international marketing: common pitfalls**

1 The home country's products may be too expensive, too sophisticated or wrong in some other aspect of the specifications (e.g. colour, flavour, appearance etc.).
2 Customs, traditions, religion, beliefs and other ethnic factors may not be understood or allowed for sufficiently.
3 Inadequate assessment of product-market possibilities.
4 Political motivations, institutions, objectives may have been misunderstood or misinterpreted.
5 Product-market development plans may have been sequenced incorrectly.
6 Inaccurate interpretation of words or symbols.
7 Incorrect assessment of promotional restrictions, rules and regulations.
8 Ignorance, or the ignoring, of political requirements.
9 Failure to comply with legal requirements.
10 Failure to adhere to ethical, social and religious practices and standards.
11 Initiating company may have failed to develop an indigenous image (as against its own 'foreign' image).
12 Failure to identify with national aims and aspirations, especially economic ones and the desire to improve the quality of life as well as the standard of living.
13 Trade channels may have varied with that of the 'home' market and may not have been fully understood.
14 Attempting operations that are too far in advance of the stage of development reached by the 'host' nation.
15 Failure to develop local nationals to take executive positions in the operation.
16 Mistakes in estimating long-term investment requirements and risks, correct strategies, information flows and controls.

9.6 INTERNATIONAL MARKETING: METHODS

Consideration will now be given, briefly, to the methods available to those wishing to develop overseas business.

(a) Direct exports
This is usually the first stage. It involves selling and shipping abroad products made in the home country. As mentioned, this poses problems when the needs and characteristics of overseas markets differ from those of the home market. Sales potential may be limited unless costly modifications are undertaken. The different usages (and hence values) of the product must also be appreciated.

For example the bicycle in Western Europe is normally used for fun or recreational and sporting purposes. In developing countries (e.g. India and Africa) it is an essential mode of transport, probably the only one that most people can afford. It is a workhorse too, used to carry an astonishing range of products. When the author was in India in 1972 on a United Nations assignment, he was astonished to find two beds and mattresses were delivered to his apartment on bicycles!

Electric washing machines, which are expensive, are ostentatious luxuries enjoyed only by the relatively rich in poor countries with uncertain electricity supply and lots of cheap labour. Most would make do with hand-washing either doing it themselves or employing very cheap labour to do it. Ordinary soap, or none at all, may displace expensive detergents and powders.

The usual method of entry is through appointed agents. These should have the necessary experience and skills, especially if regular maintenance is needed or if the products are technical ones. Their selection requires careful consideration and visits, perhaps numerous, to the country to interview and chose them. Their financial strength and integrity should be sufficient for the work they will do and the stocks they should hold. What is helpful here is advice from other firms already operating in the country, the commercial sections of foreign embassies in the home country and commercial attachés of the home country in foreign countries. Reports by major banks, especially the commercial or industrial ones, government departments and agencies at home and trade and industry associations all provide useful information and guidance. Regular 'servicing' visits to appointed agents are also important.

(b) Local facilities
As business increases, or because of difficulties in exporting finished goods (host governments may discourage or embargo this), local assembly plants can be set up. In the case of cars and some other equipment, complete

kits are shipped out and assembled locally. Sometimes local manufacture of simple components can be used with key components shipped out from home. Or if the business is substantial but not big enough to justify local assembly, the firm may set up a marketing (only) subsidiary or office. This could work independently of the original agents who may still carry on the agency, or, more usually, in conjunction with the original agents. The latter is preferred when host governments are particularly keen on local involvement and investment. Only with highly technical products and where the necessary skills are not available would a firm be permitted to go it alone with a marketing subsidiary.

Then when the conditions (sufficient demand, necessary skills available, economic and political factors and experience) are right, manufacturing and marketing subsidiaries can be set up. These may be wholly owned or be in partnership with local nationals and capital as the laws of the land demand. Joint ventures with relatively sophisticated local firms is another variation in more developed countries.

(c) Multinational operations

For the successful firms, the final stage will be evolution into multinational enterprises. This results when a company has several overseas organisations, now usually a mix of wholly owned subsidiaries, minority shareholdings in local companies and joint ventures, operating in several countries. Also usually 50 per cent or more of the group's trading profits come from overseas operations rather than the original home market. Trading of components between the different units may go on freely as the enterprise uses the most economical (low-cost) countries for the manufacture of different items.

Multinationals face many marketing and other management problems. The main one centres around the control of the group's activities including policies on the raising and transfer of capital and the remittance of profits to the initiating, or parent, company. Then there is the question of the multinational balancing its policies for profit, sales and return with the economic and other goals of the host countries. Further, because of their size, the total business can be many times greater than the gross national product of the smaller host nations and political pressure can result from this.

Then there are the decisions that have to be reached on the standardisation of pricing, products, distribution and method of selling and promoting the products. The method of operation can range from totally centralised planning by the home, or parent, unit to some generalised statement of intent and financial planning based on a sharing of ideas and values between the different units. In the latter case, the individual companies are left to implement the agreed objectives in their own way, as efficiently as local conditions permit. Thus there would be considerable variations in the detailed activities each would implement.

The above gives some idea of the nature of the problems faced by multinationals. Fuller discussion on them is outside the scope of this book.

9.7 FURTHER THOUGHTS ON DEVELOPING COUNTRIES

In addition to the comments made earlier, it is worth noting here that marketing has a further role to play in developing countries. By its successful use in the rural environment it must improve the total distribution in rural areas. There is need for more efficient distribution of agricultural products as well as fertilisers, pesticides and basic equipment needed by farmers. This will improve the productivity and real income of rural areas. Then there is the distribution of manufactured goods to the rural population to stimulate greater consumption as a result of improved productivity and incomes.

There is also the humanitarian aspect. Despite recent advances, something like 30 per cent of all children in the rural areas of developing countries die young because of malnutrition and lack of medical and other essential supplies. Marketing can make a useful contribution here. However, attempts to serve the agricultural producer should not be planned so blindly as to damage the natural infrastructure of the agricultural market. Finally, there is the very real contribution that successful marketing can make to economic growth and the creation of much needed capital.

9.8 ATTAINING AND HOLDING MARKET LEADERSHIP

Many companies find it difficult to attain and hold market leadership or standing. This is so particularly during hard economic times as experienced in the period 1979 to 1983. It is less difficult to achieve if certain key factors are remembered.

First, the marketing problem is essentially dynamic. It is subject to change, almost continually, for the better or worse. Because of this there is need for greater conceptual skill. This requires the ability to see the enterprise as a whole and to understand how its various functions and activities interact or depend on each other's success for corporate success. Third, there is need for inbuilt flexibility in marketing plans and actions to permit response to market and technological change.

The more common causes of loss of leadership are, first, designing products and services in isolation from the market and hence its demands or needs. Second, there is little or no customer/consumer research to identify changing needs. Third, there is inadequate investment in the development of existing and new markets. Fourth, promotional campaigns are misdirected to the wrong target markets and have inadequate budgets. Finally, changing market conditions may require changes in the selling methods used or these are only implemented slowly and reluctantly, long after they should have been. These changes include movement away from a few large customers concentrated in a region to many smaller customers scattered throughout the country. Existing middlemen being used may lack the necessary experience to handle this change and the company may be unable to adapt its selling and merchandising operations accordingly. Failure to adapt can prove disastrous.

9.9 FURTHER THOUGHTS ON CUSTOMER/BRAND LOYALTY

Marketing executives set great score on the fact that many customers appear to maintain loyalty to a brand or manufacturer. However, they consider, too often, that loyalty is a static attribute of markets. It is not, and it is hardly ever absolute. Therefore, to hope that loyal customers may form a substantial market segment can lead to bad marketing decisions. Evidence shows that rather than having unchanging preference, consumers make their selection from a group of acceptable products and service. Convenience is often the final, over-riding criterion. Consumer behaviour can be a highly dynamic phenomenon. It is rarely stable or undivided. Hence the marketing of similar and competing brands, products or services can be a means of ensuring profit and sales stability when brand or product switching occurs.

9.10 SCENARIO FOR THE 1990s

The scenario for the rest of this century will depend on two distinct sets of developments. First are the predictable trends of demographic characteristics, technological change, institutional structures and attitudes towards the use of scarce resources. Second are areas of major uncertainties such as the economic options available, attitudes towards the protection of the world's ecology, the division of time between work and leisure (which itself will be influenced by the level of unemployment), and what will be the dominant social values of the period. It is therefore advisable for executives to work out the alternative scenarios that may develop for marketing and also management as a whole.

Changing social values could place greater emphasis on quality rather than quantity. There may be a willingness to recognise free time, as well as work, as sources of satisfaction. If this happens, leisure activities could grow faster than consumer spending as a whole. So leisure could attract not only greater public interest but also greater business attention and activity. The pattern of working hours would be determined by consumers' and workers' leisure interests and not only the needs of production. The result could be greater flexibility in the use of time and the breakdown of the conventional pattern of work.

9.11 IN CONCLUSION

Thus it will be seen that basic marketing concepts and techniques can be applied to big and small companies, to manufacturing and service industries, developed and developing nations and non-profit making enterprises. What executives have to do is study and understand the special needs of each case and learn to modify basic techniques to match them. Careful selection of appropriate techniques is also necessary. Full scale application of every technique, willy-nilly, will just erode existing profits and lead eventually to business disaster.

ASSIGNMENTS

1 As marketing manager of a major group in consumer goods you are not satisfied with current activities in after-sales work nor with the warranties and guarantees being used. What points would you recommend need study and consideration and how would you bring into consideration the subjects of consumerism and codes of practice?

2 If your company diversified into industrial products what changes, if any, would you recommend re the above?

3 If the company expands its international business what additional consideration has to be given to the above?

4 If your cousin has similar responsibilities in a service industry (say travel and tourism or any other – specify) how would her approach to this subject vary?

5 A few years later you move to a company to open up its (non-existent) international business. You are asked to review the various methods that could be employed and the many considerations that have to be taken into account. Prepare a paper for submission to the Managing Director, who is taking a personal interest in this development.

APPENDICES

A.1 GLOSSARY OF THE MORE USUAL MARKETING TERMS

Above-the-line
: Commission paying media (see Table 7.5).

Account executive
: Advertising agency executive who looks after a client's requirements (see also Section 7.3(e)).

Advertising
: Paid form of promotional activity (see Section 7.2).

Advertising schedule
: Details the planned advertising, its cost, size and timing and the media to be used (see also Section 7.3).

After-sales service
: See Section 9.1.

Agent
: Organisation or person appointed to sell a product or service (see Section 9.6(a)).

Analysis
: Examination of marketing research intelligence (see Chapter 4).

Artwork
: Illustrative part of an advertisement (see Sections 7.2 and 7.3).

Attitude research
: An investigation of people's attitudes by personal interview or group discussion (see Section 4.4).

Audit
: Periodic check to measure the movement of products through outlets. Also detailed study of resources (manpower, skills, plant, finances etc.) and performance of a firm (e.g. Figure 3.8).

Below-the-line
: Media that do not pay commission to advertising agencies (see Table 7.5 and Section 7.3(b)).

Bias
: Distortion of intelligence (see Section 4.8).

Block
: Metal or other plate, engraved, moulded or cast for printing purposes.

Blow-up
: Big enlargement of photograph etc.

Brand or market leader	Product with the greatest share of a market (see Sections 6.5(b) and 6.5(a)).
Brand name	Distinctive name by which a product or group of products is identified (see also Section 7.5(a)).
Brief	Summary of objectives and instructions governing the creation of a marketing research exercise or advertising campaign (see Section 4.5(b)).
Brochure	Stitched booklet often with a prestige connotation (see also Section 7.4).
Budget	Estimate of future expenditure for a stated period of time. Not to be confused with *target*, which see (see Section 7.7(a)).
Buying motives	Motives which create a desire to buy a product or service (see Section 1.9(e)).
Call rate	Number of calls made on customers or potential customers, e.g. daily or weekly. See also *Sales call*.
Captive market	Purchasers who have to buy a particular product or service because there are no other practical alternatives.
Catalogue	Describes and details (with/without illustrations) a range of products/services. See *Brochure* and also Section 7.4.
Circulation	Total number of distributed copies of a publication (see also Section 7.3(b)).
Check list	Related questions to verify all that must be known, investigated or done (e.g. Tables 4.1, 4.4, etc.).
Classification (of information, products, markets, etc.)	Arrangement of data and information in some predetermined way or category; also similar arrangement of research interviews (e.g. Figure 5.5 and Table 6.1).
Coarse screening	Initial (rough) check, at any early stage, on viability of a new product idea.
Cold calling	Call made by salesperson without prior appointment having been made; an uninvited call.
Column millimetres	Area in a publication: the no. of columns of type multiplied by the depth in millimetres.
Commission	Incentive payment or remuneration based in some way on sales achieved.
Competition	Direct competition: rival products or services

sold in the same market; indirect competition: alternative or dissimilar products or services on offer that can reduce demand for the original offering.

Concept testing	Checking the possible acceptability of a new product idea before manufacture.
Control question	Question which checks the correctness of other answers (see Section 4.7 also).
Controlled circulation	Circulation is controlled in some specific way relating to the status of the reader.
Copy	Text of a publication (see Section 7.3(a)).
Copy or press date	Date when advertising material must be with publisher or printer.
Copy platform	Main theme of an advertisement (see Section 7.3(a)).
Creative task	See Section 7.2(c)(i).
Customer need	In the broadest sense, potential customer's requirements which have to be satisfied.
Data collection	See Section 4.3(e).
Data processing	Arranging data into some systematic form to facilitate analysis.
Declining market	Market for a product or service whose total demand is falling (see Section 6.2).
Demand	Total amount required of, or number of customers for, a product or service (see Sections 2.8 and 6.2).
Depth interview	Investigation in depth of a subject where researcher works within broad guidelines and respondent is free to develop views/ideas (see also Section 4.5(d)(iii)).
Desk research	Study of secondary data and information not requiring field studies (see Sections 4.3 and 4.5(c)).
Direct mail	Mailed literature to selected prospects (see also Section 7.4).
Diversification	When company enters an entirely new field of activity which it has not tackled before. Involves introducing new products/services into new markets. Products need not be 'new' to the industry (see also Section 5.4(d)).
Editorial publicity or 'free editorial'	Editorial matter describing product/service or activity published without charge to the initiating company (see Sections 7.4 and 7.6).

Extrapolation	Projection of historical data to identify possible future trends (see Section 4.9).
Feasibility study	Study which ascertains whether a proposed course of action is possible.
Feedback	Information (usually sales and customer reactions) passed back to company and used to update intelligence and plans.
Field selling	Direct selling by salespersons in the market, to all prospects (see Section 7.8).
Fieldwork	Research carried out in the field (see Section 4.5(d)).
Galleys	Rough proofs, or 'pulls', of typesetting before the make-up of pages.
Group discussion	A group of people who express their views freely on a given subject, usually under the guidance of a group leader (see Section 4.5(d) (iv) also).
Growth market	Market in which demand for product/service is increasing (see also Section 6.2).
Handout	Cheap leaflet for handing out at exhibitions, sales conventions, etc.
Historical trends	Changes which have taken place in previous years; indicated by study of past performance. Used as basis for extrapolations.
House style	Standardised graphic form used throughout by a company on its letterheads, publications, packaging and advertisements.
Image	How customers view a company and its products/services.
Impact	The effectiveness of a selling message or promotion (see Section 7.3).
Insert	Piece of sales promotional material (loose or bound) placed between the pages of a publication.
Key factors	Essential elements of a situation that affect the achievement of specific goals.
Key prospects	Important potential customers; buyers in a market who have the greatest potential purchasing power.
Keyed advertisement	One where enquirer indicates the source of their information by reference to a code number or particular department.

Layout	Accurate position guide for an advertisement or publication.
Leaflet	Printed paper, folded to form 4 pages; may be stitched or stapled to others to give more pages (see also *Brochure*).
Local press	In the United Kingdom, local newspapers covering a borough, rural district or similar region.
Logotype	Or 'Logo'. A company symbol, badge or name.
Longrange planning	Forward plan involving projections for five years or more ahead.
Mailing list	Classified list of names and addresses used for mail shots. Often compiled from membership lists of clubs, trade and professional associations/institutes, local council rates lists etc.
Mailing piece	Leaflet etc. sent through the post.
Mailing shot	A single mailing operation.
Manual	Printed document (any number of pages) usually containing specific instructions (i.e. service manual, sales manual etc.).
Margin	Difference between total cost of a product (or service) and its market price, i.e. the profit before tax.
Marketing	See Sections 1.1 and 1.5 *et seq*.
Marketing intelligence	Sum total of all the marketing data and information available or obtainable.
Marketing services	All activities, other than direct selling, that assist marketing activities (e.g. marketing research).
Medium/Media	Channel/channels of communication (see Table 7.5).
Merchandising	See Section 7.4(b).
Mix	Planned mixture of all elements of a specific marketing operation for optimal effect (or greatest effect at minimum cost). For example: *market mix* = selection of markets and the volume of business attained/to be attained in each of them; *marketing mix* = all the various marketing operations and the amounts of them that will (or have) been used, when and where they will be (or were) used, etc.

Mix (*contd*)	*product mix* = selection of all products and the quantities of each to be sold/have been sold to give the best return for any given resources/capabilities situation (see also Section 5.3); *product-market mix* = selection of the products and markets and their combination or permutations to give optimal return in any given resource/capability situation (see also Figure 5.5); *sales mix* = the quantities of different products or services sold and the incidence and timing of such sales.
Motivational research	Investigation of motives influencing buying and other decisions.
National press	In United Kingdom, daily and Sunday papers with mass circulation throughout a country. Many countries do not have this (see Section 7.3(b)).
Observational research	Research information gathered by observation of a situation etc. (see Section 4.4(c) also).
Open-ended question	A question where choice of reply is not restricted (see Section 4.7(b)).
Opinion leaders	People who because of their status, position etc. are considered to influence the views of others (see Section 4.4(c)(iv)).
Outlet	A distribution or selling point, e.g. shops, wholesalers, retailers, departmental stores etc.
Penetration	Normally, the market share or extent to which market potential has been realised (see Sections 6.2 and 6.5(a)).
Physical distribution	Means by which goods are moved from point of manufacture to point of sale or buyer's base or home. With travel and tourism, distribution refers to despatch of information, reservation details and tickets and the movement of the traveller to and from the *destination* (see Chapter 8).
Pilot study	Short study carried out before main research to test accuracy of assumptions etc.
Point of sale (point of purchase)	Place where sale or purchase occurs.
Policy	See Section 1.7(a).

Postal check	Postal method of checking validity of answers to questionnaires, using a percentage of total questionnaires returned.
Postal questionnaire	Questionnaire posted to those comprising the sample of a survey for completion and return without the aid of skilled interviewers (see Section 4.5(d)(i)).
Pre-selected	Interviewees in a sample selected beforehand according to some pre-determined formula (see also Section 4.6).
Press	All newspapers and periodicals of all kinds.
Press relations	See Section 7.6.
Price/demand or Price/volume ratio	Relationship between the price of a product and the demand for it.
Price elasticity	Measures the incremental change in demand with every incremental change of price.
Price sensitivity	Measures consumers' sensitivity to different price levels and changes of price.
Pricing strategy	and policies (see Sections 5.6(a) and (c)).
Product life cycle	See Section 5.3(d); also Figure 5.3.
Product mix	See *Mix*.
'Product plus'	Unique property of a product (see also *USP*).
Product screening	Process whereby new or modified products are evaluated against company/marketing objectives, future potential and other critical factors.
Profit	See *Margin* and Section 5.5.
Profit objectives	See Sections 5.5 and 5.6.
Prompted response	Reply to a question where respondents are aided by a list of possible answers.
Prospect	Potential purchaser or customer.
Provincial press	Newspapers circulating in a restricted region (town etc.) other than in the capital.
Public Relations	See Section 7.6.
PRO	Public Relations Officer - person responsible for public relations activities.
Publicity	Process of securing attention and imparting a message.
Purchasing influences	All factors which affect a (favourable) buying decision.
Qualitative	Unquantifiable factors describing the quality, value etc. rather than size or amounts in numbers.

Quantify	To express in numerical or measurable terms (either units or money).
Quantitative factors	Those that can be quantified, e.g. revenue, sales units, profit, return, no. of customers or competitors etc.
Questionnaire	See Sections 4.5(d) and 4.7.
Quota sample	See Section 4.6 and Table 4.8.
Random sample	See Section 4.6 and Table 4.8.
Rate card	Card or leaflet showing the different charges for different sizes and types of advertisement; issued by the various media.
Research	See Table 1.1 under MARKETING RESEARCH and Chapter 4.
Research mix	Refers to the various research activities to be used in a marketing operation or project, to achieve research objectives at minimum cost. See also *Mix*.
Respondent	Interviewee in a research study; person from whom information is obtained.
Response rate	Rate at which successfully completed interviews are being achieved in a research sample.
Ruling market price (or market price)	The price currently being paid in the market. The value purchaser's place on a product/ service.
Sales aid	Any element of sales promotion (leaflets, slides, samples, showcards etc.) which back up face-to-face selling activities.
Sales call	Visit to potential customer for purpose of achieving a sale, apart from calls simply to maintain contact or continue customer's awareness of company or its products.
Sampling	See Section 4.6.
Segmentation	Breakdown of a total market into discrete and identifiable parts (see Section 6.4).
Share	See *Penetration*.
'Skew'	The bias given to data, or way it has been distorted by bias accidentally or deliberately injected into any study.
Size	A characteristic of a market, or market segment, usually expressed in quantity or value.
Static market	One of relatively unchanging size, i.e. not subject to growth or decline or any fluctuations. See also Section 6.2.

Strategy	See Section 1.7(a).
Strengths and weaknesses	Positive and negative features of a product, service or organisation.
Structured interview	Interview using a questionnaire in which questions are specifically indicated and diversion from them must not occur. See also Section 4.7.
Tabulation	Presentation of data in tables for further evaluation and easier assimilation.
Target	Quantity or thing to be achieved by specific activities, e.g. sales target. Not to be confused with *Budget* (which see).
Technical press	Publications dealing with technical subjects. Also those dealing with professional or specialist subjects, e.g. accountancy, travel etc.
Test marketing	Method of testing a marketing plan on a limited scale by implementing the plan in at least two areas typical of the total market. All planned activities are used. One area is the 'control' and in the other experimental changes in some activities are tried and the change in results measured. Areas used should not be close to each other to avoid cross effects (see also Section 9.2).
Trade press	Strictly, publications dealing with a trade rather than a technical subject, e.g. *Travel Trade Press*.
Unique selling proposition (USP)	A special benefit or property offered to customers that is unique to the product/service.
Universe	See Table 4.8.
Unprompted response	Open or unaided reply by a respondent to a question.
Unstructured interview	Interview in which interviewer is not restricted by a particular question or sequence of questioning.

A.2 PRODUCT SCREEN (QUALITATIVE)

When screening a new product idea for viability, the following factors are usually evaluated.

Group	Factors
Profit objectives	Size; growth; level of profit; stability.
Market stability	Durability; breadth; captive market; difficulty to copy; stability in recession and wartime.
Growth	Unique character of product/process; export prospects; demand/supply ratio; rate of technical change; improved opportunities.
Marketability	Relationship with existing markets; image; ease of market penetration; competition; user stratification; no seasonal fluctuations.
Production techniques	Ease of development; value added; favoured purchasing position; availability of materials.
R and D	Utilising existing know-how; future development needs; availability of R and D personnel.
Engineering	Reliability of process; utilisation of standard equipment; availability of skills.
Manufacturing	Utilisation of idle equipment, surplus services; upgrading of by-products; availability of resources; absorbs hitherto waste materials; hazardous operations; familiar processes etc.

The usual procedure is to give each factor a 'weight' (ranging from 1 to 5 or more) which reflects the skills, resources, capabilities and methods of the company. These are changed only if some change occurs in the company on these counts. Then each is given a rating according to its importance to the success/viability of the idea. These can range from −3 to +3; −5 to +5 etc. '0' = not important; (0) = don't know. Weightings and ratings are multipled and summed. The score resulting is scaled to indicate the idea's chances of success.

A.3 MARKET SCREEN

With new markets it is advisable to screen them also to check their viability. The approach is similar to that for product ideas but the factors screened are as shown below.

Group	Factors
Market size	E.g. Under £1m. p.a.; £1–3m.; over £3m. etc.
Growth	E.g. Declining, static; growing by −% etc. (usually measured in £ and units)

Long-term growth	E.g. Certain decline; static; growth by $-\%$ etc.
Customer class	E.g. C2, D, E; C2, D; C1, C2; C1; B, C1; A, B; A etc.
Age groups	E.g. All over 60; 45–60; 35–45; 25–35; etc.

And any other relevant groups (e.g. Market share).

Weightings and ratings are given as for the product screen but in this case the 'weight' applies to the (whole) group. Ratings are given to the various factors according to their importance. However, both the weighting and the rating are fixed and are altered only when the nature of the company (resources, skills etc.) change. Ratings and weightings are multiplied and the resultant scores are summed. In this case the ratings range from '0' (not important) to +5 or more. (Unlike the product screen there are no '(0)' = don't know. While '(0)' signifies the areas in new product ideas which require further study, by the time a market is screened, all the necessary information i.e. factors, are known.)

According to the total score achieved, the viability of the market can be judged. For example over 80 points = immediate exploitation possible; 70–80 points = rechecked key factors; 60–70 points = leave for x years; under 60 points = abandon. The actual scaling used will vary from market to market, the above being purely indicative for purpose of explanation of the method.

A.4 PRODUCT-MARKET SCREEN

Before a decision is finally taken to develop and launch a new product idea or to enter a new market, it is advisable to screen the proposed product-market situation. This screen combines the key factors and groups taken from the product and market screens (Appendices 2 and 3) such as the groups shown below.

Profit	*Market size*
Marketability	*Long-term growth*
Growth	*Customer class*
Manufacturing	*Market shares*

and whatever others are deemed to be critical

The weighting, rating and method of calculating the final score are carried out in the same way as indicated in Appendices 2 and 3. The final total score is measured against the usual scaling scheme and the viability of the final product-market proposition is thus evaluated.

A.5 SELECT BIBLIOGRAPHY

Boone, L. E. and Kurtz, D. L. *Contemporary Marketing*, 3rd edn (Ill., Dryden Press, 1980).

Delozier, W. M., *The Marketing Communication Process* (New York: McGraw-Hill, 1976).

Foster, D. W., *Planning for Products and Markets* (London: Longman, 1972).

Foster, D. W., 'Distribution: The Achilles Heel', ch. 33 in J. B. Westing and G. Albaum (eds), *Modern Marketing Thought*, 3rd edn (New York: The Macmillan Co., 1975).

Foster, D. W., *The Management Quadrille* (London: Pitman, 1980).

Gilligan, C. and Crowther, G., *Advertising Management* (Oxford: Allan, 1976).

Harvey, J., *Mastering Economics* (London: Macmillan, 1982).

Kotler, P., *Marketing Management: Analysis, Planning and Control*, 4th edn (Englewood Cliffs, N. J.: Prentice-Hall, 1980).

Kotler, P., *Principles of Marketing* (Englewood Cliffs, N.J.: Prentice-Hall, 1980).

Livesey, F., *Pricing* (London: Macmillan, 1976).

Livingstone, J. M. *International Marketing Management* (London: Macmillan, 1976).

Skinner, R. N., *Launching New Products in Competitive Markets* (London: Cassell/Assoc. Business Programmes, 1978).

Spillard, P., *Sales Promotion*, 2nd edn (London: Business Books, 1977).

Stone, M., *Product Planning; An Integrated Approach* (London: Macmillan, 1976).

Wilmshurst, J., *The Fundamentals and Practice of Marketing* (London: Heinemann, 1980).

INDEX